KU-744-134

Comprehensive Schooling
A Reader

WITHDRAWN

LIVERPOOL POLYTECHNIC LIBRARY
I M MARSH CAMPUS
BARKHILL ROAD, LIVERPOOL L17 6BD

LIVERPOOL POLYTECHNIC LIBRARY

3 1111 00150 8595

Ball, S.J
Comprehensive schooling
M M 373.25 BAL 1984

WITHDRAWN

Issues in Education and Training: 1

Comprehensive Schooling
A Reader

Edited By
Stephen J. Ball
University of Sussex

 The Falmer Press

A member of the Taylor & Francis Group
London and Philadelphia

UK	The Falmer Press, Falmer House, Barcombe, Lewes, East Sussex, BN8 5DL
USA	The Falmer Press, Taylor & Francis Inc., 242 Cherry Street, Philadelphia, PA 19106-1906

© Selection and editorial material copyright
Stephen J. Ball 1984

All rights reserved. No part of this publication may be reproduced, stored in a retrieval system, or transmitted in any form or by any means, electronic, mechanical, photocopying, recording or otherwise, without permission in writing from the Publisher.

First published in 1984

Library of Congress Cataloging in Publication Data

Main entry under title:

Comprehensive schooling

Bibliography: p.
Includes index.
1. Comprehensive high schools—Great Britain—
Addresses, essays, lectures. I. Ball, Stephen J.
LA635.C684 1984 373.2′5′0942 84-6096
ISBN 0-905273-90-7
ISBN 0-905273-89-3 (pbk.)

Typeset in 11/13 Bembo by
Imago Publishing Ltd, Thame, Oxon

Jacket design by Leonard Williams

Printed in Great Britain by Taylor & Francis (Printers) Ltd, Basingstoke

Contents

Introduction: Comprehensives in Crisis?

Stephen J. Ball

In his recent book examining the contemporary problems of the
comprehensive school David Hargreaves (1982) portrayed the development of these schools in the following way:

> The comprehensive school had a difficult birth. It was always
> an unwanted child for some, who impatiently awaited an
> opportunity to commit a discreet infanticide. For others it was
> an infant prodigy which needed to be carefully nurtured and to
> be defended against serious enemies. It survived. (p. 161)

The question is whether Hargreaves' judgment on the still immature
child was in fact premature. Even in the short time that has elapsed
since the publication of Hargreaves' book there has been ample
evidence of a continuing process of weakening and undermining of the
comprehensive basis for secondary education in this country. The
survival of the comprehensive system, such as it is, remains in doubt.

It is usual to take 1965 as the most significant date in the history of
comprehensive education in this country, the year in which Harold
Wilson's Labour Government issued Circular 10/65 requesting local
authorities to submit plans for comprehensive reorganization. But
overemphasis on this date can serve to perpetuate confusion on at least
three points. First, several comprehensives had been established in local
authorities across the country from as early as 1947 (see Rubinstein and
Simon, 1969, for a full account). Secondly, the extent of support for
comprehensive education in the Labour Party in 1965 and the particular
view of comprehensive education upon which that support was based is
by no means clear (see Parkinson, 1970). It must be borne in mind that
the Labour Party had an opportunity to introduce comprehensive
education in 1945–51 but chose instead to go ahead with the implementation of the tripartite system based on the 1944 Education Act (see
Vernon's, 1982, biography of Ellen Wilkinson, first Minister of

Education in the 1945–51 Labour Government). Also, in the period 1951–64 a considerable proportion of the comprehensives which were established were set up by Conservative-controlled authorities (even if not always on purely educational grounds). Edward Boyle, the Conservative education spokesman, interviewed in the late 1960s, seemed to have accepted the inevitability of total comprehensivization of the state sector (Kogan 1971). Finally, it is easy to forget in discussions of comprehensive education that 5–6 per cent of school age children are educated in the private sector, that a number of local authorities have continued to resist reorganization in the state sector and that others have managed to maintain selection despite the appearance of having reorganized. In 1965 240,000 (8.5 per cent) pupils in the maintained sector were in comprehensive schools, by 1979 this figure had risen to 3,061,597 (84.9 per cent).

Clearly, one of the problems in talking about the comprehensive school in general terms is that the concept of comprehensive education has no commonly agreed meaning either for its advocates or its opponents. The Labour governments which introduced Circular 10/65 and passed the 1976 Education Act made no attempt to define or lay down guidelines for the provision of a comprehensive education. Caroline Benn (1979) makes the point that:

> It was impossible to ensure equality of opportunity without a definition of those minimum opportunities which should be available to all boys and girls in any school called 'comprehensive'. To try to define them would have conflicted with the *laissez-faire* policy of governments in implementing the reform since 1965, a policy adopted by both political parties in the vain hope of appeasing two different kinds of political opposition. (p. 197)

The consequences of lack of direction and lack of definition have been, first, a piecemeal and uncoordinated process of reorganization; apart from those authorities which managed to resist entirely the introduction of comprehensives, there are some which have comprehensives existing alongside grammar schools and others which have 'super-comprehensives' taking a selective intake within a reorganized system (for example, Bromley). Second, in those schools which have been reorganized as comprehensive, with a few notable exceptions, the expectations of parents, the demands of the examination system and the increasingly critical attitude of successive governments have tended to reinforce an emphasis on internal selection and differentiation among pupils. They have been 'grammarized' (Elliott, 1983); see for example Burgess's (1983) account of the development of Bishop Macgregor Comprehensive, which was established as a purpose-built comprehensive but whose organization (in the head's view) was to be based on the best aspects of the tripartite system. The vast majority of schools called 'comprehensive' are in effect pursuing educational policies which to a great extent reflect the notions of meritocracy and separate provision embodied in the 1944 Norwood Report (see Ball, 1981, pp. 138–41).

Within the schools themselves opposing definitions of the concept of comprehensive education have been in competition to define the school and to determine policy (see Ball, 1981, pp. 11–13). But over time the meritocratic lobby has tended to predominate and it is only in a handful of innovative schools that alternative 'radical' conceptions of comprehensive education have found their way into the organization of teaching and learning. Apart from a brief and heady period of educational optimism between 1965 and 1970 the 'radical' conceptions of comprehensive schooling have found only limited support or encouragement either inside schools or from outside groups and agencies. Certainly the late 1960s did provide an innovative gap for newly established comprehensive schools to experiment with new pedagogies and new forms of knowledge. Indeed few subjects were not affected in one way or another by the need that was felt to re-examine the curriculum and teaching practices. Group work, integrated studies and discovery learning, along with many other 'progressive' educational innovations were, for a short time at least, on the educational agenda in many of the new schools. And some schools began to experiment with the possibilities of mixed-ability grouping, a form of organization which was seen by many teachers as being in line with the spirit of comprehensive education and greater equality of opportunity. Also, as the raising of the school leaving age was anticipated, with dire warnings of disastrous consequences emanating from some newspapers and teacher union conferences, the new possibilities of Mode III examining were taken up on a large scale for the first time (see Whitty, 1983).

However, the CCCS (1981) review of educational policy in the 1960s makes it clear that the 'noise' of educational reform was often not necessarily matched by 'real' changes in educational practices (see Goodson in this volume.) They also argue that while 'There was a distinctive social democratic "moment" in the formulation of policy', in the 1960s, 'it was always caught within sharp limits' (p. 111). And they highlight the incoherent nature of the policies and reforms being advanced in this period, which were 'uneasily adjacent, often incompatible and held loosely together by ambiguous key terms' (p. 106). Their conclusion on the 1960s is that while the implementation of circular 10/65 'encouraged a national movement towards comprehensives ... the meaning of the movement was never in any way radical' (p. 129). Indeed one simple point that puts the 'radical' period of the 1960s into perspective, as regards both the changes being attempted in schools and the subsequent conservative backlash, is that when the Conservative government assumed office in 1970 still only 10 per cent of secondary age children were in fully comprehensive schools (that is, in schools which were not being creamed by grammars, and which were not redesignated secondary moderns). In summing up this first stage of reform of secondary education the CCCS group suggests that 'Comprehensive schools did remove forms of separation to some degree; they did allow a greater autonomy of teachers and pupils. Yet they were not encouragd even to begin to implement stronger definitions of equality, nor was the public support for them secured' (p. 129). In general terms this summary can hardly be disputed but like all generalizations it does do some injustice to the truth. There are a few schools and a few LEAs where the stronger definitions of equality have been and continue to be taken seriously. Recent initiatives in the Inner London Education Authority certainly provide one example. The ILEA has committed itself to improve the performance of girls, working class children and children from the ethnic minorities in order to eradicate 'gross inequalities of outcome'. A new Equal Opportunities Unit is to be set up, although an authority spokesperson has been willing to recognize that 'there are many teachers [who] feel that they have little time or energy to undertake major initiatives of this kind' (Frances Morrell, ILEA school conference). At the same time the ILEA is engaged in a major review of the comprehensive curriculum, an exercise being carried out by a committee chaired by David Hargreaves.

A Crisis of Confidence

The beginning of the end of the period of optimism, the 'moment' of educational innovation, of 'radical' potential for the comprehensive school, may be seen to be marked neatly and symbolically by the publication in 1969 of the first Black Paper, *Fight for Education* (Cox and Dyson, 1969). While this pamphlet was dominated by concerns about the 'collapse of community' in higher education, following the events of 1968, it contained the first of a series of trenchant attacks on the idea of comprehensive education, egalitarianism and 'progressive teaching methods'. These attacks were articulated through a number of basic themes which were to be echoed and reinforced in the remaining Black Papers and which were quickly taken up in the press and later by television (and more recently by the Social Affairs Unit). Three themes were to the forefront in these attacks: 'declining standards of education', 'political indoctrination' and 'classroom violence and pupil delinquency'. In the same way that advocates of comprehensive education were pointing to the achievements of comprehensive reform and confusing 'noise' with change, the opponents of the comprehensive school saw these schools as being responsible for a fundamental redefinition of the educational process. It was asserted that 'ideologically the comprehensive school represents a socialist society in miniature' and that reorganization was associated with 'fanatical egalitarianism'. Angus Maude, writing in the 1969 Black Paper, saw 'the egalitarian' as decrying 'the importance of academic standards and discipline — and indeed of learning itself. He will advocate a variety of "new teaching methods", which in fact absolve anyone from teaching and anyone from having to learn' (p. 7). In the same paper, R.R. Pedley (headmaster of St. Dunstans College) asserted that 'The move to the establishment of total comprehensivization seems to be part of that sinister attack on excellence' (p. 47). In the 1975 Paper (Cox and Boyson, 1975), G. Kenneth Green (Schools Council Field Officer and ex-comprehensive headmaster) wrote:

> In terms of reorganization, too much has been attempted too fast in a context of threatening imposition from some education committees and, from time to time, from central government. Too little evaluation of what has been done has taken place and we are stumbling along blindly, hopefully, leaving chaos and confusion behind us. (p. 26)

He went on to portray comprehensives as beset by rampant indiscipline and truancy and achieving poor educational standards. Ironically he sees these problems as stemming, in part at least, from the lack of an 'academic top' in most comprehensives, the parents of the 'academic children' having retreated into private schooling; 'the flight from the reorganized, maintained sector has not only begun, it is becoming a flood' (p. 25). The Black Papers set out an agenda for educational debate which was to run throughout the 1970s, but which had little or no substantial relationship to the realities of comprehensive schooling (Wright, 1976).

By the early 1970s, fuelled by press and television 'horror stories', the level of 'public concern' about the state of the nation's schooling had reached the level of a moral panic. And the events concerning William Tyndale school provided a central focus in the backlash against 'progressive' teaching methods and underlined once again the major themes of 'the Conservative education offensive' (CCCS, 1981) — standards, discipline and the political motivations of teachers. Tyndale 'offered "progressive" teachers who were at best "sincere but misguided" and at worst "dangerous" and "politically motivated", parents who were kept out of school decisions and managers and inspectors who were failing in their statutory duties' (CCCS, 1981, p. 195). William Tyndale also demonstrated clearly for the first time, through the activities of local Labour activists, that 'radical' attempts at a reformulation of teaching and learning in schools were unlikely to gain support from a Labour Party still committed to a view of comprehensive schools as, in Harold Wilson's phrase, 'grammar schools for all'.

More specifically, newspaper and television coverage of educational matters began to associate 'progressive' methods of various kinds with allegations of declining standards in reading among schoolchildren and increasing numbers of illiterate school leavers. As early as 1968 Dolores Moore was writing in *The Daily Mail* (28 October):

> Read the numbers, published now and then, of illiterate school leavers each year. Notice at an open-day, just how few seven-year-olds, and even eleven-year-olds, can actually write and spell correctly. Look at the standard of reading books. It is generally low. Sometimes very low. Yet more money is spent each year on educating our children.

Further ammunition was provided for the attack on 'progressive' methods in 1972 when an NFER report was published which seemed to indicate a measurable decline in reading standards in the late 1960s, among certain groups of children (Start and Wells, 1972). The public furore which ensued led the Secretary of State for Education, Margaret Thatcher, to respond by setting up a Committee of Inquiry, chaired by Sir Alan Bullock. 'to consider in relation to schools all aspects of teaching the use of English, including reading, writing and speech'. But when the findings of the Bullock Committee, *A Language For Life*, were published in 1975, *The Daily Mail* at least remained unconvinced, with an attempt at comic irony it commented: 'WHITEWASH spells whitewash. Sir Alan Bullock's report on the teaching of English shrouds the reality in trendy pieties' (19 February).

Throughout this period further Black Papers were published at regular intervals, and out of this apparently uncoordinated series of attacks, critiques and diatribes, an ideological rationale began to emerge which would provide the basis for Conservative Party education policy in the 1980s. Many of the populist proposals being tested out in the DES under Keith Joseph and Rhodes Boyson (voucher schemes, student loans, teacher accountability, and the assisted places scheme) first found an airing in the pages of the Black Papers. But in the first instance it was the Labour Party which attempted to cash in on the public disenchantment with the 'state' of education and 'to steal the clothes of the Conservatives' with 'the creation and agenda of the Great Debate on education' (Dale, 1983, p. 243). The main platform of the Labour Party initiative was set out in Prime Minister Callaghan's Ruskin College speech and Shirley Williams' DES Green Paper *Education in Schools* (1977). The main argument was that comprehensive schools (and colleges and universities) had failed to take adequate account, and service the needs, of British industry. It was claimed that 'the cultural ethos of Britain's schools had contributed to the decline of the industrial spirit' (Beck, 1983, p. 225).

In the forefront of the debate which followed was an emphasis on the need to make schools and teachers more accountable. A prime role in the discussion about the future direction of education policy was given to industrialists who had been dissatisfied with 'the products' that the schools system had been turning out. Beck, in looking back at the outcomes of the Great Debate, charges that 'Perhaps the most damaging educational legacy of the Callaghan Government's policy of linking education to industrial regeneration was the legitimacy it gave to forms of educational practice which substitute political socialization for evidential education' (1983, p. 229). In the background to the Great Debate other changes were set in train which were in time to have a major impact on the balance of control over the education system, in particular a significant shift in the role of the DES and HMI in relation to the school curriculum. For the first time since the 1920s the DES began to assume a role of direct intervention in curriculum decision-making. More specifically, a curriculum review was initiated (DES, 1978), the role of the Assessment of Performance Unit (set up by Mrs Thatcher) was altered and expanded, the Department of Industry's Industry/Education Unit was set up and changes were instituted in the constitution of the Schools Council which had the effect of reducing the influence of the teacher representatives and increasing that of the DES and LEA representatives. All these initiatives in their different ways provided à framework for the implementation of the Conservatives' 'radical' education policies when they returned to office in 1979. The Great Debate also had the effect of giving government legitimation to the media-based campaigns aimed at the comprehensive schools and it crucially undermined the already waning confidence of parents in their children's teachers. (This lack of confidence in teachers is now being fully exploited in moves to establish closer centralized control over teacher certification.) The teaching profession was placed firmly on the defensive. More tentatively, it could be argued that The Great Debate and its aftermath provided legitimation for the education cuts which were soon to come.

A Crisis of Cuts

According to Donald (1979), the Green Paper of 1977 set in train a process of redefinition and restructuring of the education system which was to fit education into 'new patterns of state expenditure'. Schools were to become subject to the same 'market forces' that were affecting industry and of necessity they were to become accountable to the economic requirements of the social system. 'The financial constraints are portrayed as the inevitable consequence of "market forces" and the "natural" consequence of a failure to "live within our means". Schools must therefore take a "share" of the "cuts" and teachers must work harder and to better effect' (Wallace, Miller and Ginsberg, 1983, p. 113). Schools were to be expected to be more efficient and the allocation of finance in education to be more closely tied to specific policies. The low ebb of parental confidence in state schooling combined with the coincidental decline in school rolls in many parts of the country provided exactly the sort of 'slack' in the system which allowed the Conservative government to extend its policy of cutting public expenditure into the previously privileged arena of spending on education. This was achieved for the most part through cuts in the monies paid to local authorities by central government, specifically cuts in the rate support grant (see Hunter, in this volume). The 'savings' (as they are known) were to be decided upon and implemented by the LEAs concerned, although given that by far the largest proportion of recurrent expenditure for any authority consists of teachers' salaries, it was in this budget that the bulk of 'savings' had to be sought. Thus, the

HMI report, *On the Effects on the Education Service in England of Local Authority Expenditure Policies — Financial Year 1980–81*, presented findings which recorded, in nine-tenths of the LEAs surveyed, that 'there was an overall reduction in teacher numbers in November 1980 as compared with November 1979 that in total amounted nationally to just over 10,000 full-time equivalent posts after allowing for those LEAs where there were small increases in numbers' (p. 2)

The widespread fall in the school population meant that posts were being lost without significant worsening of teacher-pupil ratios. But the report notes that 'The overall picture is of a stricter application of teacher staffing formulae than in 1979, with, on balance a marginal bettering of ratios in primary schools and a marginal worsening in secondary schools' (p. 3). These aggregate figures obscure the vast range of effects that resulted from schemes of natural wastage, early retirement, voluntary and compulsory redeployment and in some cases redundancy (some of these effects are discussed in the papers in this volume, those by Sikes, Hunter and Ball in particular). Cuts were also made in the funds available for book and materials provision, school trips and visits, painting and maintenance of buildings, support facilities and staff (for example, the school psychological service, the school meals service, provision of auxiliaries and peripatetic teachers) and attempts were made to increase the range of activities (swimming and music tuition for example,) for which parents were expected to pay. In-service training and secondments for teachers were also cut and schemes for the induction of probationary teachers were run down and the HMIs found a reduction in advisory services in just over one third of the authorities surveyed. The Report also draws attention to two other factors that cannot be estimated in quantitative terms but which are nonetheless vital to the standard of education being offered in schools. First,

> In their visits to institutions the HMIs' strong impression is of professional commitment and resourcefulness. Nevertheless there is evidence that teachers' morale has been adversely affected in many schools. Its weakening, if it became widespread, would pose a major problem in the effort to maintain present standards, let alone improve them. (p. 13)

Several papers in this volume address this issue. Second,

> Most of the above comments relate to effects in terms of the maintenance of school provision as it now exists. They need to

> be considered also in relation to the likely capacity of teaching staff and advisers to engage in that reappraisal of the curriculum, development of an improved system of assessment and of appropriate public examinations, and response to changing educational needs which are widely recognised as desirable. (p. 13)

In effect the autonomous process of development within the comprehensive school was brought to an end. From this point on it was the task of comprehensive teachers to respond to the increased demands being made directly or indirectly from the DES, with special funding being provided for schemes seen as relevant to national needs and priorities, for example the Department of Industry scheme to get a computer into every school. In the period from the initiation of the Great Debate in 1977 to the arrival at the DES of Sir Keith Joseph, the whole relationship between schools and their various 'client-audiences' — parents, local authorities and the DES — had undergone a vital shift.[1]

The Minister Intervenes

A major element in this shift has been the steady and deliberate reassertion of an active role, in matters of school curriculum, by HMI and other officials and units in the DES, and the Secretaries of State for Education which has resulted in a much closer specification of the comprehensive school curriculum. To a great extent this process of reassertion has been clouded by contradictory statements and marked by an emphasis on indirect influence rather than, with some exceptions, direct action. It is a process which is by no means easy to interpret. Referring to the period between 1974 and 1979, Lawton (1980, p. 50) argues that a 'major characteristic of the DES was a tendency to operate by stealth rather than by open discussion of policy and policy changes'. (An alternative interpretation would be opportunism rather than stealth.)

One of the clearest examples of this 'change by stealth' is the development of the Assessment of Performance Unit. The setting up of the APU was announced in 1974 in relation to an original concern with the problems of the educationally disadvantaged. By 1976 it was being described in the DES Yellow Book as a small group under the leadership of a staff inspector with access to the department's research budget. The concerns were now identified as following up the Bullock Report work on the testing of reading and the development of mathematical aptitude testing. The 1978 pamphlet *APU: An Introduction* provided an altogether much broader definition of the Unit's role.

> The last ten years have seen changes in school organization and curriculum. We need to be able to monitor the consequences for children's performance in school. We need to know how our schools are serving the changing needs of children and society. This is why the Department of Education and Science set up the APU.

Thus far the work of the APU has not, as some commentators feared, become a matter of laying down national standards for pupils' achievement across a range of subjects.[2] However, Lawton clearly sees the approach of the APU, and its reliance on testing, as anachronistic and possibly dangerous in terms of its 'backwash effects'.

> ... having moved away from the Scylla of *laissez-faire* the DES show no sign of possessing an adequate theoretical base for curriculum change and is in danger of getting too close to the Charybdis of behaviouristic, mechanistic approaches to curriculum and evaluation. (1980, p. 48)

In the popular phrase of the late 1970s the DES (the HMI and the Secretaries of State) were seeking to walk once more in 'the secret garden of the curriculum', to break the teachers' monopoly of curriculum control (always assuming that such control existed in the first place). In a speech to local education officials in 1977, the senior chief HMI, Sheila Browne, explained the official view of the work of the Inspectorate in the following terms:

> At this stage I would merely say that, by right and by obligation, the HMI does walk in the secret garden of the curriculum and passes comment on it: but, contrary to the assertions of some critics — critics that is, of either the garden of the curriculum or of the inspectorate — he does not personally plan it or plant it, still less strew it with weeds.

The 1977 Green Paper, *Education in Schools*, set out an essentially similar view of the role of the Secretaries of State:

> It would not be compatible with the duty of the Secretaries of State to 'promote the education of the people of England and Wales', or with their accountability to parliament, to abdicate

> from leadership on educational issues which have become a matter of lively public concern. The Secretaries of State will therefore seek to establish a broad agreement with their partners in the education service on a frame-work for the curriculum, and particularly, on whether, because there are aims common to all schools and to all pupils at certain stages, there should be a 'core' or 'protected part'. (para 2.19)

The main issues at this point were the question of a common curriculum and more broadly the accountability of schools. The aim was to establish a common, agreed core curriculum in all secondary schools, at the same time opening up the schools to greater community influence, the concern of the Taylor Report. The work of the Inspectorate reflects both these issues but also indicates a more general attempt to identify a set of 'concerns' about school practice and establish examples of 'good' and 'bad' practice. One indication of the change of emphasis in the HMI came with the reorganization of the Inspectorate in 1977 which involved withdrawing about one quarter of the locally assigned inspectors for work at the centre on national studies and surveys. In a letter to Chief Education Officers, Sheila Browne explained that 'We have decided that a proportion of the Inspectorate will be made answerable primarily to the centre and will not be available for territorial assignment in a general or specialist capacity'.[3] Also in 1977, Circular 14/77 announced a review of existing LEA arrangements for the school curriculum, involving LEA officers directly in a process of curriculum review in schools.

Another of the manifestations of the more active HMI role has been the publication, beginning in 1977, of a series of *Surveys* and *Matters for Discussion*. The *Matters* series began with the pamphlet *Ten Good Schools: A Secondary School Inquiry*, and most recently produced *The New Teacher in School*. For the most part these documents are carefully and moderately worded commentaries on observed practice with occasional bursts of forthrightness. The sixth pamphlet on *Mixed Ability Work in Comprehensive Schools* is arguably the most critical in tone. Indeed *The Times Educational Supplement* dealt with the initial circulation of the paper under the headline 'Inspectors wade into mixed ability'. And in the sections on mathematics, science and languages there is little encouragement for teachers attempting mixed ability in these subjects. The language group reported that 'There seem to be no grounds for believing that mixed-ability grouping can offer an advantage to the modern language class even in the hands of an able teacher;

in the hands of those less skilled or experienced it can have positively harmful effects' (p. 118) The science group found 'In numerous cases ... that in the early years able pupils are underachieving (for example in quality and range of writing as well as in their grasp of concepts)', and forecast that 'With present levels of expertise there may be a serious decline in standards and progress if mixed ability science extends beyond the second year' (p. 139).

The actual effects of such statements are impossible to measure but clearly 'authoritative' reporting of this kind is likely to make itself felt in debates going on in schools about methods of grouping and to provide backing, in this case, for those who oppose mixed-ability grouping. The recent pamphlet *The New Teacher in School* has had more concrete outcomes, laying as it did the groundwork for the White Paper on 'Teaching Quality'. The HMI pamphlet based on the observation, for two lessons each, of 294 probationary teachers (by 130 HMIs) found that some 25 per cent lacked adequate mastery of basic teaching techniques. (It should be noted that the evidential basis of this and other HMI surveys has come in for considerable criticism). The publication of these 'findings' again provided some powerful material for newspaper headlines. *The Times* reported 'Too many teachers lack skills for the job, school inspectors say', *The Guardian* that 'School Inspectors report on new teachers says they lack training and temperament', while the *TES* reported 'one in four poorly equipped for the job' and went on to say 'HMI blames teacher training for not weeding out weak students'. Here then there are two targets under attack, not only the technically deficient teachers but also the institutions of teacher training which had prepared them inadequately. This leads on 'naturally' in the White Paper to guidelines for new forms of training, for the DES approval of training courses, and for HMI inspection of university education departments.[4] The White Paper also provides a vehicle for underlining the principle of specialist subject training for secondary teachers and introducing age specialist training for primary teachers. It is also clear that the Secretary of State hopes to proscribe certain subjects as being inappropriate as background for teaching — for example sociology.

Finally, and briefly, in examining the influences on comprehensive curriculum it is important to mention the change in control of and eventual disbanding of the Schools Council. Again the Labour government provided the first move, wresting control of the Council from the teacher unions by revising the constitution, and giving effective leadership to the LEA and DES representatives. The Conservative opposition to and distrust of the Council was already well established and Rhodes Boyson's oft quoted 'fulmination' is worth recalling again. 'My objection [to the work of the Schools Council] is root and branch. It includes the humanities programme of Mr. Stenhouse [HCP]. Not many people are neutral about that programme, although the teacher in charge of it was supposed to be neutral' (Hansard, 21 July 1976). In April 1982 Keith Joseph wrote to the acting chairman to inform him of the decision to disband the Council. Colin Lacey, research director of the Council (1975–79) commented that: 'It is clear that the weakening of the Council and the now fractured coalition between the teacher unions and local authorities had allowed the Black Paper educationalists in Government and the DES to produce a new winning coalition. Central coordination and direction are the issues on which they agree' (1983, p. 15).

Despite the innovatory work done by the Schools Council and the curriculum developments attempted in the schools themselves (or it might be said, because of it) and irrespective of attempts, by Conservative or Labour governments, at political intervention, the 'deep structures' of the comprehensive school curriculum continue to reflect the basic assumptions of the tripartite system. Forms of streaming, banding and setting in the schools reflect and maintain a hierarchy of status among subjects and courses. Those high status subjects and courses which provide access to higher education derive from the traditional academic grammar school curriculum and are reserved for pupils whose 'success' at school has shown them worthy. Practical or vocational subjects and the new Mode III CSE courses which breach the strong divide between academic knowledge and the 'action' knowledge of everyday life, are low status. They are reserved for those pupils who have failed in the traditional curriculum. These assumptions are conveyed clearly to the pupils in the implicit message systems of school organization.

> The hidden curriculum of the formal curriculum transmits a message that schooling is principally ordered around a particular constellation of knowledge, skills and abilities, the intellectual-cognitive domain of propositional knowledge, which constitutes the central content of the main school subjects and which is assessed in public examinations. Other forms of knowledge, skill and ability are not by any means always ignored or excluded, but they are accorded a secondary position and are therefore less important. (Hargreaves 1982, p. 59)

Current Trends and Future Prospects

Despite the increasing level of state intervention perhaps the greatest threat to the continued development of comprehensive education in Britain lies not in attempts to redefine or circumscribe the comprehensive school curriculum or the practices of teachers but rather in the restructuring work begun by the Conservative government of 1979–83. The assisted places scheme on the one hand and the Manpower Services Commission pilot schemes for education and training packages, including work experience, for 14 to 18-year-olds, on the other, may be seen as a move back towards a form of tripartite schooling. The assisted places scheme, aimed at identifying and sponsoring academically gifted working class pupils — whether these are the pupils who actually get on the scheme is another matter — both serves to reinforce and revitalize the private school system and to impoverish the comprehensive system by reducing further, admittedly on a small scale, the range of pupils in the state schools. Also in terms of measures of academic achievement the odds are weighted more heavily still against the comprehensive system. The comprehensive schools have been indited and attacked at regular intervals since the late 1960s for producing poor academic results while being compared with grammar schools and private schools which cream off from the comprehensives the academically most able pupils. It seems likely that the transfer of examination passes, through the assisted places scheme, from the comprehensive schools to the private sector will be used in the future as a further indicator of the failure of the comprehensives to measure up to the attainments of their unequal rivals.

At the other end of the scale the MSC training schemes mark the first stage in a separation of training from education, for Keith Joseph's 'bottom 40 per cent', and the creation of a separate group of 'worker-pupils'. According to the DES this scheme is intended 'to stimulate technical and vocational education for 14 to 18-year-olds as part of a drive to improve our performance in the development of new skills and technology'. The *Times Higher Education Supplement*, anticipating many of the subsequent criticisms, noted that: 'The danger of Mr Tebbit's proposal is that some 14-year-olds would receive an impoverished education which left them with inadequate skills to achieve the social autonomy that is their right as citizens and the economic adaptability, that is their duty, and safeguard, as workers' (19 November, 1982). In the event, in a situation of scarce resources in schools and increasing problems of motivation and commitment among pupils facing up to the prospect of unemployment there has been no shortage of applicants for inclusion in the pilot scheme. This is a further illustration of the way in which funding is being attached to specific educational policies and schools are losing autonomy in their curriculum planning.[5] It may be that some loss of autonomy is inevitable if a response by schools to technological and industrial changes in society is to be achieved. The important issue ultimately is perhaps not centralization itself but the concerns, values and motives of those who control the centre (as the Swedish case illustrates very well).

It is also important to place this initiative in the context of earlier debate within the MSC and the DES about the purposes and scope of vocational training and preparation. The CCCS (1981) noted that earlier schemes laid great emphasis on the necessity of fitting young people into the established social relations of production and 'concentrated not on technical competences but on the moulding of worker initiative' (p. 236). And again it is suggested by the CCCS that the development of the MSC is further indication of 'Labour's particular appropriation of a part of the new right's agenda' (p. 238). In these earlier schemes (WEEP, YOPS, TES, etc.) a paradigm for a 'new model of capitalist training was visibly on offer' (p. 238). The possibilities of this new model are now to be extended into the arena of schooling.[6]

Alongside these developments we may note Sir Keith Joseph's refusal to approve reorganization schemes, such as those put forward by Croydon and Manchester, which attempt to establish, via a tertiary college structure, the 'logical' extension of the comprehensive principle to the 16–19 age group (Edwards, 1983). 'Study' and 'work' are to remain separated here also and the elitist, academic conception of 'the sixth form' is to be preserved.

To an increasing extent the government is involving itself in the management of the school-work transition (and to some degree in the transition from further and higher education into work). As a result the articulation between school and the labour market and the preparation of pupils for work is becoming more closely defined. And within this closer relationship of school and work 'there is an age segregation effect which feeds back on the attitudes and expectations of young people' (Williamson, 1983, p. 152). The outcomes and full effects of the assisted places and work training schemes remain to be seen and the development of the latter beyond the pilot stage is unclear at this time. What is clear is that selection in secondary education and the differentiation of routes through schooling are being firmly re-established in the structure of educational provision, as Dale (1983) points out:

> Thatcherism is very much in favour of selectiveness, of allowing the natural differences between people to grow, both as a reward to the talented and successful, the intellectually and morally deserving, and as a spur to the less well endowed, successful or responsible, to make the most of what we have. (p. 249)

In general policy terms the theory of 'human capital development' which fuelled the expansionary period of the 1960s (by positing a general relationship between education, the development of human skills and productivity, and economic growth) has been superseded by a commitment to a much more careful 'manpower planning' theory which views the education system as the provider of specifically trained personnel (matched by level of education and in numbers, to the particular needs of the economy). Thus Dale again makes the point that 'Thatcherite education policy might be seen as not so much anti-statist, as anti-universalist and anti-social democratic. While the state is to be rolled back — or at least cut back — that is to be done selectively' (p. 249).

If the comprehensive school system has any future that future now lies, more than ever, in the hands of those who work in the schools. The system itself is under attack and teachers find themselves confronted by politicians, employers, parents and pupils who are, in different ways dissatisfied with the existing forms of educational provision. This provides a situation in schools where a thorough-going reappraisal of existing practices is urgently required. The process and outcomes of this rethinking could provide a new impetus, despite intervention, for a creative response to changing economic and technological conditions. If the challenge for the comprehensive school, as Hargreaves calls it, is not taken up inside the schools then increased centralization and state control of education may be inevitable.

Case Studies of Comprehensive Schooling

It is easy to overdo the rhetoric of *crisis* in contemporary educational discussion, to emphasize all the negative factors, bad signs and problematic issues and to ignore the successes, the continuity of routine and the mundane 'dailiness' of teaching that constitute the reality of comprehensive schooling. It might be argued that my discussion has fallen into that trap. The long term intentions of the present government are still unclear, the contradictions inherent in the DES attitudes to comprehensive education practice are evidenced in the range of publications which they address to teachers, the role of the APU has not turned out to be as sinister as was first thought, and the interventions of the MSC are supposedly short term. But it is difficult to sustain a view that all is well in comprehensive schools or that the issues and problems identified above are not beginning to percolate down into and affect the classroom work of the average teacher. The relationship of schools and teachers to their local authority, and the DES, has changed; the relationship of the LEAs to central government has changed; the relationships, formal and informal, between teachers and parents have changed; the attitude of certain sections of the press is aggressive towards comprehensive schooling and progressive practice wherever it may be found, and the attitude of teachers is defensive.

The question mark in the title of this introduction is intentional, the evidence which would allow a clear cut answer is probably as yet inadequate but it is against the background outlined above that the papers in this volume need to be set. In each of the papers the particular issue addressed is examined using case study materials. As a whole the volume attempts to move beyond the existing debate about comprehensive education, which is so often conducted in terms of the empty rhetorics of entrenched proponents and opponents. It is important that debate becomes more clearly focused on the actual processes and problems of comprehensive schooling. In this way issues may be removed from the arena of abstract speculation, which so often leads to trivializing and the ritual quotation of extreme or atypical examples. We are concerned here with the day-to-day work and experiences of pupils and teachers in a range of ordinary schools. The case study materials in each paper draw upon recent research carried out through the direct involvement of the writers in the schools they studied. (In most cases the papers concentrate on one school, but Denscombe, Sikes, and Davies and Evans each use two case studies for between-school comparisons, Hunter takes one local authority as his case and Goodson presents the case of one subject.) The schools themselves represent a cross-section of types of comprehensive — some well-established, others just beginning to become comprehensive, inner-city and suburban, purpose-built and split-site, LEA and church-controlled, mono and multi-racial, and innovative and conservative. A variety of settings in England are also represented: the North, the North-east, badly hit by unemployment, the Midlands, London, the South-west and a new town in the South-east.

The first five papers are concerned with aspects of comprehensive schooling as experienced from the pupils' point of view. The paper by Measor and Woods examines the process of transition from middle to secondary school, and follows one group of pupils from their last term in a middle school through to their third term in a comprehensive. The fears and anxieties which accompany this move are vividly captured, as are the processes for coping which the pupils evolve. Coping with transfer means coming to grips not only with the formal demands of the school but also with the informal demands of the peer group culture. Status and friendships are crucially dependent on achieving a careful balance between the formal and the informal. Coping is also intimately related to patterns of work and behaviour that pupils display in the classroom as teachers and subjects are evaluated and 'tested out'. The first year in the comprehensive school is very much a period of establishing and sorting out identities; the processes of differentiation which are crucial to the long-term school careers of pupils are begun here. Deviant and conformist, male and female and 'thick' and 'brainy' are crucially divided off from one another as stable friendships groups are formed. Even in the first few weeks of the secondary school the interaction between the formal demands of the institution and the informal processes of the peer group is beginning to produce a firm academic and behavioural separation among the pupils.[7]

Davies' paper takes up two aspects of those separations, those based upon gender and upon behaviour. Specifically she presents an analysis of the 'identity work' done by deviant girls in a mixed-comprehensive. Reputations are shown to arise from the interplay between the institutional interpretations of behaviour and personality and the range of preferred styles, postures and responses which the girls explore. Davies is anxious to demonstrate the ways in which deviant girls are able to experiment with a variety of personal reactions to school life and are not the powerless victims of sex-typing as they are sometimes portrayed. She also argues for the need for analyses of gender in school to recognize the fundamental relational nature of femininity and masculinity and the social class differences that are inherent in these concepts.

In some ways Yates is making a similar point about the relational nature of identities in his exploration of inter-ethnic images in a New Town comprehensive. He examines the mutual ignorance which white teachers and pupils and Asian parents and pupils have of the culture of the other group. In some cases the white stereotypes of Asian culture lead to forms of personal and institutional racism, in other ways both the white and Asian communities simply misjudge and misunderstand the values and behaviour of the other group. Yates' study shows both aspects, racism and misunderstanding, at work in the school — in the staffroom, the classroom and the playground.

Buswell's material draws upon work done in a north-eastern comprehensive sixth form; she plots the impact upon the school regime and teacher-pupil relationships of the increased number of pupils staying on in the sixth form as an alternative to unemployment. At the heart of the changes she describes is a process of increased bureaucratization within the school, which once again is linked to the separation between pupils (and teachers) by gender and status. Teachers are very aware of the increased numbers of pupils in the sixth form who are not doing A level examination courses and the sixth form careers of A level and non-A level as well as male and female pupils are perceived and constructed by their teachers in significantly different ways. The reactions and adaptations of the A levellers and non-A levellers to work, and their relationships with their teachers, are also clearly very different. The A level pupils find that life in the sixth form fails in many respects to live up to their expectations.

Finally in this first group of papers, Miles takes us to another critical point of transition for pupils, that from school to work. Several of the themes and issues raised in previous papers are picked up once again. Miles' work focuses on the job aspirations of, and employment opportunities available to, groups of Asian girls nearing the end of their school careers. Many of the common assumptions about the views and concerns of Asian women are shown to be inapplicable to these girls, who, almost without exception, have hopes of establishing themselves in careers. The levels of unemployment among female Asian school leavers however, suggests that the majority will be disappointed. The girls are caught in a mesh of sexism, racism and ageism, being poorly perceived both by prospective employers and their own teachers. They seem ill-prepared by their school for the realities of the job market; the transition to work which they hope will enable them to get a better job than those of their mothers is in fact tinged with disillusion and despair.

The next group of three papers is addressed to teaching and curriculum issues. Denscombe's paper is a response to controversies over the extent of violence and disruption in the comprehensive school classroom. Through a careful examination of available evidence he rebuts the newspaper picture of a crisis of control in the secondary school. In contrast to the 'popular myth' of widespread violence occurring daily, it would seem that attacks on teachers and other major incidents of this kind are rare. Furthermore, teachers themselves are primarily concerned not with the likelihood of major confrontations with pupils but rather with the mundane problems of misbehaviour in their classrooms. Drawing on data from two London comprehensives, Denscombe illustrates the kinds of disruption which are 'normal' on a day-to-day basis, in the process of classroom management. He also examines the ways in which this 'normal' disruption is dealt with by the teachers, and the systems of pastoral care which give them support. But teachers are shown to be under considerable pressure not to call upon outside support to maintain control in their classroom. By 'referring' pupils to the pastoral staff, teachers risk being dubbed as incompetent by their colleagues. While problems of control have been wildly exaggerated by press reports they do emerge in more mundane forms as a major institutional concern in the comprehensive school.

In recent years another area of comprehensive schooling to have received a uniformly bad press is mixed ability grouping. But as Davies and Evans point out in their paper here, again the media have tended to misrepresent and radically over-estimate the extent of mixed ability within the comprehensive system: 'in crude national terms, the whole curriculum, mixed ability secondary experience has never touched more than a third of our pupils at 11+ entry'. The whole mixed ability issue seems to be massively misunderstood. While in the minds of its opponents it is associated with rampant egalitarian idealism, the motives expressed by practitioners for 'going mixed ability' tend to be related either to the technical problems of pupil transfer or to attempts to eradicate the disciplinary problems associated with streaming. The major issue thrown up by mixed ability is not so much its adoption as a way of grouping pupils but rather its implementation as a system of teaching them. In the two London schools described by Davies and Evans, the practice of mixed ability teaching is both hedged in by fears about the academic performance of the 'more able child' and lacking in any coherent classroom pedagogy. The stock response of some kind of individualized worksheet system seems to do little more than replace one set of learning and management problems with another, equally poorly understood, set. Davies and Evans suggest that in those schools where areas of mixed ability grouping have been abandoned we are witnessing 'an acceptance of pedagogical failure'.

In the third paper in this group Goodson examines the 'curriculum history' of one school subject — rural studies. He uses this history to raise important issues about the nature and origins of the comprehensive curriculum. Rural studies emerged and developed as an elementary/secondary modern subject *par excellence* — practical, applied and even vocationally oriented, but also non-literate and unexamined. In the era of comprehensive reorganization these attributes have proved to be a major stumbling block to the spread of the subject; indeed it appeared at one time as though rural studies faced total extinction. Only by a radical recasting of the subject as an examinable 'academic' discipline, renamed as environmental studies, was survival guaranteed. But the question that Goodson asks is 'survival at what cost?'. Rural studies was forced to come to terms with a comprehensive curriculum where status, resources and planning priorities are monopolized by 'academic' subjects whose origins lay in the grammar school. Even with these compromises rural/environmental studies finds itself as a poor relation in a differentiated system, destined to attract the 'less able' pupils who are turned away from the more 'authentic' and more negotiable grammar school subjects. In this differentiation by subject, separation continues to flourish within the comprehensive school.

In the final group of four papers the current problems and travails of the comprehensive school are viewed from the perspective of the teachers. In the first of these Burgess takes us into a crucial but virtually unexplored area of comprehensive schooling, the role of the headteacher. While commentators are unanimous about the importance of the head in determining 'what a school sets out to do and the extent to which it achieves those aims', headteachers have to a great extent avoided the attention of educational researchers. Using case study material from one school and an analysis of further particulars accompanying advertisements for headteacher posts, Burgess attempts both to illustrate the degree of control and definition available to the headteacher in the running of a school and to plot the limits to that control. Increasingly local authority committees and officers are taking decisions which preempt the headteacher's responsibility in matters of curriculum, staffing and resource allocation. The role of the head is now highly problematic and further dramatic changes in headteacher-staff relationships are likely as the 'management revolution' sweeps through our schools. Burgess provides a first step into an area of practice which is in urgent need of attention from school researchers.

My own paper attends primarily to the problems of falling rolls, as experienced by the teachers of a recently created comprehensive school.

This is a deliberate attempt to counterbalance the emphasis given in much recent literature to the management of falling rolls by portraying instead the perspectives of the managed. Redeployments, lack of promotion and lack of staff mobility are shown to have compounding effects on the morale of the teachers and the ethos and structure of the school as it struggles with the task of becoming comprehensive.

The effects of comprehensive reorganization on teachers' careers is taken further in Sikes' paper. In comparing two schools and their very different responses to the process of reorganization, she demonstrates the way in which teacher morale and satisfaction are intimately bound up with the sense of community and degree of participation available to the teachers involved. Reorganization is shown as equally traumatic for grammar and secondary modern school teachers. The degree of trauma experienced is related very much to the extent to which those concerned feel themselves prepared for their new tasks and identified with the new institution. Schools in which there is no agreement about aims and which 'stream' their teachers seem unlikely to produce any sort of adequate response to the demands of comprehensivization.

In the final paper in this group Hunter takes us out of the school to examine recent changes in school-local authority and local authority-central government relationships. He describes the way in which changes in local authority funding have both reduced the funds available for spending on education and created increased constraints upon the financial planning and policy-making of the authorities. Using material from a report drawn up by headteachers in Bradford, the breadth and depth of the impact of spending cuts on the work of schools is displayed — curriculum, staffing, materials, teaching methods, support services, extra-curricular activities and buildings are all affected. The range of central government interventions into schooling and school provision are itemized and Hunter points out that present indications suggest that such intervention is likely to increase.

Notes

1 Clearly, there are some local authorities which continue to pursue policies aimed at achieving greater equality in secondary education. The ILEA, for example, has announced a new Equal Opportunities Unit with teams concerned both with multi-cultural education and race relations, and opportunities for women and girls.
2 So far the APU has produced two *Primary Survey Reports* on 'Language Performance in Schools' and two *Secondary Survey Reports* on the same

topic. The impact of the Reports in the press in no way matches the heat and controversy which accompanied the publication of the original study which seemed to indicate declining standards in reading. In the review of the second secondary survey in the *TES*, it is noted that the Report 'does not support the often-stated contention that many secondary pupils face more fundamental difficulties in reading and understanding written texts' (21 January 1983).

3 Subsequently the balance between locally and centrally attached inspectors has been readjusted.

4 In its meeting in July 1983, the Advisory Committee for the Supply and Education of Teachers (ACSET) recommended the setting up of a National Advisory Council to judge the suitability of courses for the preparation of teachers. This is clearly in line with thinking in the government's White Paper on *Teaching Quality*. The *THES* described the proposed council as 'a new powerful form of central control on all teacher training courses' (22 July 1983).

5 There are parallels to this move to a closer specification of planning priorities in higher education. The 1980 UGC distribution of funds to universities and the 1983 'new blood' appointments scheme are both examples of increased centralized control over university spending.

6 At the annual conference of the Council of Local Education Authorities, in July 1983, the Chairman of the MSC, Mr David Young, announced that the MSC had found extra money for a second round of Technical and Vocational Education Initiative (TVEI) pilot schemes for 14–18 year olds. A number of CLEA members were critical of the ease with which the MSC was able to find finance for its schemes when the local authorities were having to cut back on spending on education. Ms. Ruth Gee of the ILEA is reported as saying: 'You are in fact belying us if you are suggesting that we can work in partnership, because what we have seen in TVEI is a real erosion of our powers and responsibilities'. Mr Young is reported to have denied that MSC had any role in schools, or that the MSC would remain involved in schools in the long term. A resolution was passed at the conference which called upon the government to deny unequivocally any intention of centralizing the education service through the MSC (*THES* 22 July 1983).

7 Here Woods and Measor identify the earliest phases of the processes of polarization and differentiation, which are plotted further up the school by Hargreaves (1967), Lacey (1970) and Ball (1981).

References

BALL, S.J. (1981) *Beachside Comprehensive: A Case Study of Secondary Schooling*, Cambridge, Cambridge University Press.

BECK, J. (1983) 'Accountability, industry and education' in AHIER, J. and M. FLUDE (Eds) *Contemporary Education Policy*, London, Croom Helm.

BENN, C. (1979) 'Elites versus equals: The political background of educational reform' in RUBINSTEIN, D. (Ed) *Education and Equality*, Harmondsworth, Penguin.

BURGESS, R.G. (1983) *Experiencing Comprehensive Education: A Study of Bishop MacGregor School*, London, Methuen.

CENTRE FOR CONTEMPORARY CULTURAL STUDIES (1981) *Unpopular Education*, London, Hutchinson.

COX, C.B. and BOYSON, R. (Eds), *The Black Paper 1975*, London, Dent.

COX, C.B. and DYSON, A.E. (Eds) (1969) *Fight for Education: a Black Paper*, London, The Critical Quarterly Society.

DALE, R. (1983) 'Thatcherism and education' in AHIER, J. and M. FLUDE (Eds) *Contemporary Education Policy*, London, Croom Helm.

DEPARTMENT OF EDUCATION AND SCIENCE (1977) *Education in Schools: A Consultative Document* (Green Paper), Cmnd 6869, London, HMSO.

DEPARTMENT OF EDUCATION AND SCIENCE (1978) *APU: An Introduction*, London, HMSO.

DONALD, J. (1979) 'Green Paper: noise of a crisis', *Screen Education*, 30 (Spring).

EDWARDS, A.D. (1983) 'An elite transformed: Continuity and change in 16–19 educational policy', in AHIER, J. and M. FLUDE (Eds) *Contemporary Education Policy*, London, Croom Helm.

ELLIOTT, J. (1983) 'A curriculum for the study of human affairs: The contribution of Lawrence Stenhouse', *Journal of Curriculum Studies*, 15, 2, pp 105–23.

GREEN, G.K. (1975) 'Why comprehensives fail', in COX, C.B. and R. BOYSON (Eds) op. cit.

HARGREAVES, D.H. (1967) *Social Relations in a Secondary School*, London, Routledge and Kegan Paul.

HARGREAVES, D.H. (1982) *The Challenge for the Comprehensive School*, London, Routledge and Kegan Paul.

HER MAJESTY'S INSPECTORATE (1977) *Ten Good Schools*, London, HMSO.

HER MAJESTY'S INSPECTORATE (1979) *Mixed-ability Work in Comprehensive Schools*, London HMSO.

HER MAJESTY'S INSPECTORATE (1983) *The New Teacher in School*, London, HMSO.

KOGAN, M. (1971) *The Politics of Education*, Harmondsworth, Penguin.

LACEY, C. (1970) *Hightown Grammar*, Manchester, Manchester University Press.

LACEY, C. (1983) 'The Schools Council: An Evaluation from a Research Perspective' Unpub. Faculty Research Paper, Education Area, University of Sussex.

LAWTON, D. (1980) *The Politics of the School Curriculum*, London, Routledge and Kegan Paul

MAUDE, A. (1969) 'The Egalitarian threat', in COX, C.B. and A.E. DYSON (Eds), op. cit.

PARKINSON, M. (1970) *The Labour Party and the Organization of Secondary Education, 1918–65*, London, Routledge and Kegal Paul.

PEDLEY, R.R. (1969) 'Comprehensive disaster', in COX. C.B. and A.E. DYSON (Eds), op. cit.

RUBINSTEIN, D. and SIMON, B. (1969) *The Evolution of the Comprehensive School, 1926–66* London, Routledge and Kegan Paul.

START, K.B. and WELLS, B.K. (1972) *The Trend of Reading Standards*, Windsor, NFER.

VERNON, B. (1982) *Ellen Wilkinson*, London, Croom Helm.

WALLACE, G., MILLER, H. and GINSBURG, M. (1983) 'Teachers' Responses to Cuts' in AHIER, J. and M. FLUDE (Eds) *Contemporary Education Policy*, London, Croom Helm.

WHITTY, G. (1983) 'State policy and school examinations 1976–82' in AHIER, J. and M. FLUDE (Eds) *Contemporary Education Policy*, London, Croom Helm.

WILLIAMSON, B. (1983) 'The peripheralisation of youth in the labour market' in AHIER, J. and M. FLUDE (Eds) *Contemporary Education Policy*, London, Croom Helm.

WRIGHT, N. (1976) *Progress in Schools*, London, Croom Helm.

Coping with Transfer: Pupil Perceptions of the Passage from Middle to Upper School

Lynda Measor and Peter Woods

The Significance of Pupil Transfer

Transition between schools has become, arguably, for most pupils a more common experience than settled state within any one educational institution. With first, middle and upper schools, and sixth form colleges in many areas, there are now two or three major breaks in the pupil career where formerly under the tripartite system there was one. In addition, within internally differentiated upper schools, the ages of 14 and 16 have become increasingly significant transition points. Since the prospect and effects of transfer reach forward and back in time, the pupil career has become increasingly characterized by change, and has made increasing demands on the pupil's powers of adaptation.

Among these transitions, none is more traumatic and consequential than that which takes place at age 11 or 12. It is an emphatic break, involving for the most part new tasks, new teachers, new forms of school organization and learning, a new curriculum and new cultures. It also marks an advance from 'primary' to 'secondary', with all that that implies in terms of the quality and status of one's work and one's self, and of the implications for future career. The transition therefore is crucial, and how pupils cope with it is critical for some of the professed aims of comprehensivization. Are social inequalities to be modified, as the rhetoric would suggest? Are pupils to be more socially integrated? Are educational opportunities to be afforded and experienced on a more equal footing? Are pupils to be won over to the comprehensive ethos, with a clear commitment to school? Are they to engage with the curriculum in a free and equal manner?

It is also critical for pupils' own powers of coping. For pupils do not arrive at comprehensive school as 'blank cheques'. They have their own interests, some in accord with teacher aims, some not. How, then, do they adapt to these new demands? Not all will take them in their stride. In fact, it is almost certain that the majority will have to compromise in some way. They will have to juggle their interests and negotiate with teachers, in their attempts to find a form of adaptation that maximizes both their own and the teachers' interests. We know little about the process of initial adaptation and the factors bearing on it, despite its significance for the whole issue of pupil attitudes and motivation.

These then, are two good reasons why we should study pupil transfer at 11 or 12 years of age — for what it tells us first, about pupils' experiences of change, and second, about how they come to terms with the comprehensive school. There is a third reason, namely to find out how their own identities — as male or female, as pupil, and as adolescent — develop. It is at the age of 12 that most pupils experience the onset of puberty, involving profound emotional and physical changes. The pupils at our research school saw the transfer as a decisive step away from childhood. The upper school ('Old Town') was defined as more 'grown up', it 'prepared you for life' whereas the middle school just prepared you for upper school. The middle school 'treated you like a baby', whereas the upper 'treated you like adults'. The transfer thus marks in the pupils' eyes, a significant advance toward adulthood, but also manhood and womanhood, for sexual identities now begin to become established in earnest, together with socialization into gender cultures. Possibly, then, there are clues here to the development of gender inequalities, or at least to their assumption by pupils, and to how they might be repaired.

Above all, it is in the interaction among these various elements — identities, cultures, strategies — that transfer at 11 or 12 has to be understood. But there is another important interaction, for cutting across these elements is a formal-informal distinction. By 'formal', we refer to those matters that relate to goals, values and organization specified by teachers acting in their official roles. By 'informal' we refer to aims, interests, values, beliefs, codes of practice and groupings generated and sustained by pupils independently of school. Again, though analytically distinct, they have considerable influence upon each other, and that interaction may hold important keys to pupil attitude and commitment to comprehensive school.

In order to study these matters it was necessary to consider pupils' views and experiences on a day-to-day basis over a lengthy period covering transition. Accordingly, we made an ethnographic study of a group of pupils over their last term at middle school, and their first year at upper, transferring in this case at age 12 plus. The school was a large, mixed comprehensive on a modern housing estate in a semi-industrial town in the East Midlands. Full details of methods and results of the research are given in Measor and Woods (1984). In this article, we outline the major consequences as we see them for comprehensive schools.

Transition

The most notable feature of pupils' attitudes towards transfer while still at the middle school was one of anxiety. Expressions of being 'frightened', 'worried', 'scared' and 'nervous' about going to the new school were frequent: 'I'm a bit worried about how big the school is. I sat and thought what a change it would be to go there, it looked giant compared to Hayes' [The middle school]. While anxieties have been noted before (Murdock, 1966; Bryan, 1980), their source has not been properly located. We believe that pupils see their whole identities at risk in the coming transition. Pupil identities, like teachers' (Hargreaves, 1980), have three main elements — status, competence and relationships — and we found these at the bottom of much of the pupil anxiety. In content, this revolved around five major issues: the size and more complex organization of the new school, new forms of discipline and authority, new demands of work, the prospect of being bullied, and the possibility of losing one's friends:

> *Keith:* It is so big — so many places I have to go see. It will take me a whole year to learn all the places and it will take me longer than that to know all the people there.

The comfortable, homely, secure environment of primary education will be exchanged for a brash, impersonal, more cosmopolitan environment, where they must find their own solutions.

Pupils feared loss of self and more distant treatment from teachers in the new, huge bureaucratic organization. Harder forms of work threatened their self-image as a competent person, internalized during earlier years, but now suddenly fragile. For some, their status as high achievers appeared in jeopardy. One said, 'I like being best, and I want to come near the top' but was worried there would be increased competition in the new school. For others there was a fear of not coping at all, that it would be 'too hard for me' and that 'sometimes, when we learn new things I won't learn it straightaway'. Homework threatened to encroach on pupils' private space and time, and hence to interfere with the expression of preferred identities. It was not simply a matter of temporary anonymity therefore, but a real threat to self. For some, games and sport offered the prospect of a humiliated self, being forced to do things beyond their capabilities. Basic security appeared threatened by coming up against older pupils who thronged the maze of corridors and classrooms in the new school. Here again, status was involved, for there is a pecking order in the pupils' informal culture, ranked on a seniority principle. Pupils' projected low status in the informal culture in the new order was felt to be the more acute compared to their high status within their current, middle school. They were 'at the top' of their middle schools, but in the comprehensive they would be reduced to 'silly little 1st years'. All the paraphernalia supporting conception of self would have to be constructed anew — private spaces, reputations (for example, as a 'fighter'), appearances, and, most importantly, friends. The fear that they would be split up from their friends was their greatest anxiety. Friends provide support and reassurance, but they also help in defining the world, in making sense of situations and in developing one's own identity.

Despite these fears, pupils at times employed a longer time perspective, seeing the move as a step towards the coveted status of adult. Pupils saw the transfer as 'moving up' and saw symbolic value in all sorts of things — even school uniform:

Andy: Going to Old Town, it seems more grown up.
Ros: Wearing school uniform seems very grown up.
Mark: Here you just get a drink of water out of the taps, but there they've got a coffee machine, with chocolate, like a proper job.

Also, pupils reasoned that they had successfully managed the earlier transfer in their career from primary to middle school.

A rather less hard-headed resource helping them to cope lay in the phenomenon of pupil myths. We would argue that myths take on particular importance for people undergoing a status passage (Glaser and Strauss, 1971), and that their significance lies within the perspectives and life-worlds of the pupils. They provide a kind of anticipatory socialization, preparing the pupil for the tougher and more impersonal realities, the status hierarchies and peer group subcultures of the informal area, and the mysterious unknown of sexual development.

They act as a kind of cultural blueprint, or social charter (Malinowski, 1926) for future behaviour, which contains both hints on norms and rules to observe, and clues as to what kind of identity will be most appropriate in the new circumstances. Their power rests in the fact that they operate at both a conscious and subconscious level, and affect both the intellect and the emotions.

The myths fell into three broad areas which match the stated causes of anxiety — 1 situations and activities making new demands of harshness and toughness in the new secondary school world in both formal and informal cultures; 2 sexual development, and 3 new forms of knowledge and work. Most of the myths in the first two categories were told by boys, though the third was shared by girls. There were stories of 'having your head flushed down the loo on your birthday', marauding gangs who were 'after yer', of going on '5 mile runs', of being hit with 'corner flags' for failing a physical test, of a 'homosexual teacher'. Many of these can be related to the inculcation of gender identities. They convey information of attitudes, feelings and behaviour appropriate for masculinity. Those relating to work convey appropriate feminine codes also. Thus boys expressed delight at the prospect of the grizzly ritual of rat dissection, while girls were repelled. Though the surface detail of these myths was not realized, the inner message was proved to be correct, as we shall see. (For a more detailed analysis of pupil myths, see Measor and Woods, 1983a.)

To belay these anxieties, and to initiate pupils into this particular school ethos, teachers operated a principled induction scheme (Hamblin 1978; for a discussion of the 'ethos' in question, see Measor and Woods, 1983b). They aimed to present the school as an attractive place, with reasonable, humane people in it. They stressed that they enjoyed good results, academic and behavioural. There was firm discipline, but within a caring environment that was alive to pupils' personal problems such as being bullied or lost. Similarly, though certain rules and expectations were made very clear, it was also apparent that there was also room for manoeuvre. Certain modifications to school uniform were permissible, and they were allowed to discover the full range of the discipline framework of certain lessons. For example, though the myths about the severity of games teachers was confirmed, they discovered that they could enjoy immensely a game of non-stop cricket — as long as they observed the basic rule-structure. Elsewhere, they discovered that some of the more difficult work, like maths, would be revised, that upper school teachers could be 'a laugh' (the English department acted an hilarious play) and that learning could be fun and exciting (the science staff arranging a number of 'magical' experiments).

In this way pupils were cushioned from the full shock of transition and on the whole they expressed enthusiasm about going to that school. But despite the induction scheme pupils were still apprehensive about some teachers, and about what crimes merited what punishments. Above all, little was done to help ease pupils into the informal culture. This was a mistake, for the two areas, as we shall see, are inextricably intertwined.

Initial Encounters

When they arrived at the school in earnest, there was an 'initial encounters' period (Ball, 1980) lasting from two to three weeks. It contained two phases — a 'honeymoon' phase, during which teachers and pupils presented their best 'fronts' toward each other; and a 'coming out' phase, in which the seamless fronts began to disintegrate, and truer identities emerge.

The pupils presented a front during the first two days of silent attention and rigid conformity. They were desperately anxious to get things right and unwilling to risk initiatives. They rushed to obey commands, did all their homework, and even volunteered for more. In class, teachers met a 'forest of hands' when they asked a question. Pupils also presented a circumspect appearance, with traditional hairstyles, new, unadulterated uniforms, and tightly tied ties. They were, however, reluctant to ask anything of a teacher whom they did not know — more through pressure of the informal peer group culture than fear of the teacher. And they had considerable difficulty switching from the 'task oriented' activity of the middle school to the 'time oriented' of the upper. In middle school the day was split into large blocks of time and a 'project' was done within these blocks. If pupils finished quickly, they were allowed to do something else, or finish off work from another area. Thus their learning was individualized, and oriented toward the completion of tasks. The regime in the upper school was divided up into discrete one hour sessions. Work thus became 'time oriented', and pupils had to learn to respond not to their own progress, but to the bell, which governed the activities of the whole cohort. Many pupils found it difficult to stop working when the 'bell went'. One girl said, 'I don't think you get long enough with that hour. I think if you had about two hours in every lesson'. Teachers appeared to experience this as a discipline problem.

Two weeks into the term, the 'front' began to disintegrate. Many pupils' appearances began to change radically. Uniforms were adjusted, aprons and books emblazoned with graffiti. Pupils also began to test spaces and places during the school day for degrees of freedom. Registration, for example, was soon identified as an appropriate time for deviance, and some lessons and subjects were afforded lower status than others (see Measor, 1984). Art and music, for example, provided space for 'messing around', expressing identities and cementing ties within the informal culture. English and maths, however, were highly rated, because of their marketability. In these subjects, pupils accepted the general rules of conduct but had to discover appropriate modes of working. In English, for example, there was a limit to the amount of chatting required — a 'working noise' and an 'unacceptable noise' — a distinction which pupils had to learn, and for which the teachers had a fine ear.

Gender differences also soon began to assert themselves. In domestic science, while the girls were ultra-conformist, the boys were passive. In the second week, this passivity turned to more active deviance. In contrast to initial ultra conformity elsewhere, this often took the form of *over*playing the pupil role. In science, the girls were much less enthusiastic than the boys. More of this later (and see Measor 1983).

By the fourth week, some pupils, by continually trying to push the rule boundaries further back, had established identities of 'ace deviants'. Others emerged with the initial front almost intact — they tried to influence others to do the same. They were concerned to do well, and to signal their 'brightness'. They did this by answering questions and getting them right, finishing work first, and scoring high marks. Those who did the exact opposite soon became known as 'really thick'. These, however, were not blanket responses to all situations. The conformists could turn deviant in subject areas they rated of low value, and 'thick' pupils could turn remarkably bright in particular areas.

In the informal culture, the initial encounters stage was marked by the pupils making new forms of relationships among themselves. We have noted the intense anxiety caused by the prospect of losing friends and status, and being bullied by older pupils. So rapid developments here were to be expected. Part of the initial front presented by pupils was an attitude of polite civility toward each other. Pupils, girls in particular, tended to form mutual support groups which were exclusively single gender and based largely on middle school contacts. These groups met the first need of security, but were an inadequate basis for identity construction. As pupils came to feel more secure after the first few days, the civility was replaced by the public trading of insults, the dissolution of middle school groupings and their replacement by new alignments on the basis of similar identities.

Need and identity were reflected in the re-emergence of cooperative groups — groups of pupils among whom it was legitimate to ask for and to give help. These groups had certain implicit rules. You only asked for help from someone you could rely on for a sympathetic response and who was worth asking. If they came from the same middle school, that gave you a right to ask, but not at this stage if they were of an incompatible identity. They were also single sex, except in cross-gender curriculum areas, where status was not lost by consulting a member of the opposite sex, as, for example, a boy consulting a girl in needlework. Some pupils soon became established as powerful resources in these groups, and hence acquired status as leaders. One boy was observed showing himself willing to give help, thus gaining the identity he sought and a network of relationships. Identities within these groups gradually became confirmed by the repeated asking for and giving of help.

Shortly, however, friendship groups, involving stronger ties, began to form. Some middle school associations were retained, others were dissolved as personal incompatibilities were discovered. Identities were judged in the first instance, paradoxically, on reaction to the *formal* culture, pupils becoming established as 'brainy' or 'thick' and so on. Pupils of similar dispositions appeared to make overtures to each other within cooperative groups, and then proceed to a deeper level of relationship by discussing more personal matters, such as interests and family. Soon they would be walking together through school and sitting together in classes. The friendship escalated to association outside school, girls visiting each others' homes, while boys seemed to develop more of a street culture — predictably, given what we know about adolescent subcultures.

In addition, girls tended to develop still stronger liaisons with one other girl in best friend bonds. These would include all the elements of other friendships discussed above, but at greater intensity. Best friends, for example, might stay the night at each other's house, and there were strong loyalties involved. Identity concerns were uppermost here, for best friends reflected one's chosen image back on oneself.

Orientation to school remained the prime criterion of identity, but for boys, how one responded to the demands of the informal culture was also an important factor. Here, the myths, which had warned of the need for 'toughness', were borne out as boys began to be more aggressive toward each other, and pecking orders were established. One 'weak' boy was shunned by the others. Two polar stereotypes of toughness and weakness came to be established, with certain boys acting as 'markers'.

For girls in the informal culture, fashion and make-up were a major indicator of identity. But first year girls soon found that older girls acted as a check in this area, exerting pressures if they used 'too much make-up' (see also Ball, 1981, p. 260). Again the myths are seen to have been accurate with their invitation to and warning about the youth culture, and their indication of differential power between age grades.

The myths had also laid down codes of behaviour for boys and girls, and as they learnt these behaviours in the early weeks of upper school, pupils became almost completely sex segregated, not only sitting apart, but demonstrably avoiding each other. However, a few were soon experimenting with cross-gender interactions, signalling their interest in the opposite sex and seeking to establish whether others judged them to be successful within that sphere. Attitudes to cross-gender relationships were associated with attitudes to school. Conformist boys were unlikely to 'go out with' girls, but deviant boys did. Similarly, going out with boys mattered a great deal to the deviant girls. Much status was at stake in these relationships. The sexual interest soon came to exert an influence over appearances, uniform, with hair styles in particular being adapted in accordance with the dictates of fashion. Pupils found themselves confronted with several conflicting demands — from peer group, older age-grades in the informal culture, parents and teachers — and were to devote much time and ingenuity to solving them in the coming months.

Rebellion and Purge

By the beginning of the second term, pupils had successfully adapted to the formal demands of their new school. Their anxieties had dispersed, and in some cases were considered to have been unfounded. On some aspects of their middle school lives they now looked back with contempt, whereas initially nostalgia had been more common. Thus they now welcomed a wider range of teachers. These teachers were more 'professional', they 'knew more'. Subject divisions were an indication of more advanced knowledge, and hence of greater status, and anyway were neater and tidier. The great anxiety about friends had also been dissipated, many pupils expressing their appreciation of new sociability networks. They had found, too, that they could cope with schoolwork. It was harder, certainly, but some enjoyed being stretched, with a new sense of purpose. Discipline was certainly tighter than in the 'family-centred' middle school, but this again was indication of new purpose, and in any case, pupils had discovered there was room for negotiation.

At the beginning of the second term, this was exploited by some pupils in a series of attempted 'take-overs' in which they tried to wrest control from teachers. They found themselves confronted by new situations, with a large number of supply and student teachers, and staff absences, entailing 'doubling up' of classes. With their own new-found confidence, the time was ripe for some pupils to attempt to win more space. Typically, the deviance would begin on a moderate scale within the limits of the space already generally negotiated, and then escalate to challenges for the centre stage. The status of the subject was not relevant to whether or not this occurred. Nor could some senior teachers successfully cope with some of these situations without resorting to extreme punitive measures, regarded as an indication of failure by other teachers.

In reply to this 'rebellion', the teachers calculatedly instituted a purge. Previously tacitly agreed limits were tightened, and the need for discipline stressed. Some older pupils were sent home for minor transgressions of uniform. House and form teachers laid emphasis on good manners and self-discipline. In lessons, teachers employed five major strategies: restating the rules and instituting strict enforcement of them for a period; clarifying the boundaries between formal and informal area, and the teacher conception of the pupil role; 'exampling', that is to say making an example of one or two miscreants *'pour encourager les autres'*; threatening extreme penalities, especially violence, and, finally, 'making a scene', or what Furlong's pupils referred to as 'causing trouble', which pupils tried to avoid at all costs (Furlong, 1977). Skill was needed in the deployment of these strategies, if they were to work. For instance, it was counter-productive to make an example of a 'conformist' rather than a deviant. And it was possible to overstep the mark of general fairness, even in a purge, by such devices as public humiliations, like caning in front of the class.

By this stage, pupils were beginning to experiment with a range of role distancing techniques. Three of these had become particularly prominent. The first was an advancing of the informal culture into formal areas, such as lessons. Pupils knew that in art and design lessons there would be the opportunity to talk and discuss their own concerns for much of the lesson. In music lessons, they could demand to hear punk music rather than classical, and could beat out heavy metal rock rhythms on their tambourines and triangles. The blending of formal and informal allowed pupils to be 'themselves' and to resist any pressures to mould them into 'pupil types'. The second strategy was the appropriation of school uniform to their own identity concerns — both pupils and teachers fully realized the symbolic importance of appearance. Pupils altered items of clothing like jackets, coats and shoes to approximate more closely to fashion than school uniform. Boys began to wear their ties in huge, oversize knots, or tied very loosely half way down their jumpers.

The third ploy was overplaying the pupil role, intentionally exaggerating some responses and actions and thus subtly mocking formal requirements. For example, they could ask questions of a teacher, but the questions were of that species known as 'silly questions'. They could sit to rigid and satirical attention in a lesson for a few seconds only, and then refuse to cooperate at all, or offer insistently to complete work tasks or jobs for teachers, only to 'mess them up' completely.

In this second term, shifts in friendships occurred as pupils continued to 'come out'. Pupils were able to make more realistic judgements on who they wished to be friends with. The important criterion was attitude to the formal culture. Some girls, for example, maintained attitudes of ultra-conformity beyond the initial fronts stage, and were rejected by the rest of the groups who moved into a phase of negotiating for space for the play of the informal culture. One girl, for example, who did not adjust her appearance had 'unfashionable flat shoes!' yelled at her derisively by a group as she waited at a bus stop. Different sets of values came to be applied to situations, as when some thought unisex goggles should be worn in science as a safety measure, whereas others objected to them because they were unfeminine. Again, some girls 'liked a laugh, like the boys', seeing themselves as more deviant than other girls, and revealing again the underlying gender codes.

At the same time as groups were re-forming on the basis of mutual identities (as opposed to mutual need for security), they began to distinguish themselves more sharply from each other. They established their own seating patterns in classrooms, which teachers found difficult to alter when the nature of the lesson required it; and they also showed enmity toward each other, as if to reinforce particular group memberships.

There were developments, too, in the 'best friend' bond among the girls. There was clearly strong emotional content, and there was great upset when any 'broke up'. There was also strong identity investment. They shared much time, activities and equipment, both in and out of school, staying at each other's houses, borrowing each other's clothes. They dressed, and had their hair cut in the same style. In short, in some respects they were almost mirror-images of each other.

The boys were encountering more of the demands for toughness in the *macho* hierarchy. In February, there was a 'fights fever' involving older boys and girls from other schools. The deviant first year boys expressed great interest in these, signalling their involvement in the informal culture and sense of male identity. A kind of status network based on toughness began to evolve within classes. The pattern of one individual maintaining dominance within a group continued, but also, now, status between groups, and especially the leaders, became an additional factor. Conformist boys could not avoid the *macho* hierarchy. One such boy asserted his toughness with some deviant boys, but shrewdly did not tangle with those he was not sure of beating.

Pupils generally began to feel their new status of being more 'grown up' and the need of more recognition of it. Certain activities, language and behaviour were proscribed as 'childish'. There was a difference in presents asked for by the girls on birthdays, clothes now taking precedence over games. Discos replaced parties, dancing replaced games, teenage magazines replaced comics. This feel for new status applied to curriculum and school practices as well as playground activities. Both boys and girls welcomed situations where they could feel older, trusted, and responsible, and denigrated those that did not allow for this. Music, art and needlework lessons were particularly culpable of instituting 'childish' projects. Although domestic science ironically was valued for the space it gave, it allowed pupils to handle large knives, light the gas and learn adult skills like breaking eggs easily.

Consolidation

By the third term, there was a more lasting consolidation of positions. Early in the year they had had the rules stipulated. They had responded and tested for elasticity. In the second term, they had attempted take-overs, and brought on a purge. They had discovered differences among teachers, subjects and situations. They knew how far they could go in most cases. It remained for them to work out within these perimeters adaptational modes which were in line with their own interests.

By now, the cohort was showing clear differences in adapting to the formal area, the most distinctive being a conformist deviant one. Deviant attitudes had hardened. School was 'rubbish' and 'boring', and individual teachers were criticized. There was a marked difference, however, in the strategies used by boys and by girls, the former being active, the latter passive, the difference emerging, we would argue, from perceived gender roles.

In general, deviant boys developed more subtle forms of deviance, manipulating the meanings and implications of teacher discourse, exploiting ambiguities, twisting the rules and redefining situations. They developed their skill in repartee, for example, in giving 'silly answers'. Successful jokes brought status and also, at times, asserted the boys' own adolescent, media-related culture. Many of these strategies involved centre-stage challenges, but stopped short of provoking absolute breakdown. Space for 'talking' was secured, beyond that already negotiated as legitimate. Boys created or stole time for themselves, and operated a range of work avoidance strategies, exploiting slack space around the edges and in the crevices of lessons, working to exaggerated rule, recapturing space school had threatened to take over (for example through homework). The most deviant began to 'skive off' school altogether. There were curriculum variations in the scale of deviance, 'talking' for example, a comparatively minor offence, being considered more grave in important subjects like maths or English, than 'mucking about', a more serious offence, in home economics, a low status subject.

Conformist boys indulged in occasional acts of deviance, for example, all boys were opposed to teachers who did not treat them as grown up. But in general, their identities were more bound up with the formal culture. They preferred this school, felt they knew their teachers better than those at middle school. They competed with each other to finish their work, showed a high level of interest and commitment, answered questions, were concerned about the appearance of their work and to get things right.

None of the girls was as extreme as the 'ace' boy deviants. Their deviance differed in character from the boys' generally, in that it was passive, and rarely brought any teacher reprimand. It might involve simply daydreaming, chatting, or 'doodling'. They might practise 'being upset', shy quietness, answering questions inaudibly, being demure, giggling in mock embarrassment. All these often covered a resistance to doing set work, but the cover was sufficient to avoid 'trouble'. Girls who made centre-stage challenges and were noisy brought rebuke not only from teachers, but also from boys — yet another commentary on the underlying gender codes, and an illustration of how pupils socialize with each other. Occasionally a girl would give an insolent answer, but this was always in response to what they perceived as illegitimate challenges to their passive work avoidance strategies from a teacher. (See also Buswell's discussion of Judy, in this volume.)

Certain curriculum areas continued to be seen as non-feminine, and by the same token, to offer opportunities to reinforce the girls' femininity. Thus science, wood and metalwork invited more deviance from girls, but of a 'feminine' nature — doing hair, practising with make-up. Their evaluations of these subjects on gender lines hardened. Thus science made some 'sick', 'afraid', 'squeamish', 'disgusted', and metalwork was 'dirty' and 'noisy'. Girls also emitted messages about their incompetence with machines and technology. In some of these lessons they received conflicting messages. For example, in design, the teacher told them they were as good as the boys and urged them to compete, but his form of humour with them conveyed impressions of female inadequacy in these areas.

Girls utilized their school equipment, uniform and rough books in distinctive ways to intrude the informal culture into the formal. They occupied strategic sites to conduct their informal activities, forsook the traditional formality of school dinners, which initially they had acclaimed, for illicit snacks out of school, and some began to abscond in varying degrees.

They were also learning how to secure favours from male teachers by exploiting their femininity. Already, however, they had a strict sense of proprieties. Some teachers were universally unpopular, one in particular offending girls by his insidious sexual remarks. Another, popular among the boys, was resented for his self-indulgent playing up to the *macho* hierarchy. Women teachers were often judged in terms of their femininity. Some were seen as lacking certain qualities, others as having a surfeit, which was equally reprehensible. All this, again, illustrates the importance of the informal culture in shaping pupil perspectives on teachers. If girls tended to overdraw the characters of their teachers, and to concentrate on certain aspects with phobic zeal, we suggest this was because they were not making objective appraisals of their teachers, but using them as role models for the construction of their own feminine identities. Ball (1981) has shown how the demands of school and the culture of femininity conflict. The data here demonstrates some of the ways in which girls try to resolve this conflict.

By the third term, pupil identities in terms of ability and attitude toward school were fairly clear, and enabled a conformist-deviant distinction in general terms to be made. Key events such as the parents' evening, and especially the introduction of setting for particular subjects had hardened conceptions of the academic hierarchy. Pupils themselves had clear views on who was 'brainy' and 'thick', who the 'good' and 'quiet' ones were, and who were the ones who 'mucked about'.

Among the boys, friendship groups remained stable on the whole, though there were some new developments. Cooperative groups continued with the same rules, but it was now noticeable that there could be variations in leadership according to curriculum area. Setting fragmented some groups, and made cooperation difficult for others. It also had the effect of overcoming the gender-exclusivity rule, for in the top set, though not in the lower one, there was increased interaction between boys and girls, suggesting that positive academic orientation took precedence over gender codes. Between individuals in separate cooperation groups, hard bargaining for help was now observed, indicating that the boundaries of these groups had become clear, ruling out proffers of friendship. Some — those members of the 'pupil mafia' — had earned the right to break general rules applying to these groups, as a result of their toughness.

Boys' friendship groups, unlike the girls', remained stable, depending on shared interests, and with no 'best mates' (best friends was seen as a female concept). With increased identification within these groups, enmities between them grew stronger. To deviants, the conformists worked too hard, and were 'soft'. But their attitude to leisure interests was important too, and they did not go to discos or go out with girls. This syndrome of factors was seen as non-masculine — another illustration of how a gender code militates against academic success.

However, most boys aligned themselves somewhere between the polar extremes of ultra conformity and deviance, which they found useful to personalize in the shape of certain boys who had general notoriety, and who were shunned and derided for being too 'weak' and 'goody-goody' or 'too thick'. For most boys, the ideal pupil was neither too conformist, nor too deviant, neither too clever nor too thick. Maintaining a balance between these poles was a delicate task requiring knife-edge strategies. Thus some deviant boys who were not really 'thick' soon hoisted themselves out of the 'dummies' set. Some began to excel at selected things. They might not usually work hard, but they established the point that they were capable of doing well if they chose.

Similarly, conformists began to engage in the occasional deviance in 'safe' spaces already mined by the deviants. These strategies qualified them for membership of the informal culture, without threatening their basic identity. So they also played down their academic success, not 'showing off', and diverting praise with pantomime gestures, derived from the media input into the informal culture, and they adopted deviant infringements, not wholesale readjustments, to their uniforms. Conformist boys saw this as indicating more maturity, perhaps in the sense that it was a step to more independence and self-assertion. Some deviant boys also saw their occasional expression of conformity in a similar way, guided by a growing awareness of ultimate masculine responsibility.

Girls' identities, also, were increasingly influenced by how they related to school and the academic hierarchy. It was clear that, while girls may have the resources to be academically successful, there were problems in their *choosing* to be, for the feminine gender code operated against them. This caused some girls a great deal of pain and misery as their conformity elicited teasing and social isolation. These girls welcomed setting for it meant fewer social sanctions. The deviant girls saw conformists as 'goodie-goodies', who did good, neat work, were 'no fun', spoiled it for others, were bossy, posh, stuck-up, know-alls, always wanting to be 'it'. They always did things by the book, ate their school dinners, dressed traditionally. The deviant girls, by contrast, liked to 'have a laugh', wore fashionable clothes and make-up, made do with lunchtime snacks, went out with boys and sported a profound knowledge of sexual matters. Ignorance was unforgivable in the latter — it was better to pretend that you knew.

The boys in general disapproved of conformist and 'brainy' girls, and did not see them as desirable. They supported the deviant girls' views on womanhood. The fact that girls were 'always talking' was peculiarly feminine, and their future wives would not go out to work — that was the man's responsibility.

Some girls managed this problem of opposing influences by employing, like the boys, knife-edge strategies. They engaged in strategic deviance in areas where their basic identity was not under threat. Language, woodwork and technical drawing lessons were considered appropriate for this. Generally such strategies were designed to just avoid teacher censure, but the finest knife-edge move was to earn rebuke from a teacher of low status, such as a supply or probationer, since this gave it the acclaim of 'teacher certificated deviance' without seriously affecting identity.

On the other side of the knife-edge, such girls took a middle line on youth culture, wearing nail varnish but no make-up, having moderate pictures on their rough book covers, going out with one boy, or letting it be known they were not averse to doing so. They retained some friends from middle school who might now be taking a deviant line, joining them in outside activities. And they disassociated themselves from the ultra-conformists, mocking the associated tendencies of 'bossiness'.

Conformist girls, for their part, were dedicated to the formal culture, interested in their work, and anxious to do well academically. They wanted a good job eventually and a career, as well as marriage and a family, while deviant girls tended to think primarily in terms of the latter. Conformists objected to wasting time in lessons, and, while usually docile and cooperative, could complain vociferously if teacher malfunction threatened their academic chances. They worried at home about their work. They disapproved of the priority given to the youth culture by the deviants, with their preoccupation with make-up, boys, and magazines about appearance. Diaries that these girls completed over a half-term holiday revealed that they spent their time with their families, whereas deviants were with the peer group.

Conclusion

This research into transfer shows the problems of pupils adapting to secondary school, from their own perspectives. At our research school they were required to make three important transitions simultaneously — through formal and informal cultures, and also through the profound physical and emotional changes associated with puberty. Transfer at 11 plus would appear more sensible, for it allows a year to adjust to the new institution before the set of pressures associated with puberty begin to be felt. Friendship bondings are crucial for the child's development. At 11, these friendships are still fragmentary, insubstantial and fleeting; but at 12 plus, and especially for girls, they are more stable and have a deeper emotional investment. Transfer at 12 plus therefore disrupts many of these friendships and makes their task of adapting to a vastly different situation that much harder.

The research demonstrates the value of carefully devised and programmed induction schemes. This one had considerable impact on easing the transition to the formal area of the upper school, but almost totally ignored the 'informal' transition. We have seen the close connection between the two areas, and it is to here, arguably, that much of the 'crisis' in comprehensives can be traced. For pupil cultures exert profound influence on attitudes to the curriculum, to learning and to pupil roles, and ensure a massive 'no' to the questions about the efficacy of comprehensivation posed in the introduction. If this school is typical, as we feel it is, then, despite the fact that by all the usual standards it would be considered a 'good' school, social inequalities are not being modified, there is no greater educational equality of opportunity, and there is no greater commitment to school. In fact, one of the most prominent features of the research is the huge reservoir of talent that is forcibly suppressed among pupils through gender and social class codes. Yet in the one instance where informal pupil groupings actually promoted learning in line with the official programme — in cooperative groups — it was invariably interpreted by teachers as deviant activity.

We would argue that schools must move further to recognize and to meet the informal culture if they are to promote their aims more successfully and if they are to begin to tap this reservoir of talent. This has implications for school ethos (see Measor and Woods, 1983b) and for the curriculum (see Hargreaves, 1982).

However, perhaps the most important message from the research is a recognition of the complexities involved at this particular juncture of the pupil career. There are no easy solutions, and indeed one might argue that there should be no easy solutions. For most rites of passage involve some kind of trauma to aid the psychology of transition. Also, comprehensives reflect society more integrally than tripartite schools, and in making their adaptations, pupils are learning one of the most important lessons of life — how to adjust to society, with all its inequalities, inconsistencies, irrelevancies — and how to make the best out of one's own interests. Too much direction and succour might subvert this lesson. In any kind of school there will always be things pupils have to learn for themselves.

References

BALL, S.J. (1980) 'Initial encounters in the classroom and the process of establishment' in WOODS, P. (Ed) *Pupil Strategies*, London, Croom Helm.

BALL, S.J. (1981) *Beachside Comprehensive*, Cambridge, Cambridge University Press.

BRYAN, K.A. (1980) 'Pupil perceptions of transfer between middle and high schools' in HARGREAVES, A. and L. TICKLE, (Eds) *Middle Schools; Origins, Ideology and Practice*, London, Harper and Row.

FURLONG, V.J. (1977) 'Anancy goes to school' in HAMMERSLEY, M. and P. WOODS (Eds) *School Experience*, London, Croom Helm.

GLASER, B.G. and STRAUSS, A.L. (1971) *Status Passage*, Chicago, Aldine.

HAMBLIN, D. (1978) *The Teacher and Pastoral Care*, Oxford, Blackwell.

HARGREAVES, D.H. (1980) 'The occupational culture of teachers' in WOODS, P. (Ed) *Teacher Strategies*, London, Croom Helm.

HARGREAVES, D.H. (1982) *The Challenge for the Comprehensive School*, London, Routledge and Kegan Paul.

MALINOWSKI, B. (1926) *Myth in Primitive Psychology*, London, Routledge and Kegan Paul.

MEASOR, L. (1983) 'Girls and science' in HAMMERSLEY, M. and A. HARGREAVES, (Eds) *Curriculum Practice: Sociological Case-Studies*, Lewes, Falmer Press.

MEASOR, L. (1984) 'Pupil perceptions of subject status' in GOODSON, I.F. and S.J. BALL (Eds) *Defining the Curriculum: Histories and Ethnographies of School Subjects*, Lewes, Falmer Press.

MEASOR, L. and WOODS, P. (1983a) 'The interpretation of pupil myths' in HAMMERSLEY, M. (Ed) *The Ethnography of Schooling*, Driffield, Nafferton.

MEASOR, L. and WOODS, P. (1983b) 'Teachers and middle ground culture', *mimeo*.

MEASOR, L. and WOODS, P. (1984) *Identity and Culture: the Sociology of Pupil Transfer*, Milton Keynes, Open University Press.

MURDOCK, W.F. (1966) 'The Effect of Transfer on the Level of Children's Adjustment to School', Unpublished MEd thesis, University of Aberdeen.

Gender and Comprehensive Schooling

Lynn Davies

All too often in generalized collections, the topic of gender can fall prey to what Postman and Weingartner (1971) term the 'vaccination' theory of education: once you have 'done' gender, you are then immune, and need not 'do' it again — at least until the next burning issue of the moment. There might appear the danger that 'gender and comprehensive schooling' will become just one of a long line: 'gender and glue-sniffing', 'gender and the Falklands crisis', 'gender and the London Transport fares policy'. However, in this book 'gender' is not in fact relegated to one token discussion, to the now compulsory acknowledgement to the feminists or the eagle eyes at the Equal Opportunities Commission. It is instead a substantive component of discussion throughout, and the broad title of this particular chapter does not indicate a claim to sovereignty over the issue. Ironically, what I shall be doing here is to insist that gender cannot actually be tackled as a separate and distinct issue — either in concept or in practice.

To claim this is, of course, to undermine many of my own early stabs at sex role analysis in the heady days of the early seventies. Hence this paper will need first of all to trace the evolution of concerns about gender and education — the blind alleys, the arguments, the tunnel vision about 'girls' — in order to locate a position where we might profitably view the relationship of gender with comprehensive schooling in particular. Later I shall draw on some of my own more recent material on deviance and sex roles in school, and try to tease out general points about power and resistance which might have implications for the classroom teacher. Those working in comprehensive schools in the 1980s may sense they have enough to think about without being made to feel guilty about sex-typing or failure to consciousness-raise; but the point I want to make is that gender-related behaviour in school is part of a whole package of status and identity concerns, and that a teacher would be wise, in the interests of both pupils and herself, to identify the complex sources of power strategies used in the classroom.

The Story So Far

As in any scientific search, the history of thinking about gender and education is not so much one of solving problems as identifying new ones. While girls were denied access to formal education, the problem was getting them into school. When girls received free education, the problem was differential curricula for the sexes. When the Equal Opportunities Commission instigated legislation against discrimination in access to subjects, the problem was the hidden curriculum of expectations and attitudes. When the hidden curriculum was exposed as being inextricably derived from economic and political structures, the problem was patriarchy, capitalism, or indeed, patriarchal capitalism.

Underlying all this was still the same seemingly simple query: why do girls tend to have lower educational achievements than boys, and different employment opportunities and aspirations? In the 1970s much analysis was to centre round school socialization — overt and covert. In terms of the official curriculum, boys and girls were seen as forced, persuaded or allowed to take different options which served to confirm expectations about the 'suitability' of certain knowledge areas for the sexes. 'Hard' sciences and 'hard' crafts were for boys; 'soft' sciences and 'soft' crafts were the female domain. Most schools now avoid this by common timetabling (at least in the early years) regardless of sex; we are, however, still a long way from the kind of compulsory core curriculum including maths and science up till 16 which might partially account for the large numbers of women engineers and doctors in the USSR.

Cracking open the timetable meant also some examination of curriculum content, and in particular textbooks distributed as supposedly gender-free representations of knowledge. We are now in possession of a wealth of studies of sex-typing in everything from pre-school picture books to A level sociology texts. Some of these are predictable — history is patently about men — while others require some quite rigorous numerical and linguistic analysis to expose the persistent bias towards, and celebration of, the male (see Whyld, 1983) for curriculum analyses particularly relevant to the secondary level). While the major difficulty in such studies is the parallel examination of how these 'messages' might be received and interpreted by pupils (if at all), the research has certainly had an impact on writers and publishers. Contributors to volumes such as these will receive as routine a checklist of guidelines for avoiding sexism. An eager student might have fun at Falmer's expense going through this book — or even this chapter — for any horrors such as 'the inequality of man' or 'the sociologist ... he' which might have slipped through the net.

The hidden curriculum has of course been a rewarding, if uncertain, area for scrutiny. Working out how a school might convey messages about sex-appropriate behaviour means excavating a whole range of possible sites. There is the authority structure of the staff — how a preponderance of males in positions of responsibility, or dominating certain knowledge areas, can imply 'natural' male superiority and confirm the concomitant female deputy/helper subservient role (see Ball in this volume). There is the enormous arena of teacher expectancies — teachers may hold conscious or unconscious beliefs both about different aptitudes of the sexes for academic achievement and about their 'normal' classroom behaviour (see Miles in this volume). The mechanisms by which such beliefs might be conveyed to pupils still need much concrete research, but we have clues when we monitor teacher strategies such as handing out tasks, setting achievement goals, commenting on pupils' behaviour and appearance, the personal use of body language and eye contact, and the spatial ordering of the sexes in various contexts within the school. Distinguishing between the sexes in our culture is of course acceptable in a way that distinguishing by race (officially) is not. A teacher cannot say 'Good morning blacks and whites', even less 'you two blacks, stop talking'; but in schools we use gender to differentiate pupils routinely in addressing them, registering them and even seating them. The difficulty is knowing whether such taken-for-granted, and often non-judgmental, distinctions actually influence pupil behaviour and future orientations.

More persuasive in terms of socialization is data such as that which show that the majority of teachers, if forced to choose, would actually prefer to teach boys (Fuller, 1980; Davies, 1979). Apparently they find them academically more rewarding, outward going and easier to discipline than girls, in spite of the boys' more immediate roughness or 'cheekiness'. Girls are perceived as more insidious, insolent, devious and, while initially conformist, harder to control once aroused to deviance. Such perceptions parellel the growing body of evidence that teachers interact more with boys than girls in the classroom, spending more time on them in controlling and monitoring both work and behaviour (Brophy and Good, 1974). The comparative neglect of girls in mixed classrooms *must* have an effect on self-concept, achievement and orientation to school, and hence there is now the re-emerging debate on the respective merits of single sex versus coeducational schooling (see Shaw, 1980). While, as Dale (1971) claims, mixed schools might be better all round for *social* development, girls, it is now thought, might be disadvantaged *academically* because of the teacher orientations just mentioned and also because of their own need to demonstrate and reiterate femininity *vis-á-vis* the boys. Traditional deference to the male and unease about displaying academic forceful-ness would be key aspects of 'femininity' here to influence classroom achievement.

Distractions and Distortions

Until comparatively recently, analysis has, I think, been clouded by two somewhat misleading images. One is the implicit portrayal of 'girls' and 'boys' as discrete categories, like gerbils and hamsters, where the perceptions is of a 'gap' between them, or of their occupying different 'levels' in the Great Cage of Life. The policy aim has been to 'narrow the gap' of educational achievement, or to 'bring girls up to the level' of boys. It has taken the political analysts, the feminist inroads into family structures, to demonstrate effectively that male and female denote the two sides of a *relationship*. That this relationship may be asymmetrical, and sometimes a relationship of power, does not invali-date the fact that the sexes are locked in a mutually interdependent symbiosis, and that one can never tackle the education of one sex without considering the function of schooling for gender reproduction as a whole. The popular term 'sexual divisions' is in effect unhelpful: the differences between men and women are *not* the same as those deriving from a division of labour, as those between spot-welders and centre-lathe turners. Whereas it is possible to have a job specification for, say, a lorry driver which could exist independently of other job outlines, the definition of 'masculine' is conditional on being 'non-feminine', and *vice versa*. To be a boy, it is necessary *not* to be a girl; if we change the expectations of what it is to be a girl, we are also shifting the notions of what it is to be a non-girl, i.e. a boy. All this sounds a truism, but it is curious how much research on sex roles has ignored the *relational* imperative of gender in order to emphasise *difference*.

Studies of sex roles and education have understandably stemmed (implicitly or explicitly) from concern about girls rather than boys, or boys-and-girls. Although the aim was to highlight the female position, paradoxically the result has been often to dehumanize women. The second misrepresentation in gender studies is of the woman as passive victim/subject. She is confined by the biological imperative; she is socialized, conditioned, sex-typed; she is 'exposed' to the hidden curriculum; she is oppressed by the state, the economy, her mother, men, history, the Harpic advertisements. Rarely do girls and women come through as active participants and negotiators. Education is something which is 'done' to them, from which they are 'channelled' into domesticity or low-level employment. Work on the 'education of boys' might well have had similar emphases; but the fact that gender work has concentrated on discrimination against women has served to relegate females in particular to the status of jelly beans being moulded. We need to see what women and girls *do with* the constraints they find themselves in, how they shape their contexts, before we can even begin to make any recommendations for what education, or comprehensive schooling, should *do for* them.

At a political meeting I attended recently, the ward chairperson was asked whether he would be doing anything specifically to involve the 50 per cent of the voting population comprising women. Indeed, he said proudly, women form one constituent of a 'nine-pronged plan of attack'. The derisive laughs from the women present conveyed their frustration at being relegated once more to a minority group along with blacks, gays and the handicapped. Denoting women as a 'problem area' does little to describe their status as participators, and it also fails to distinguish between women in terms of social class, occupation or any other strategic position. In order to 'bring women back in' we need to demonstrate their variety and their richness of experience, not their marginality. An interesting example of the 'problem' approach came recently from Zambia. There, well-meaning positive discrimination policies have produced the decision to set a lower examination pass mark for girls to enter secondary schools, in order to balance the current inequitable sex distribution at higher levels of education. The result has been to confirm teacher stereotypes of girls as being 'less able', and even to induce direct hostility from teachers towards girls for taking the places which should have 'rightfully' gone to the boys (Martin, 1983).

There is then a dilemma. While applauding initiatives by author-ities such as ILEA to attack 'gross inequalities' in the three groups, working class, ethnic minorities and girls (see *The Guardian*, 3 May, 1983) I am doubtful about the highlighting of one side of a relationship only. Can one tackle 'the working class' without recognizing its status as conditional on the existence of a ruling class? Does ILEA's leaflet on 'Education for Girls' not give the false impression of girls as a 'special' case, a group of Category A prisoners?

The Political Framework

The notion of women as a discrete homogeneous group, 'subject' to stereotyping, has of course been countered by at least two of the directions in contemporary work on gender. The first to mention is the macro theoretical analysis which seeks to locate women's 'subordination' in the economic underpinning of society. It is not 'tradition' alone which keeps women in their place, but the power of those directing the economy to maintain asymmetrical roles. This is not a perceived plot, not conspiracy theory run riot, for it is difficult to identify a group of Politically Motivated Men who decide this week's sex roles. Instead, family and work relationships are seen to derive from the broad requirements of 'the economy' — with the finger usually pointed here at the capitalist economy. The present day family is crucial to the continuation of unequal profit-sharing; the woman provides a haven and a rationale for the potentially discontented worker; she socializes the next work force into acceptance of selling its labour for wages, thereby creating surplus value; she happily and competitively purchases the consumer products of capitalism. The current espousal of the 'Victorian' values of family life by the Conservative Party brings these apparent generalizations into stark relief; the emphasis on hard work, thrift, respect for authority and self-reliance, while sounding uncontroversial, can be seen to disadvantage women particularly. Their role is even more firmly sited in 'proper' child-rearing; it is they who will be responsible for caring for the elderly and disabled, not the state nor the euphemism of 'the community' which will really mean individual women at home. Blame for any malfunctioning of society such as implied by crime and unemployment can be laid even more squarely at the feet of women: it is their job to stay at home, both to release jobs for men and to socialize the children properly.

The debates between the theorists centre round whether such ideologies are primarily the product of capitalism or patriarchy, whether they are to do with the concentration of capital ownership in the hands of the few, or to do with the control of work, marriage and property being in the hands of men. An interesting exercise is to identify what patriarchal socialism reveals itself to be, or to envisage a

society based on matriarchal capitalism. The great usefulness of political analyses of gender is in highlighting contradictions in ideology — for
example between adherence to 'equal opportunity' in education and the
reality of such opportunity patently not existing — whether in class,
race or gender terms. It is such contradictions which provide the space
for individuals to negotiate their position, to create unique interpretations of their social world. And it is this space which will enable
women to be 'brought back in' as active sentient beings, *influencing*
their world as well as being constrained by it.

Inside the Secondary School

The second strand within contemporary work on gender is the micro
case study investigation of gender processes in classrooms. The process
of identifying political mechanisms at work in the school is of course
fraught with problems. While the official and the hidden curriculum
can be seen to act to 'confirm' current political ideologies for the sexes,
this is complicated by the obvious fact that not all teachers transmit or
operate in the same way; that pupils respond (or even do not respond)
uniquely; and that gender is but one of the many interlocking dimensions of possible inequality in the school. I want now to use just two
sources to illustrate the complexity. The first is presented because it is
probably as yet relatively unfamiliar here and hence stimulating; and
the second because it is the most familiar to me — i.e. my own
research.

Making the Difference (Connell *et al*, 1982) is an Australian investigation of the different relations between home and school for 'ruling
class' and for 'working class' groups. There are enough parallels with
the independent versus the state sector in this country to make the
study a rewarding one for any comprehensive school teacher. What the
authors point to is the inextricable linkage between social class and
gender (which indeed make generalizations about 'the education of
girls' impossible). 'We can see that it was in response to class dynamics
that the education system as a whole was organized as a system of
academic competition. But once it was organized that way, it became
available to women to improve their position *vis-à-vis* men' (p. 182).
We have to look not simply at 'the school' but the fact that the
secondary school is the embodiment of organized (masculinist?) competition. In independent, sex-segregated girls' schools, the combination
of academically successful, career-oriented female teachers and girls

with pressure from home to do well academically 'opens up unprecedented possibilities'. Previously such schools had tended to see as their main task the production of femininity which complemented the masculinity dominant in the class *milieu*, addressing themselves to sociability, to the interests and skills to grace a well-appointed home. The study suggests there is nothing about segregation or coeducation which *by itself* produces a given result:

> Historically the educational segregation of ruling class women has been the means of marginalizing them and preparing them for subordination to men. Precisely that segregation is now helping to erode that subordination. Second, one of the major determinants of the impact of a given organization of gender in schools is the class context in which it occurs. The effects of segregation in independent girls' schools are closely bound up with their class *milieu*; in particular, its stress on competition and achievement, and the recently changed relations between ruling class women and the top end of the labour market. It seems to us unlikely that coeducation has done much to advance the interests of working-class women. (p. 113)

Yet the presence of female teachers in mixed working class schools did provide a model for something different from economic dependence on a husband; some female teachers were questioning sex role conventions and were fighting put-downs from men; and with 'bright' and 'cooperative' girls at least, such teachers were involved in a 'project of social mobility'. What seems to happen is a split in models of femininity among working class girls, closely connected with mobility in class terms. Having women teachers in nearly equal numbers is undercut, as here, by the fact that positions of responsibility are held mostly by men. And the presence of women in the school was handled by the boys through their concluding that there was something wrong with them as women, since they had gone beyond their real role in life.

Not only, then, are there differences between ruling class and working class schools in 'expectations' for girls, but in state schools themselves there are different models of femininity — and, I would infer, no one set of 'sexist practices'. What is more, this interacts with the many different forms of gender relations in the home, where pupils may or may not be part of a patriarchal set-up, which in turn they may either accept or use the school to escape from. Femininity is then something to be *constructed* from all the available (and often conflicting) sources. Similarly, the study undermines any single notion of 'masculinity' and instead points to a hierarchy of forms of masculinity constructed by the school. In the world of high-powered business competition a particular kind of masculinity is needed: motivation to compete, confidence in one's own abilities, ability to dominate others and to face down opponents in situations of conflict. Elite schools are very effectively organized to produce that kind of character, even if they do not teach the specific techniques of modern business. Masculinity is often given expression through competitive team sports in school, although the school does not abolish diversity, and strengths can be displayed in a number of ways (athletics, or study), even if these are not of equal status. What becomes interesting is the potential clash between the forms of competitive masculinity constructed by the schools and the versions of femininity which also include personal achievement and mastery of knowledge. Businessmen fathers thought about daughters following in their footsteps, but wondered whether the men 'would stand for it':

> Male resistance, then, is likely to exclude women from that sphere where capitalist authority fuses most completely with masculinity, *management*, and therefore deflect career-oriented girls towards the *professions*. It is notable that that is already where the schools are pointing them in their academic programmes, while in their non-academic curricula there is no equivalent of the boy's training in dominance through heavily-stressed confrontation sports and the like. In both the change and its containment we see how the ruling class is an active agent in the construction of masculinities and femininities and the relations between them. The process has a dynamic growing out of diversity and conflict. (p. 97)

Working class schools, too, are an arena for different types of masculinity: there is, as with elite schools, the version which is centred round competitive achievement in study and/or sport, and there is the *macho* mould, often achieved through resistance to school. Girls can choose resistance to the school through femininity, or by a double break with convention, abjuring both the school's individualized work ethic and the family version of domesticated compliance. But the shifts in women's employment and hence economic independence have meant anyway a real change in power relations in the family, independent of the school. The school may, by promoting social mobility for academically successful working class girls, split certain kinds of women away from that *milieu*, but it does not of itself reconstruct gender relations there. Versions of femininity are almost as varied as the families that produce the females: the most telling and summarizing assertion of the book might be 'Class and gender don't just occur jointly in a situation. They abrade, inflame, amplify, twist, negate, dampen and complicate each other' (p. 182).

Deviance and Gender

The notion of resistance just mentioned was central to my own research (Davies, 1980). This set out to probe whether girls' and boys' deviance in a comprehensive school was different, either in quantity or in kind, and if so, what explanations could be found for such differences. The case study school, where research was carried out over a period of two years, was a 1500 mixed, streamed comprehensive in a heavily industrialized, predominantly working class area of the West Midlands. The first complication was the basic finding confirming the old line 'When she was good she was very very good and when she was bad she was horrid'. Girls appeared more compliant in general, but when difficult, presented more problems to the teachers than did deviant boys. So the framework theory had to explain both greater conformity and special forms of resistance from girls. I played around with biological imperatives, socialization practices, subcultural formations, labelling by teachers, and economic/social structures — and inevitably found that they all interacted. Home backgrounds were far too rich and diverse, and subject to interpretation by participants, to warrant any factor analysis of causes of difference. Pupils did form peer groupings, but — especially with the girls — these were not predictable determinants of values and norms, merely a backcloth against which identities were tried and played out. The school was indeed found to have official and unofficial differences in treatment for boys and girls — but there was little uniformity among teachers in terms either of the ideology of schooling or the practical administration of discipline. And while the school could be seen willingly to 'reproduce' certain aspects of sex roles, at other times the emphasis on ability and achievement took precedence, so that the 'good pupil' was ideally androgynous, or at least sexually neutral. While the 'objectifying' of women might be central to patriarchy, the sexualizing of contact between male and female caused particular problems for male teachers disciplining female pupils (especially for male teachers who would have liked to beat them all indiscriminately). And the contradictions between the economic or domestic results of capitalism and ideologies of equality of opportunity meant a range of interpretations by teachers and pupils as to expected positions in the social structure.

The way I coped with all this was through the notion of 'scripts' and 'typescripts'. While a typescript is the broad social expectation for a particular category of people, a script is the more personal imposition of identity on the scene as one views it. It is the momentary expression of what Cohen and Taylor (1976) call 'identity work'. When a person says 'There's no way I'm ever going to put up with that', they are making a statement both about themselves as a person and about their definition of the situation. Our scripts are our favourite projections of ourselves: 'My door is always open' boasts a headteacher, and the fact that this may be patent nonsense, either literally or metaphorically, is immaterial, for through the script this person is saying 'I am an accessible friendly type who supports democracy and the breaking down of barriers' — and in the end believes it herself. It is important how articulation of a script not only describes but further defines action. Repeatedly saying 'I am the sort of person who ...' will condition behaviour far more than any physiological traits. The 'deviant' girls in my study who would assert 'that's me all over', or 'I can't help it, I have to join in' provided not only a justification but a forecast of action.

While there are parallels with the notion of 'strategy' which has been effectively used elsewhere (Hargreaves, 1978), I prefer script analysis because it allows for the concept of lines being written for others — as in the school's typescript for the good pupil — and also because it can cover the whole range of expression from throwaway one-liners 'I don't care what they think of me' — to entire life scenarios. Strategy is sometimes too grand a word for the idle experimental bits of repartee through which pupils try out different possibilities for interaction, some to be instantly discarded, others to be polished and refined, and lovingly preserved for future use.

What happens in a mixed comprehensive school seems to be simultaneously a confirmation of and a blurring of sex role identities. While one could see 'traditional' expressions of power relations between male and female, with the boys being *macho* and aggressive, the girls submissive and neat, the girls especially seemed able to call on a whole range of other scripts. They could be as aggressive and loud as the boys; they could use 'bad' language and sexual innuendo; they could 'objectify' the lads and use telling put-downs; they could portray themselves as more 'mature' than the boys (or even than some of the teachers); and they could joke and tease and confidently use humour to defuse, to debunk, to control. In commenting on the girls' generally more 'lenient' treatment by the school, boys in turn vacillated between the *macho* script 'we can take it better' and the 'equal opportunities' script expressed as injured indignation at unfairness.

Most interesting to watch was how experimental pupil scripts could coalesce to become a preferred style. This is where the peer group has its importance, to provide photocopied handouts of possibilities for action. Kath explains the start of her school 'reputation' thus:

> I dunno, how did it start off? Mr. C — we put the basket on the door and all the rubbish fell down on his head — we kept doing things like that, like the other kids used to do, so we just tried it, didn't we? The fifth years used to tell us what they used to do. When you mix outside.

Both she and her mate Terri had also been coached in masculine scripts by their fathers, who always insisted they 'stand up for themselves' — 'they've toughened us up', explained Terri. Yet they also had feminine scripts as well, being fashion and boy conscious, and not above a feminine wile in the classroom (as the teachers wryly noted). In fact, a proportion of the difficult girls had in reserve a 'settling down' script for their final year, claiming to have 'quietened down'. It was as if they recognized the impending need to embrace a mainstream feminine script, to consolidate a mature female image. The abandoning of old lines frequently bewildered teachers:

> *Mr. T:* 'Why is it you can be so charming?'
> *Linda:* 'I've settled down, I have.'

In turn, teacher typescripts for pupils varied according to pupil age and ability as well as gender. Through use of a bi-polar construct questionnaire, I elicited that the 'good pupil' typescript was not in many ways significantly different for boys and girls: all were supposed to exhibit the selected masculine qualities of achievement orientation and initiative while displaying the traditional feminine qualities of helpfulness, neatness and obedience. Deviant pupil typescripts did, however, vary according to gender: the deviant boy was cast as rough, untidy, but taking punishment well; the deviant girl characterized as emotional, resentful, aggressive with the mouth and even immoral. Pupils 'deviant' in terms of achievement — i.e. the 'less able' — were also subject to gender typescripts from the school, with the boys seen as good at craft subjects, the girls 'optioned' into child care. Such typescripts only crystallized in the fourth and fifth years, for earlier on there was a common timetable; it was as if pupils had been given their chance to be cleverly neutral, and now had to fall back on sex.

The central pivot of all these scripts seems to be the question of status and power. Achieving pupils are given consistent 'star' scripts by the school; the less able barely merit a walk-on part. It is small wonder that the latter draw on a range of cultures to give dramatic impact to their lives. Debbie casts herself as the 'black sheep of the family', tells of threats to 'have her put away', and announces finally, and somewhat triumphantly, 'I'm a criminal' (sic). Hers was the ageing starlet role: she would have a cigarette 'to calm me nerves down'; she would claim, seriously, 'I'm dying. My life ain't worth living'. Her preference for a woman-of-mystery script to support this dramatic and deviant role meant the frequent reiteration of lines such as 'nobody understands me', or the dark 'you don't know me. They don't know the half of it'. Such scripts are just a few from a myriad of pupil methods to gain or control an audience. If certain types of femininity work to manipulate teachers, in terms of eyelash-fluttering or turning-on-the-waterworks, fine; if that does not impress, then there are the more overtly sexual forms of dress, make-up or posture which can be guaranteed either to outrage or charm. For boys, the display of tough masculinity both celebrates the male working class culture and provides a forum for interesting diversions to the otherwise boring school day. But gender-derived scripts are not the only ones to constitute a pupil's repertoire: scripts will be borrowed from the other sex, and also combined with social class, ethnic and age variants to give a unique Identikit battery. One girl, usually renowned for her explosive confrontation scripts, was then described with her sister at a school production:

> the way she was speaking was *incredible* — she's normally got the Scrapton dialect accent, and she was speaking perfect English, and being so refined, such a lady in front of her sister — it was incredible, the change in her. I do feel that this minority of girls who are like this in the school really want to give off this tough image, and not being interested, when they're outside live up to a totally different image, whereas the boys are more consistent.

The greater range and unpredictability of girls' scripts may partially account for the teacher preference for boys (better the evil you know . . .); yet it is not that girls are any more 'superficial' in their responses, for the scripts may be deeply experienced while they are occurring.

Another teacher located the sex difference not in the actual lines, but in the depth of the characterization:

> Boys might even say the same things, but they would say it in a different way, which might pass it off as a joke, rather than downright insolence. Tone of voice ... I was thinking of the remedial science group, there are girls and boys in that set who are equally capable of making what could be seen as offensive remarks, but on the whole it would be the girls who would say it in an insolent and surly way, the boys would say it in a joking way, and I wouldn't mind so much.

Here the boys, by semi-joking, are not fully changing the direction of the play, merely temporarily providing comic relief. Theirs is a role distance, a natural break, rather than a different script; the girls would say the same lines 'for real', and by tone and body language convey the emotive meaning behind the words. These are Goffman's 'character contests', and the script is about honour, not just diversion: 'Honour can be engaged, namely the aspect of personal make-up that causes the individual dutifully to enjoin a character contest when his rights have been violated — a cause he must follow in the very degree that its likely costs appear to be high' (Goffman, 1969). Low-achieving girls, those with the fewest rights in the school (and those most likely to be subject to 'bitch and slut' immorality typescripts from teachers) are the ones most likely to see no holds barred in the defence of honour.

Teachers similarly choose scripts which enhance their personal ways of maintaining control, of winning or avoiding the character contest. These may be consciously gender-based in cross-sex interactions: 'The boys see me as a sort of auntie, really'; 'I'm like a grandfather to these girls'; and they may even underly the use of physical coercion by females — 'It's like their big sister hitting them really'. With same-sex interactions, there are the seemingly excessive displays of male brutality towards male miscreants — 'You don't cane in fury; but you don't lay it on soft either'; and also the parallel recognition that female power scripts are only countered by those who know the lines: 'That's why they [the girls] play up men more than they play up women. The men don't know how to deal with it. Being a bitch myself, I know exactly how to deal with it. Don't try beating me, I can do better!'

The 'successful' teachers are of course the ones who have a large repertoire of scripts at their disposal, and do not rely only on gender strategies. It sounds too obvious a platitude, but the difficult kids were better with teachers who saw them as unique individuals rather than as representatives of stereotypes, with teachers who had the flexibility to call up a range of responses to deal with personalities rather than fall back on a few stylized responses. Such teachers were not afraid to have different rules for different classes, and admitted openly to seeing teaching as an 'acting game'. Above all, for pupils of both sexes, the important thing was for a teacher to be 'someone you can have a laugh with'. Humorous scripts are not, as Willis (1977) appears to claim, confined to male working class shopfloor culture.

The difficulty lies in trying to summarize the implications of all these momentary and habitual scripts, plus their interaction, in school. Certainly it is more complicated than teachers 'sex-typing' their pupils, or pupils exclusively drawing on 'cultures of masculinity' or 'cultures of femininity'. We may be talking more of 'cultures of powerlessness': all power corrupts, but it is absolute powerlessness that corrupts absolutely, and leads to the plagiarism of scripts from all manner of sources. What appears to happen is that participants may draw on gender-based scripts if these are useful or creative, but will replace them if they become counterproductive, or inconsistent with their current identity work. Schools do not simply 'reproduce' sex roles to maintain social structure; a school will *select* certain aspects of gender expression which suit its own particular control and achievement functions. Girls would be permitted a mature, lady-of-the-manor interpretation of femininity but preferably not the objectified sexual, the dominant matriarchal, or the underdog versions. The competitive, team spirit, stiff-upper-lip side of masculinity would be favoured but not the aggression or the violence. This means potential contradictions for all concerned. Pupils of either sex, wanting to achieve, will have to cope with the fact that the good pupil must simultaneously display both female and male attributes (boys being neat, girls incisive in class). 'Less able' pupils may be given typescripts at odds with their gender cultures of home and neighbourhood, the cultures which become more impor-tant as the school comes to have less meaning in their lives. Teachers will have to face the use of a whole range of gender scripts by pupils without themselves being able to compete with similar strategies — for teachers, I found, were expected by the pupils to be morally beyond reproach. The male teacher involved with a female sixth former, or a female teacher too blatantly sexual was frowned on. Nor can female teachers call on the helpless 'little woman' script without being taken to the cleaners by the pupils. The only really safe gender roles for teachers are the familial ones.

Lynn Davies

Policy

Drawing attention to complexity and contradiction does not of course help in the attempt to make recommendations for gender policies in comprehensive schools. Let us examine some of the possibilities. At the legislative level, compulsory differential curricula for boys and girls have virtually been outlawed. This leaves the phenomenon that girls will tend to opt out of maths and science as soon as the core curriculum ends. The problem is being tackled head on by projects such as the GIST (Girls Into Science and Technology) initiative in Manchester schools, and GAMMA (Girls and Mathematics Association) in London. Both these are forms of positive action designed to convince girls (and their teachers) of their potential ability in the 'hard' areas of knowledge, and also to open up career opportunities through persuasive work on employers. In a simple script analysis, the aim would be to replace a girl's 'I've never been any good at maths' script or a head's 'the girls are very good at maths, considering' script, with a long term career scenario that sees a future for girls in hitherto 'masculine' fields. I welcome the thought of a parallel BICC (Boys Into Child Care) project, or even, Boys And Learning Languages Society. But without being flippant, I would want to challenge the assumption that sex-typed curricula disadvantage only the girls: especially with current unemployment levels, we should be countering rigidities in school socialization for *both* sexes, so that work-sharing, flexi-time and equal parenting could be accepted realities for women *and* men. If one accepts the value of 'positive discrimination' programmes, then one will need parallel projects to realign the orientations of boys as well as girls. Then such initiatives would be beneficial in extending the range of scripts available to all pupils, reducing the likelihood of their falling back on stereotyped cultural styles — which, while effective in establishing short term status and control, may be counter-productive for long term careers or for radically different family lives.

After legislation and the shifting of attitudes towards official knowledge areas comes the hidden curriculum. Most teachers will by now be not unaware of the various checklists drawn up and strategies devised for them to reduce sex differentiation (see for example Schools Council, 1983). These include everything from perusal of textbooks and reading schemes to the organization of tasks and activities, careers advice, the language and labels used by the teacher in conversation with pupils, and even mixed sports. There is in addition the argument that it is not enough for a teacher to 'avoid' sexism, she or he must directly

62

highlight gender issues in school and society. This must be done through discussion and projects as well as through exposing the real political and power structure of the mixed classroom. Not only do (unconsciousness-raised) teachers spend more time and effort with boys, but pupils may adopt deference or dominance roles *vis-à-vis* each other. Girls have to be shown how they 'contribute' less to discussion, how the classroom is simply a microcosm of 'normal' social situations where men control anything up to 98 per cent of verbal exchanges. Dale Spender's work on language is invaluable here (Spender, 1980a), although she would be the last to claim that altering the balance and dynamics of classroom interaction is an overnight task. From my own research it would seem profitable to draw attention in class not just to the amount of talk by boys and girls, but to the quality of pupil scripts. Pupils might well analyze for themselves *why* they resort to the gender-based strategies which may in the end only serve to confirm them in limited roles. Such investigation may of course be threatening to the establishment, as it should eventually lead to questioning of authority relationships and status differentials in school, of how and why certain categories of pupils may be downgraded enough to have to fight for identity.

Discussion of gender and schooling may in fact point to something far deeper than simply 'balancing' opportunities. There is the central question of whether schooling and learning as we conceive it has inherently masculinist biases. 'Subjects' like physics are supposed to be neutral, or 'pure'. But the teaching of scientific principles without any parallel discussion of how this knowledge might be applied (the bomb, space programmes) is an incredibly partial and short-sighted stance. Girls' reluctance to do science is inextricably linked to the way 'science' is (abstractly) presented in school: I will make the inevitable plea for my own sex and claim that women, for whatever reasons, *do* show more concern about social issues, do have a greater sense of social responsibility. We do not need the Greenham women to confirm that women care more about peace, for the 'gender gap' regarding disarmament already recorded in American polls is also increasing here, as recent MARPLAN and MORI surveys show (*The Guardian*, 21 January, 1983). Discussion about girls and science should make us debate whether science should in any way be seen as separable from social science. Simply getting more girls to 'do' science distracts attention from the way we might use gender as a basis for a fundamental *critique* of the knowledge areas as they are selected, bounded and presented in school.

The same applies to the hidden curriculum of language.

> Research has indicated that although men talk more, they exert more control over talk, and that they interrupt more ... Women listen more, are more supportive when they do talk ... and have greater expertise in terms of sustaining conversations ... It is precisely these qualities which have been neither valued or acknowledged. Rathe than women learning to talk more like men it would seem to be preferable if men were to learn to listen more and to be more supportive of the conversation of others. (Spender, 1980b, p. 154)

This takes us back to my earlier point about the relational definition of gender. We are not trying to make girls more dominant, for by definition both sexes cannot be dominant. The resistant girls in my study certainly did not fit the deference patterns cited above, for they could indeed effectively control verbal exchanges not only with the boys in the class but with the teachers; but while enjoying their performances, I would not want to endorse the simple substitution of aggression for courtesy. I would want to argue for an *extension* of the repertoire, of the range of possibilities for interaction, to submit that we should value and enhance the particular skills which females may in 'normal' circumstances bring to a situation. In terms of assessment, girls have been found to do better on essay-type questions, boys on multiple choice (Harding, 1980). This may be related simply to girls' greater verbal facilities, although I would like to think it is because they are able to see both sides of a question; certainly the increase in computer assessment and hence multiple-choice will not help divergent thinking and will promote the right-answerism which boys appear to find more easy.

In the end, sadly, we must return to the competitive nature of schooling, for this is the biggest stumbling block for change, whether in gender or any other structural terms. Many all-women groups will attest that their meetings are frequently more rewarding than mixed groups, for few participants are trying to score, to make points, to dominate: the enterprise is more a genuinely cooperative attempt to solve problems or to learn. Unfortunately comprehensive schools are by and large not about cooperation and mutual encouragement but about winning and losing. More girl winners may not only mean more boy losers, but also girls having to celebrate the 'masculine' attributes of ruthless competitive point-scoring, of achieving 'success' at the cost of another's failure. We have to ask, in the final analysis, whether this is what we really want, or whether we could envisage a schooling which promoted the more 'feminine' scripts for cooperation, support and social responsibility.

References

BROPHY, J. and GOOD, T. (1974) *Teacher-Student Relationships: Causes and Consequences*, New York, Holt, Rinehart and Winston.

COHEN, S. and TAYLOR, L. (1976) *Escape Attempts: The Theory and Practice of Resistance in Everyday Life*, Harmondsworth, Penguin.

CONNELL, R., ASHENDEN, D., KESSLER, S., DOWSETT, G. (1982) *Making the Difference: Schools, Families and Social Division*, Sydney, George Allen and Unwin.

DALE, R.R. (1971) *Mixed or Single-Sex School?*, London, Routledge and Kegan Paul.

DAVIES, L. (1979) 'Deadlier than the male?' in BARTON, L. and MEIGHAN, R., *Schools, Pupils and Deviance*, Driffield, Nafferton.

DAVIES, L. (1980), 'Deviance and Sex Roles in School', Unpublished PhD thesis, University of Birmingham.

FULLER, M. (1980) 'Black girls in a London comprehensive school' in DEEM, R. (Ed) *Schooling For Women's Work*, London, Routledge and Kegan Paul.

GOFFMAN, E. (1969), *The Presentation of Self in Everyday Life*, Harmondsworth, Penguin.

HARDING, J. (1980), 'Sex differences in performance in science examinations' in DEEM, R. (Ed) *Schooling for Women's Work,* London, Routledge and Kegan Paul.

HARGREAVES, A. (1978) 'Towards a theory of classroom coping strategies' in BARTON, L. and R. MEIGHAN, *Sociological Interpretations of Schooling and Classrooms*, Driffield, Nafferton.

MARTIN, V. (1983) 'The Education of Girls in Zambia', Unpublished BPhil (Ed.) dissertation, University of Birmingham.

POSTMAN, N. and WEINGARTNER, W. (1971) *Teaching as a Subversive Activity*, Harmondsworth, Penguin.

SCHOOLS COUNCIL (1983), *Sex Role Differentiation Project Newsletters*, 1–4 *Schools Council; Joint EOC Pamphlets*, London, Longman.

SHAW, J. (1980) 'Education and the Indivdual: Schooling for Girls, or Mixed Schooling — A mixed Blessing', in DEEM, R. (Ed) *Schooling for Women's Work*, London, Routledge and Kegan Paul.

SPENDER, D. (1980a), *Man Made Language*, Routledge and Kegan Paul.

SPENDER, D. (1980b), 'Talking in class' in SPENDER, D. and E. SARAH (Eds), *Learning to Lose: Sexism and Education*, London, The Women's Press.

WHYLD, J. (Ed) (1983), *Sexism in the Secondary Curriculum*, London, Harper and Row.

WILLIS, P. (1977), *Learning to Labour*, Farnborough, Saxon House.

A Case of Mistaken Identity: Inter-ethnic Images in the Comprehensive School

Paul David Yates

Cultural Identity and the School

The following account is based on fieldwork in a comprehensive school in a new town based on a light industrial estate, in the South East of England. It is a neighbourhood school of approximately 2000 pupils with a minority population of mainly Gujerati speaking East African Asians. Most of the Asians are Hindus, originally from barber and farmer castes settled in Kathiawad. The school is strongly academically oriented and because of the limited scope of local employment it is homogeneous in social class terms. The school is divided into lower, middle and upper schools, all separately housed but on the same site. The school covers the age range 12 to 16 plus, each sub-school cohort containing two year groups. I call the school Broadmere.

What I shall discuss is the notion that comprehensive education has largely failed to develop a comprehensive view of the implications of schooling in a pluralist state. This is because the concepts of culture and cultural identity are not reflected in the social organization of schooling, and only marginally in the content.

Multi-culturalism as a problem for schooling is normally seen in terms of the relative under-achievement of members of ethnic minority groups. What I want to suggest is that the causes of varying performance may not be located in theories of cultural deficit, but may initially be understood within the complex cultural configurations of different groups. The main current response is in the area of the curriculum, with the development of multi-racial education (MRE). The potential for teaching and learning across ethnic boundaries may not be enhanced by a response from within a culture specific process, that is, the curriculum. What MRE may be doing is signalling the existence of other cultures from a particular cultural standpoint without actually incorporating other cultures or affecting pupils' general understanding of culture and ethnicity, either their own or that of others. Much of what follows will be taken up with the description and analysis of the one dimensional quality of ethnic groups' images of each other in schools, and the poverty of the cultural information available to both teachers and pupils.

Let me begin with an example of the sort of dissonance in mutual understanding which typifies the problems of understanding across cultures in school. For historical reasons physical prowess in athletic games has become an important part of schooling in Europe and America. Both boys and girls can achieve high social status through being recognized as physically proficient. This is not a universal of human society but a culturally specific fact. In the culture of the Asian immigrants, for example, sporting ability is not generally recognized or valued. It is particularly irrelevant to the status of girls.

To participate in sport requires the development and refinement of certain motor skills. For example, basic to many team games is the ability to throw and catch balls, or otherwise control their movements. Again I stress that this is not a natural human activity but limited to specific cultures and contexts. The development of such abilities depends upon their being recognized as socially significant and as necessary to the establishment of a particular valued status. However, neither the indigenous pupils and teachers, nor the Asian immigrant pupils were likely to make a cultural analysis of sport in developing their own understanding.

Thus, while it was generally understood that Asians were likely not to be good at sport, the only explanation used by the English teachers was ethnocentric and in terms of cultural deficit. It was thought that the Asian lacked the necessary physical coordination to play games well, especially the girls. This is particularly interesting as a culturally specific judgment based upon a very slender knowledge of the group involved. Had the teachers seen the grace and precision with which the Asian girls danced at the Diwali festival celebrations, then the fact that physical ability is a matter of cultural emphasis would have been very well illustrated.

Other factors which might help explain the performance of Asian girls in sport tend to be left out of account by all groups, but may be crucial to the recognition of cultural identity in a comprehensive school. First, much of school sport is team-based and the relational structure of teams, involving both competition and collaboration, with a group of people whose social ties need not extend outside of the purposes of the game, is a difficult structure to translate within the values of a communal, kin oriented social structure. Running about with balls may be a meaningless activity in some cultural contexts. More specifically sporting activity can induce a sense of absurdity or a feeling of impropriety in some girls. That is to say that far from enhancing their self image sport can produce and sustain a sense of cultural alienation.

Thus, the difference in evaluative criteria employed by the English and by the Asians means that mutual understanding does not occur, because neither group appreciates the necessity of building in cultural context to explanations of school performance. This means that a level of consensual understanding that would facilitate the productive schooling of both the majority and minority cultural groups fails to be achieved.

I shall now go on to illustrate the case further and look more generally at teachers' understanding of Asian pupils, especially in the remedial section of the school where newcomers go to bring their English language ability to a level where they can join the main school. I include a vignette of a racialist teacher to illustrate the ease with which a liberal institution can accommodate, or fail to control, individual teachers' prejudices as they become the basis for their professional conduct.

I shall then turn to the description of pupil cultures as ethnic cultures, and discuss the negative stereotypes that pupils use to make sense of those from outside their ethnic groups. Finally I return briefly to the discussion of the implications of cultural analysis for a comprehensive school system.

Teachers' Models of Asian Culture

The vast majority of the teachers I spoke to did not have what could be described as an attitude towards the Asians in school, because they had not become an object separated from the body of pupils which demanded thought. This is readily understandable. Teachers outside the remedial area only came into contact with those Asians sufficiently anglicized to cope with life in the school. As a group within school, the Asian presence was not highly developed and they were conformists. They generally seemed to be thought to represent the normal spectrum of school intelligence but as a group were probably more hardworking than the English. Thus they were ideally suited to moving through the school entirely unremarked by the teachers because they did not cause them any problems.

Mr. Steel was a teacher with responsibility for the pastoral care of pupils in the middle age range. His wife was involved in a local scheme to teach immigrant women English at home. He seemed generally sympathetic to the Asians because their behaviour, as he understood it, was laudable. He told me of an Asian couple he and his wife knew, who had succeeded in getting both their son and daughter into university. He saw this as an example of making it socially through one's own efforts, something he felt himself to have done and something that he admired in others. His final comment on the success of the children was, 'good luck to them I say, if they are willing to grasp the opportunities the lazy English kids won't take'. Thus he chose to react to, and characterize the Asians on a level at which he could value them, a reasonably positive form of discrimination.

The head of physical education said that the Asians were not 'highly motivated' in sports; occasionally a good spinner would come along or a bat for the cricket team, and there was Pramit who was an excellent rugby forward, but he was very exceptional. He did say that from time to time an 'all black' ladies hockey team had been assembled but internecine wrangles had meant the venture was short-lived. He explained that there was no such team at the moment because there was no hockey specialist on the staff. He thought Asians lacked *esprit de corps* and the necessary competitive edge to be good at sport. A female physical education teacher found the Asian girls 'pretty hopeless', her explanation of this being that they lacked coordination so that, for example, they would be incompetent if a game involved catching or controlling balls. She thought perhaps it might be something in their background that caused this. Although I have already commented on this particular problem, it is interesting to note that not one Asian girl I interviewed actually enjoyed games lessons, and several had a positive dislike of them.

One Asian girl who was considered very bright by her teachers and who was particularly conscious of being discriminated against on the grounds of her colour, dreaded physical education because when the teacher asked for captains of teams it was always white girls, and when they picked their teams the Asian girls were always left till last and, sometimes the teacher had to put them into a team. If the physical education teacher who told me that Asians girls were not very efficient was voicing a generally held view then the logic of not including them in one's own team can be seen to be based on sporting rather than ethnic criteria. However, if one were using discrimination on grounds of ethnicity as a primary source of explanation then it could simply look like a case of colour prejudice.

Of the two Asian boys who excelled in a sporting activity, one, Dipak, was the son of a divorcee and had little contact with the Asian community, while the other, Pramit, was determined, and consciously so, to integrate himself into English society. He was not considered to be particularly clever academically and had remained in the remedial unit for the four years since his arrival in the UK. He had asked to be included in a rugby trial and had succeeded in gaining a place. This had proved a very fruitful avenue of recognition and allowed him to see himself as valued by the institution and obliquely by English society.

Dipak had been in England for eleven years, spoke no Asian language and talked and behaved like an English boy though evidently physically of Asian origin. He was very confident in his manner — even aggressive, and was considered to be potentially a first class sportsman. The head of physical education mentioned him to me and said that he did not know whether or not he was an Asian, 'but he was definitely a something or other', this presumably referred to his colour although his ethnic origin was undecipherable from his speech or behaviour.

Although generally it was unnecessary for teachers to make radical adjustments to the presence of immigrant pupils, this was not the case in the remedial unit. There are three points to make about how the structure of the unit made ethnicity a concept sufficiently important to demand that the teacher held a view, and developed a notion of what ethnicity meant. First, and most obvious, the remedial unit had to deal with those incoming Asians who had a language difficulty, and it was children in this category that initially formed the bulk of the Asian school population. Nearly all the remedial teachers had first-hand experience of teaching Asian children. Secondly, the remedial unit was separate from the school proper, and the staff formed, for others and themselves, a small recognizable group with particular conditions and problems. Finally, in a school which was very highly academically oriented the remedial teachers and their charges had a low if worthy standing within the school. This may partly have been due to the fact that their work did not require a high level of subject expertise.

In each year group there were two remedial forms. The teachers described below taught pupils in the middle age range. Mrs. Bushel, a comfortable-looking middle aged women, took the 'top' form as it was recognized that she was a successful remedial teacher and that if anyone was capable of coaching the remedial children through a couple of low grade certificated examinations, it was she. Indeed her form had some limited success in examinations and this was a strong factor in her high standing in the group. It is interesting to note in passing that this fact underlines the dominance of the academic ethos which was still seen as providing the only criterion of success even in a group whose existence presumed that academic success was not universally achieved.

Mrs. Shard, slightly built and in early middle age, took the second fifth form. Mr. Gordon, a man in his late thirties took a fourth form, and Mr. Less, a young English teacher with an English as a Foreign Language (EFL) qualification, and teaching experience in Africa, took a special form of immigrant children with particularly chronic language difficulties.

One of the teachers, Mrs. Shard, was perniciously prejudiced against her Asian pupils, and indeed against Asians in general. A garrulous woman, she paraded her opinions very readily, and over many conversations, I came to understand the nature though not the springs of her attitudes.

Mrs. Shard would talk of the general run of remedial children as though they were halfwits: 'of course, poor little dears, they won't know what's hit them when they leave the shelter of the school'. She had the embarrassing habit of talking about children in their presence in the third person, even to me, an outsider. Most children, unless they had some other obvious handicap, were simply described as being in various stages of thickness, 'He of course is very thick, she is not as thick as some'. If I went into her classroom she would always turn what I expected to be a private discussion into a declamation. I went into her class one day to arrange some interviews and she immediately began declaiming. Turning to a young Sikh boy she said: 'Daljit is finding out how true is everything I've said', (*à propos* employment difficulties for the unqualified fifth form leaver). Daljit simply nodded. Inspired, she went on to explain the obvious virtue of reducing the school leaving age to 14 after which age she thought schools would only have those interested in learning staying on, the rest could be 'maturing' at work. Her use of other people seemed to be only in terms of reflectors for her unnegotiable picture of social reality. I was tolerated as I was a willing audience although she expressed no interest in what I was actually doing at the school.

Mrs. Shard had a folk history of the origins of her attitudes to Asians which she blamed on the school. Before coming to school she had nothing against Asians, 'my husband used to think I was soft', but what she had learnt since then had changed her mind. She would tell the usual mutually contradictory stories of all Asians being simultaneously rich in their own right and also a drain on the welfare services. This was substantiated by the story of a family who were living on welfare and 'getting everything', while the father was a substantial property owner in India and regularly flew out to collect his rents.

Mrs. Shard only had one overt supporter in the staffroom and that was Mrs. Bushel, who had taught in Africa and South America and had a rather old fashioned colonialist view of Asians as being perfectly normal intellectually but a little less than perfectly developed spiritually. Pantheism for her was a sign of moral ignorance if not turpitude. Thus Mrs. Shard gained some general support from Mrs. Bushel though the latter was never in my hearing openly racist in her views.

Mrs. Shard disliked Mr. Less and would often suggest that he was lazy, and imply that what he was doing with the immigrant children was a scandal on account of their being far too thick to learn anything anyway. Speaking of a child she had taught from Mr. Less's form, she said, 'admittedly he's Asian but he can't even spell his name'. Later in the same conversation she described the contents of Mr. Less's school bag as being 'running shorts mixed up with curry and old sandwiches'. She once asked me what I thought of Mr. Less. I replied, non-committally, allowing her to tell me what she thought, which was what I had been set up for. She went on to be very critical in a personal way about Mr. Less in front of me and her colleagues. This was an unusual way for a teacher to behave but the community of the staffroom was too loosely knit for any effective control of a member; also this same looseness mitigated any desire for control of social attitudes amongst the staff.

If a teacher finds that he or she is not in sympathy with colleagues, it is very easy simply to avoid them in a large institution and focus attention and energy on relations with pupils, other aspects of the school world, or with something entirely outside the school. It is possible for classroom teachers to fulfil their roles without developing any particular commitment to pupils or the institution.

Mr. Less, for his part, never actually personally attacked Mrs. Shard though he did recognize that she was less than sympathetic to the group that he was most interested in. His general manner was one of extreme vagueness, his face continually registered mild shock that events were occurring, that he was holding a cup of coffee or that someone was talking to him. He was an English literature graduate and had spent some years teaching in Nigeria.

It was suggested to Mr. Less that he pick about a dozen of the children having most problems with English and set them up in a small formroom of his own. When I arrived at the school for my second period of fieldwork there were eight children in Mr. Less's form, all of them Asian immigrants, excepting one West Indian boy. The curriculum timetable of the form included science, maths and drama although these first two subjects were taught at the most rudimentary level, and drama not at all. Their teaching was simply cobbled together; because they were outside the examination system there were no criteria upon which to decide whether, with the exception of English, they should be taking one subject rather than another.

Mrs. Shard complained that the class was 'all black' and said that she and Mrs. Bushel had been in favour of a mixed form because both thought that segregation was bad. When I asked Mr. Less why the form had no indigenous English pupils in it he said that the Deputy Headmaster had been against it in case the white parents complained. This seems a feasible though hardly laudable reason for an all-immigrant class.

For Mr. Less, whose family had a tradition of humanitarian colonial service, prejudice in its modern form, was simply not part of his conceptual world. The guiding concepts for Mr. Less were cultural continuity and the British Commonwealth of nations. His overt motives for teaching immigrants were public spirited. The notion of duty to society was real for Mr. Less. This was not, however, a consciously political stance as he would rarely make any abstract comment about his role in the life of the immigrant community, and apart from a vague notion that developing world cultures should be taught to the children, to help different ethnic groups understand each other better, he had made no analysis of the potential role of education in sustaining a multi-ethnic community.

Mr. Less was very conscious, however, of the way in which his interest in a group which was not considered very important in the school made him a marginal person and vulnerable to criticism. In my estimation, this was probably not the case; the fact that the school had employed an EFL teacher was the salient point in terms of public relations and what he actually achieved was regarded as a problem of a lower order. This of course was as far as the school, or more properly, the headmaster was concerned; to Mr. Less, however, to succeed in the eyes of his colleagues was important and he saw his having been given the immigrant class as a strong public recognition of his expertise. Mr. Less was nominally a member of the English rather than the remedial department. The next academic year the head of English was giving him some ordinary teaching for the first time, about which he remarked to me, 'It will be interesting to teach some ordinary Asians'.

In many of his attitudes to immigrants Mr. Less held views representative of the teachers. He knew there was a problem, and used his expertise to alleviate it, but otherwise did not try to understand the implications of a multi-cultural society for the community or inside the profession of teaching, except through vague notions such as the family of the Commonwealth, which may well have meant even less to his immigrant charges than to the population as a whole.

There is a problem in discussing teachers' attitudes to race relations in the school because many teachers did not come into contact with the immigrants and avoided the necessity of acting on their opinions of immigrants in their professional capacity. There were a few to whom it was an issue and here attitudes and opinions differed. English is the only subject taken by the whole school where social values can be legitimately scrutinized. The head of English, an intelligent young man with mildly progressive theories of his subject and its teaching, would not have race discussed in his classes. He took the same line as the British political parties, that is that to make race an issue would be to exacerbate a potentially disruptive situation. His private opinion was that the white children 'are for the most part probably racist'. He was against classroom debate of race because he believed that the children would simply trot out the racialist platitudes learnt from their parents and reinforce each other's racism. Several of the children I interviewed would preface a racist remark with, 'Well, my mum says that ...'. However, this generalized racism need not, and did not, stop children having friendships with members of other ethnic groups.

In comparison with the head of English, another senior member of the department, Mr. Winch, took the opposite view that the discussion of racial problems in the school had a possibly cathartic effect, and at least brings the problem into the realms of conscious thought where it might be subjected to the illumination of reason. Despite this excellent purpose, Mr. Winch who had previous experience of ethnically mixed schools in America, thought that the English children were racist in their attitudes 'to a frightening extent'.

Mr. Winch surprised me with his ignorance of the school. Although he had taught there for over a year, and was one of the most vivacious members of staff, he had not realised that the majority of immigrants were in the remedial unit nor that the remedial unit was separately, and comparatively poorly, housed. His perceptions of the immigrants were limited to his experience of them in the classroom, and what sort of professional challenge they represented. In the case of drama the challenge was not taken up.

The fact that Asian children find the role-playing that is central to school drama impossibly embarrassing is a social fact that forces itself upon the attention. In a drama lesson that I observed the Asians were allowed to sit out and not take part in the acting at all. When asked why they did not find drama easy the answer was that they did not see what good it did or what they could learn from it. This certainly was part of the explanation, that expectations of school were confounded by drama being presented as a lesson rather than a diversion: a problem of different cultural values and of ideas of what constitutes legitimate school knowledge. The teacher's choices are not easy: either pupils are forced to participate where they do not understand the nature of the game, or they are excluded, which reinforces their own sense of being alien, and their alienness and incompetence in the eyes of others.

Mr. Winch's understanding of his task in relation to the immigrant typified the general liberal stance of the English department. Society for Mr. Winch was mainly a series of communications, the most important of which were through language. Thus, to promote the awareness of the potential of language in communication was seen as the major objective, whether a child was an immigrant or not. This illustrates the tendency to put new problems into old categories where the fit may not be exact but is sufficiently undisturbing to allow one to proceed as if the fit were exact. For while the language needs of the immigrant may in some senses be similar to those of the indigenous child, the fact that there is also a lack of cultural understanding behind the lack of ability in the immigrant child might be usefully taken into consideration, at least by the teacher being conscious of the fact. For Mr. Winch the inability to communicate would have serious repercussions for the child's intellectual development, emotional relationships and more mundanely the ability to perform in job interviews. He hoped that the Asians' would be able effectively to function in all the various aspects of language when they leave ... 'we expose them to more language than they would otherwise see and try to make them aware of language as a tool'. Mr. Winch was optimistic about the future in comparison with his experiences in America. He said that the English were already eating curry and that he recognised a broadening of British culture. He saw the role of the school as very important in assimilating immigrants into

British culture, teaching them the 'non-verbal cues', as well as the verbal. Mr. Winch saw eventual intermarriage as the inevitable result of this exchange. He voiced a common complaint against the immigrant community, that it did not in his opinion organize to help immigrants to adjust to life in Britain.

This is an interesting point for I think there was a noticeable passivity (in comparison with English children) amongst the Asian children at Broadmere which was the result of their attitude to authority and belief in the legitimacy of school. Mr. Winch suggested that the immigrants should make their aspirations and needs known within the school, and teachers should know more about the background of immigrant pupils. He also thought that positive discrimination was not necessarily to the good as it confirmed the difference between the races and institutionalized it. Positive discrimination in favour of immigrants always runs the risk of an adverse reaction from the indigenous community, on the ground of maintaining parity of provision. Inevitably the more fearful the immigrant community becomes, the less likely it is to favour representing itself vigorously to white authority.

Mr. Winch was a particularly aware teacher, and if any action from the school were to be initiated then he would most likely be the instigator. Despite having a higher than average consciousness of immigrants and their problems, it was a consciousness that only resulted in the formation of an attitude rather than in action. This is only to be expected, because the institution itself kept quiet about its immigrant population and this may have been because of the fear of gaining a reputation amongst the white community as a school with a high proportion of immigrants, or a school which favoured immigrants. Thus the headmaster could appear morally spotless by pursuing the policy of treating all children equally.

When asked about the Asians in school, teachers would often answer by saying that particular Asians were very bright. Two individuals were continually mentioned as representing the top ability Asians. One young science teacher, Mr. Hume, spoke of a phenomenon which seemed to him almost exclusively Asian and certainly fitted with my general understanding, that was of the child who was conscientious and diligent but whose aspirations in the education system exceeded his ability to pass examinations. Mr. Hume mentioned particular Asian children as typifying the child in whom intelligence was seen to be unbalanced as against aspiration and motivation. I asked him whether he saw motivation and ability as generally in keeping with potential. He thought they were usually, though not invariably, matched amongst the indigenous population.

Pupil Perceptions of Ethnic Difference

Apart from the judgments that specifically related to school, casual enquiry was likely to produce a stereotypical reaction from the whites regarding the Asians. 'The women don't speak English, they believe in all these gods — they don't eat meat.' To the majority of the English, Asians are an undifferentiated mass of people. The low level of general information about the Asian population and their way of life that existed amongst the indigenous English might be thought surprising given their mutual proximity. If the immigrant population was being prejudged to their detriment then one might expect a community of active prejudice to involve some attempt to know about the disfavoured group in order to give substance to the prejudicial image. I asked the white children at school where they thought the Asian immigrant population came from? Most children thought they came from India, some children mentioned Pakistan and a minority some east African country. Ignorance at this level seemed not to relate to the child's position in the school; the elite sixth form were as ignorant as the remedial children. In fact the majority of the Asian population at Broadmere was of East African origin. Much the same picture emerged from the question, what religions are practiced by the immigrant community? Not a single child made the connection between Pakistan and Islam. Some thought the Asians were all Buddhists, others Muslims. Few children seemed to have heard of Hinduism and a minority could not name a single Asian religion.

It seems clear that we have a *prima facie* case of pre-judgment on the part of the white community. Insofar as the judgments about the social and moral qualities of the Asian community are inherited, they are not based on any personal empirical evidence. This in itself is unremarkable. In order for a change in social structure to make sense it must perforce be given an interim meaning before interaction can moderate and deepen the social understanding in the host community. In other words, the process of pre-judgment would seem unavoidable, a necessary part of the dialectic of the maintenance of social reality, and the fact that this pre-judgment is unfavourable in many cases is a separate problem relating to historical relationships and particular judgments of reality.

The first part of the relational design, the pre-judgment, might be expected to be part of the Asian consciousness of the English if it is, as I suggest, a structural social process. This is in fact the case. The knowledge of UK culture amongst immigrants, many of whom had been in this country a decade or more, was as shallow as that of the host community's knowledge of them. This was in some ways more surprising in a group that was having to learn to operate in a new culture, and is probably explained through the dominating importance of the small group, the family, in the self and social conceptions of the Asian immigrant. In matters related to the public world of work and relations with the local economy the Asian knowledge of the scene was excellent. The average male immigrant could tell one where to buy the cheapest remoulds and classify local firms in terms of their wage rates and prospects for advancement, and would have met and spoken to a good many English men, but would still think that the English do not love their children and that divorce is the inevitable result of English moral laxity.

The mutual ignorance between the two groups suggests that attitudes and behaviour may rest upon a view of society that has no empirical reality. This is not unusual insofar as we can all understand, and incorporate into our conceptions of the world, attitudes and opinions based upon very scant knowledge and no direct experience. English people will have a fairly detailed personal image of America and will form judgments about American society, its moral tone, its standards and way of life. This will be done for the most part without recourse to visiting America to check attitudes against reality. When this same orientation is used to make statements about the people living next door, to incorporate them without directly relating to them, then this reticence requires some social explanation.

One element might be the inherited racism of the imperial decline. Another might simply be the apprehension about outsiders which is a fairly constant feature of human societies, though not invariably so. This would be intensified if accompanied by feelings of being in competition with the newcomer for scarce resources. Another feature of social structure that would work against inter-relations is the quality of reserve which characterises both English and Asian culture. People are often made meaningful by being put into a family context, in Asian social relations, classificatory kin abound. A boy might say, 'we are going to London on Saturday to see my cousins'. On being questioned about the relationship further, it may transpire that he does not know whether he is related by marriage or blood to the people he will visit but just calls them cousins. In this primary relational arena which depends upon the extension of kinship as a criterion for inclusion, it is obviously difficult generally, to bring in members of the English community at this level because of the simple categorical incongruity.

There is nothing inherently sinister about communities maintaining social distance while sharing the same physical space. If one thinks of the operations of class in the English community then it would seem possible for class cultures to remain discrete yet in the main mutually tolerant. Both in suburbia and urban England it is possible to live in a house without knowing anything about one's direct neighbours. In school, however, avoidance is not a possible option because of the social organization of school activities. This does not mean that proximity fosters tolerance through continuous exposure.

For example, the idea of involuntary repatriation was very much favoured by the white children, who expressed concern within the usual range of employment, housing and social security issues, although locally none of these was an acute problem. Mr. Winch said that the white children would often refer to the Asian community as 'Pakis', used as a general derogatory term. This illustrates the lack of a desire to form an accurate or realistic picture of the newcomer. Mr. Winch also suggested that it was not only colour but also manners and behaviour that made the Asian an outsider in school. The fact that they had special uniform regulations was resented; for example the few Muslim girls were allowed to wear trousers, when the rest of the girls would dearly have loved to wear them but were not allowed. This was an obvious cause of grievance and separation.

From observation of children in and around the school, girls tended to associate in pairs or in large fragmented and stationary groups of say ten to fifteen. The boys, outside of games playing, tended to be seen less in pairs or large groups than in smaller groups of around four to six. I noticed no real difference in this pattern between the indigenous English and the Asian children. Obviously though, five Asian boys together amongst a majority of white boys will stand out.

What is undeniable is that the Asian boys and girls spend most of their out of class time with other Asians. The main reason for this is the legitimately grounded fear of rejection by the white children, which is sometimes masked by professions of superiority of manners and sensibility on the part of the Asians. A common Asian perception of the English at school is that they are frivolous and do not really want to succeed. This is in contrast to the Asian self-perception as hardworking and serious in their studies, an orientation to school which they regard as virtuous. The rather sophisticated English view of academic success, that if you have to swot to succeed, then the success is in some sense devalued, is not part of the Asian view. This rather aristocratic view that only innate rather than achieved ability is authentic was not in this pure sense obvious at Broadmere, although a strong valuation was placed on work avoidance, or at least ostensible work avoidance, by the majority of the school. The Asian attitude to study made them look like swots to the English, and swots had a low social value.

There are also sex culture differences which keep the ethnic groups apart. It was difficult to observe natural playground behaviour at close quarters as my presence as an adult authority was inhibiting. Most of my observation of conversation was made at periods when children were on the move through the school. Much conversation between the English boys was dominated by sport and mutual insult in a general aura of aggression and potential physicality. There were obviously many who did not belong to this world, but it represented standard and approved behaviour. Very few of the Asian boys fitted this model, though there were notable exceptions. In general demeanour they were not ebullient; they did not appear to develop the mock aggressive joking relationships of the English boys. They were generally much quieter in their manner and more reticent in their relationships. Conversation in school was mostly about aspects of school life and work and other members of the Asian group. There was also a qualitative difference between Asian and English relationships which was very hard to define. Perhaps it could be characterised by suggesting that English relations evolve and develop through shared experience, while Asian boys, who may well see very little of each other outside of school, are friends by declaration and are referring to a set of mutually binding emotional responsibilities towards each other, rather than saying 'he is my friend, therefore we will do things together'.

There is one other major factor which separated the Asians in school. A proportion of the Asian children spoke very little English. They therefore naturally sought out those they could talk to in their Indian language, thus appearing cliqueish and emphasizing their ethnicity.

The Asian girls were not only distinguished by their colour but also by their distinctive hairstyles and in the case of the Muslim girls by their trousers. They were effectively cut off from the culture of the English girls, in a way in which other ethnic minorities are not, by their lack of interest in English fashion, make-up and boys. The conversations of the girls revolved around the doings of members of their families, and to a lesser extent happenings at school.

Naturally, among the Asians at school, there were varying degrees of closeness to and interactions with, English culture. Some Asian boys were at ease with English boys through their success as sportsmen and their English manners. There were a few Asian girls born in this country who were able to live through the medium of English culture while at school, who did not wear long plaits, and who spent their time with the English rather than the Asian girls.

Just as the Asians thought of the English children as homogeneous, so the English failed to differentiate among the Asians. However, between a boy who was born in Broadmere town of educated westernized Asian parents and a boy recently arrived from the Punjab countryside there was very little in common. Criteria for inclusion in an Asian group were first, sex, then religion and thirdly class or caste though caste was a very vague concept to most of the Asian children who thought it was merely a matter of endogamous restriction. Thus the Sikhs in school knew all the other Sikhs, at least by sight, and were likely to choose their friends from this group. The Hindus, not being sectarian in the same sense, did not have so strong a notion of themselves as a religious community; this was most strong among the Muslims who tended to be the most orthodox and the least interested in engaging with European culture. However, perhaps by default rather than design Hindus formed friendships with other Hindus.

Thus there were within the Asian school community distinct groups. These groups were to an extent autonomous. The Asians did not behave, or conceive themselves, as a general category although they were seen as such by the English. In Asian friendships there was also a divide between those in the remedial units and those in the school proper. To the extent that this division also reflected the length of time spent in England then the difference may have been between those more and less adapted to English life.

These differences which existed within the Asian community were not recognized by the English just as the Asians did not know sufficient about English culture to make any complex judgments themselves. Neither community, English nor Asian, had any necessity to find out about the other. Social judgments at the level of the cliché are sufficient to furnish the barest meaning, and unfortunately motivation to develop this meaning is more likely to be fuelled by antipathy than a real desire to increase understanding of what it is to live in a multi–ethnic community.

This may be partly for reasons of history and the specific relations between white and other races. There is also the point to be made in the case of the English that the major social theory still operating would seem to be social Darwinism and the hierarchy of cultures. Implicit in many of the casual conversations that I had with English adults and children was the idea that the Asians were fresh from the jungle, that they lacked civilized habits. The major empirical proofs of this were the fact that their food smelled different from English food, that their women insisted on what was seen as 'native' dress the sari or pyjamas — that they could rarely speak very good English and that they put their children to work. These differences were perceived as evidence that the Asian community was below the English on the cultural ladder. The Asian habit of having large families was also cited as evidence of a bucolic backwardness.

Conclusion

What I have tried to illustrate, albeit briefly, is the general lack of cultural awareness of other groups, and the constant resort to one-dimensional images in understanding other cultures. What this means in the comprehensive school is that judgments tend to be made ethnocentrically, to the detriment of other groups, by pupils and teachers alike. This may not affect the academic performance of indigenous pupils because their natal culture is also that of the school. For ethnic minority pupils, their ability to perform successfully within the culture of school in part depends upon their understanding of the host culture, particularly in relation to their own culture.

The current curriculum response to the problem of minority cultures in school through MRE is unlikely to effect positive change because of its preoccupation with content. There are two separate problems to be addressed which tend to become confused. First, how can, or indeed should, school reflect the cultures of its participants? Secondly, if as I suggest, academic performance is a function of culture, then should we begin building a consciousness of the nature and operations of culture into the social structure and political purpose of comprehensive education? The problem is not one of knowing about, but more potently of being conscious of, culture.

A Comprehensive Sixth Form

Carol Buswell

Introduction

In 1967, approximately 11 per cent of the 16 to 18 year old age group were in sixth forms, but by 1979 this had increased to approximately $18\frac{1}{2}$ per cent in maintained schools (HMSO 1981). The growth of comprehensive education has obviously made sixth form study more available to many young people and recent youth unemployment has increased incentives to gain qualifications in the absence of any alternative. In the North-Eastern city in which this study was conducted in August 1980 there were almost 2500 school leavers registered as unemployed — about 200 young people for every job notified to the careers service, and roughly the same number were on government schemes. The unemployment rate for the city as a whole was 11.8 per cent compared with 8 per cent nationally — but in parts of the catchment area of this school the rate was 30 per cent and above.

Between 1979 and 1982 the sixth form in this school, as in many others locally, doubled in size from 58 to 107 pupils — although the balance between pupils taking two or more A levels and those doing one or none remained roughly the same with about one third of the pupils doing no A levels at all. Thus, the increasing numbers staying on did not simply increase the non A level group but increased the A level contingent also, serving to make this group more heterogeneous than previously. In the summer of 1980 concern was expressed about the fact that under two-thirds of the subject entries at A level were successful. This school reflected the national picture where, according to one survey (Dean and Steeds, 1981), more than two-thirds of pupils in sixth forms were taking A levels irrespective of the size or intake of those sixth forms. The A level subjects which occupy most sixth formers are still the traditional ones and Edwards (1983) has pointed out that in 1979 three-quarters of A level entries were in the same nine subjects which produced 80 per cent of the entries in 1960, whereas only 6 per cent of entries came from new subjects such as business and computer studies.

In spite of this fairly traditional picture it is the 'new sixth' which has gained most attention. This was a term originally used to refer to pupils who wished to pursue education beyond 16, but who are neither suited to A level courses nor sufficiently committed to a particular occupation to embark on a course of vocational training (Dean and Steeds, 1981). Dean and Steeds reveal that many such pupils take O levels, however inappropriate — earlier findings showed that the average attempt of approximately four subjects resulted in average passes of only about one and a half. But O levels have established a reputation with employers, parents and pupils and are entry requirements for many occupations; new forms of certification have, therefore, to compete with this.

In 1979 a government committee report (Keohane, 1979) recommended a new Certificate in Extended Education (CEE) intended primarily for those pupils with CSE passes at grades two to five and for A level pupils wishing to take a complementary study. It was envisaged that the former group of pupils would take about five subjects at this level. The CEE, however, although in operation in many comprehensive schools, has still not been nationally validated and the majority of pupils take only one CEE subject in conjunction with O or A levels. In common with CSE Mode Three the CEE has teacher involvement in curriculum design and all modes of examining are available, which might account for its similar lack of status.

Another development that is occurring in some regions and cities is the 'link' course between schools and further education or technical colleges. In this city the Technicians Education Council (TEC) course was being developed with sixth form pupils spending about one quarter of their weekly time on it — some of that time in college — in addition to their other sixth form studies, usually O-levels. The TEC course leads to the first year of the technician apprenticeship which has to be completed on a day-release basis from a full-time occupation. This school had developed a sixth form curriculum which reflected the national picture of extended schooling — it offered thirteen A level, eighteen O and A/O, RSA secretarial and seven CEE courses with the development of the linked TEC course underway.

Credentialism and Qualification Inflation

Much of the pressure for more and extended education is linked to the growth of qualifications for entry to any kind of occupation. As Tyler (1977) points out, the belief that there is a tightening bond between education and job lies at the heart of liberal and meritocratic models of education. The belief is that, as societies become more complex, merit becomes the criterion of success and this leads to a tighter relationship between credentials and inequalities. Most evidence, however, indicates that — with very few exceptions — the educational attainment of workers within each occupational classification far *exceeds* functional requirements for doing the job (Squires, 1979). Technical change does not necessarily lead to the upgrading of jobs. In fact, Braverman (1974) has argued the opposite — that automation and technical change are leading to the 'deskilling' of many, including professional, occupations; not only are different forms of control limiting the autonomy of many workers but that the retraining which is required to cope with technical and automated change can usually be achieved in a few weeks. The assumption that qualifications are 'necessary' leads also to the conclusion, widely employed in the rhetoric of government training schemes, that the unemployed do not have the 'necessary skills' for work, whereas, they would in fact be perfectly competent to do many jobs. The use of the diploma as a work permit closes the door to many capable workers and Sarup (1982) sees entry qualifications as ideological in the sense that they are used to differentiate and rank occupations.

Dore (1976), in discussing the growth of credentialism in developing countries, points out that the more useless educational certificates become, the stronger grows the pressure for more and more education. Qualification inflation becomes, in Collins' view (1979), a result of 'credential capitalism' — a *laissez-faire* attitude where everyone attempts to get as much education as possible to cash in on as much career advancement as possible. Employers, of course, will then tailor their requirements to match the qualifications of the new supply of labour. Qualification inflation becomes, in Boudon's term, a 'perverse effect' of the aggregate result when people pursue rational activity at the individual level, since 'there is a perverse effect when two (or more) individuals, in pursuing a given objective, generate an *unintended* state of affairs which may be undesirable from the point of view of both or one of them' (Boudon, 1982, p. 14).

Carol Buswell

Bureaucracy

The use of educational qualifications for occupational credentials emphasizes the instrumental aspects of schools and it might not be surprising, therefore, if forms of organization come to reflect these concerns. In addition schools are faced with larger and more heterogeneous sixth forms and can no longer rely on the normative compliance by pupils that served largely as the form of control in small traditional sixth forms. Schools, in common with other organizations, are bureaucratic institutions characterized by hierarchical and specialized divisions between functional positions which operate according to specified rules. At the same time, the relationship between schools themselves and local authorities has become more subject to rational controls and generalized rules. Bureaucracy, according to Weber, is the means of transforming social action into rationally organized action, allowing goals to be achieved. There are, however, different degrees of bureaucratization and the increasing application of new and revived rules as an attempt to control both teachers and pupils is a move towards a more rational bureaucracy which may have unintended consequences. Bureaucratic control establishes the impersonal force of 'rules' or 'policy' as the basis for control.

Weber himself considered that 'irrationality', rather than the opposite, could be a result of certain bureaucratic developments — a displacement of goals by means, an emphasis on procedure rather than results. His conclusion was grimly expressed (Nisbet, 1967):

> Together with the machine, the bureaucratic organization is engaged in building the houses of bondage of the future, in which perhaps men will one day be like peasants in the ancient Egyptian State, acquiescent and powerless, while a purely technical good, that is rational, official administration and provision becomes the sole, final value, which sovereignly decides the direction of their affairs. (p. 299)

In industrial organizations the increase of bureaucratic control has been documented as leading to discontent but this discontent shows itself in individual or small group responses rather than in conflictual collective action (Collins, 1975). This is partly because of the inherent properties of bureaucracy which stratify and divide the members. Increased bureaucratic control in schools might be expected, therefore, to produce individual or small group discontent amongst not only pupils, but also teachers. The split between administrative/bureaucratic management and practising class teachers is widening in schools: 'Status once depended on "mystique" but is now being replaced by a technical notion of skills. The same fragmentation and routinization that is taking place in production is also occurring in teaching' (Sarup 1982, p. 36).

The division and separation of teachers through bureaucratic controls is most marked in terms of gender. This will have effects on the teachers' interaction with pupils, resulting in pupils themselves being differentiated by gender as well as by status and function which is also a result of bureaucracy. It is these themes that will be discussed in relation to empirical data from one sixth form.

The Research

The school was a large inner city comprehensive in the north of England (1500 pupils and 100 teachers) with a predominantly working class intake. Full-time research had taken place in the school, on another project, for a term in 1979. From March 1980 to July 1982 the present research was conducted on a part-time basis.

In March 1980 a representative sample of pupils who would probably stay on at school, was picked from the fourth, fifth and lower sixth forms; the upper sixth at that time acted as a pilot group. When pupils left, new individuals — of the same gender and course — were added to the group. Altogether 57 pupils were included — 14 were in the sample for two and a half years (6 girls and 8 boys), 26 for at least one year (16 girls and 10 boys) and 17 for less than a year (10 girls and 7 boys).

Pupils were interviewed individually and observed in at least one lesson every term; teachers and form tutors were interviewed once or twice a year; internal and external school reports were scrutinized; some pupils kept diaries; and informal participation in the sixth form common room and staff room took place.

Changes in the Sixth Form

Increasing bureaucratization within the school will be illustrated with reference to the changes that took place within the sixth form over the period of the research. The changes that occurred, it will be argued, increased the separation of pupils by gender and status and led to more formal relations between teachers and pupils.

Qualification inflation and unemployment served, obviously, to increase the numbers of pupils staying on at school and nearly all parents encouraged their children in this respect. The pupils with some O level passes stayed on to do A levels hoping for better job chances at 18 than there seemed to be at 16:

> *Peter:*   Me father said as long as I don't put an overall on — not to go into a factory. Me mam's pleased I'm staying on.
> *Malcolm:*   My parents would like me to stay on and get more qualifications for more chance of a job.
> *Christine:*   If I'd gone out at 16 I don't think I'd get a job as easy as what it'll be with A levels.

Pupils with lower-grade CSEs came back to 'convert' them to O-levels or vocational qualifications and said very similar things:—

> *Judy:*   Trudy's on the dole now and has got a bit of money. But in the long run you get more money if you stay on. You get a better job 'cos you've got more qualifications.
> *Mark:*   I couldn't get a job. Me dad wanted me to come back instead of going on the dole. I always used to say I'd never stay on — but now I realize what the chances are with no education.
> *Kathy:*   If you haven't got O-levels there's not much point in leaving.

The diversity of sixth form pupils as represented by their achievements at 16 was matched by a diversity of courses which included not only two-year A level courses but some one-year A levels, RSA typing and shorthand, CEE courses and extra O levels in addition to those offered in the fifth form. In terms of intake, therefore, the sixth form became increasingly more comprehensive — a trend that most teachers endorsed in theory. In practice, however, some of them had difficulty in coming to terms with this change in the sense that their 'ideal sixth former' had more traditional characteristics, based on normative identification, as illustrated by these comments made about particular fifth formers:

> *Mr. Q.*   He's probably the type of pupil I'd like to see in the sixth form — someone who takes part in extra curricula activities, is good academically, has a pleasant personality and no disciplinary problems.
> *Mrs. N:*   Malcolm will be a super sixth former. He has a

natural politeness, he's very good at his work. He's been in football teams and clubs — an ideal 'grammar school pupil' in the old sense. He's reliable and has hardly ever been absent.

The teachers' views of what sixth formers should be like achieves importance when it is apparent that fifth formers intending to stay on, view the sixth form mainly in terms of the different treatment they will receive from teachers — and there was no difference between the intending A level candidates and the non A levellers in this respect. In the fifth year they typically expressed these opinions:

> *Dick: (non A leveller)* The sixth form looks different. I've heard they get free periods and that. The teachers accept them as adults — as equals — because they've got more time to discuss things with sixth formers 'cos there's less of them.
> *Wendy: (A leveller)* I know it'll be a lot more work, but you'll be treated better. You get free lessons and you can do what you like.

The similarity between pupils destined for different kinds of courses with respect to their reasons for staying on and their views of what the sixth form will be like was mirrored, at this time, in the easy social relations between the sixth formers themselves.

Leniency

In the summer term 1980 there were so many informal activities that it was difficult to keep track of events. There was a festival air in the sixth form common room as pupils from all courses congregated before and after their exams. The A levellers and non A levellers knew each other and there were sub-groups of party-goers, pub drinkers and sports enthusiasts who socialized outside school. Most of these groups were mixed in terms of gender and courses being taken. During this period the fifth formers who were taking exams, and intending to stay on, were allowed into the common room and there was some 'weighing up' going on by the lower sixth formers as to which ones would 'fit in'. These judgments, however, were based more on personal characteristics than on perceived cleverness or course of study. For example, a couple of fifth year O level boys — later to be A levellers — poked their heads round the common room door one day when three non-A-level sixth form girls were in the room. Judy shouted 'You're a lot of cretins' and they — not surprisingly — beat a hasty retreat. After they had gone

Amanda commented 'They're O.K. — those two — canny. I was talking to them last week.' To which Judy replied 'I know they are, I was just kidding them.'

They were aware that they were making it difficult for some fifth formers to come into the room and the game was played with much merriment. A couple of days after this incident, however, Judy brought two quiet O level girls into the room and made them coffee. 'I just wanted to show them we're not really scary', she said, after they had gone. Sue, an upper sixth A level pupil, said at this time 'I love the atmosphere in the sixth. There's a lot of different people from different backgrounds. I like a lot of the people, although I can't stand one or two! I like trying to talk to people who aren't perhaps quite so intelligent as me — they're different'.

Good-natured banter between the pupils was a common occurrence. One day Roger, an O level pupil later to be an A leveller, with a reputation for being clever, hard-working and very organized, was holding forth one day about his revision 'plan'. Kim, a non A leveller, said mockingly 'I'd hate to be like ye. I bet you've got a 90 year diary that says "January 1990 — go and see Mum" '. Roger laughed and replied that he had not, but it was a good idea.

There were also organized extra-curricula activities — a barge trip to Stratford included two non A level girls besides some A level pupils. For a week or so before the trip there was much common room discussion about which clothes and how much money to take, besides such questions as who would be doing the cooking. The week or so after the event saw the non-attenders regaled with accounts of the more exciting happenings. A play that was being produced at this time involved many pupils in rehearsals and, in the end, included many more 'helping'. At the end of term a staff/senior pupils rounders match sent pupils scurrying to the props cupboard for outfits, to little avail, as the teachers' garbs were inspired. All these social activities included teachers — and both lower sixth and fifth form pupils who intended to return to school looked forward to being involved in such things.

Strictness

During the autumn term the social pace would not have been expected to be as frenetic as the post-exam period, although Judy did have a party which some teachers attended and Kim tried to organize an 'idiot play' for Christmas. But there was some concern among the teachers about the social side of the sixth form and the 'attitude' of some of the pupils:

> *Mr. E:* Most people who stay on do so because it's more sensible than collecting dole money and drifting round the house. But I think a lot of them are staying on for the social atmosphere, although some of the sixth form do give a lot to the rest of the school — assemblies, sports and so on.
>
> *Miss H:* We've got some super kids in our sixth form, although there's a certain 'element' who are not very mature and not like the traditional sixth form student — this might have a detrimental effect. I think there are some who are taking advantage of their freedom.

There was also some concern about the A level pupils' work, which was described in terms of them 'under-achieving'. In fact, some of the A level pupils had very modest exam results at 16 and were taking two or three A levels which added impetus to some teachers' desire to extract more work and a more 'serious' attitude from them. The dual concerns regarding the 'kind' of sixth former that was emerging and that of the work of the A levellers led to increased control over the pupils — the main mechanism of this control being attempts to eradicate the 'social' from the school day. So the common room was checked at the beginning of each lesson and pupils discovered they were sent to the library or the sixth form work room; the coffee was locked away to be collected at breaks and the work room was 'supervised' each lesson by a teacher to keep talk to a minimum and work to a maximum. The fact that the pupils did not have eight 'free periods' a week but 'non-contact time' in which they were expected to work was reiterated almost daily. As far as the work was concerned, some of the A level pupils were constantly chased up regarding homework and parents were contacted in the case of the really dilatory boys. Senior staff told pupils they should be 'putting in forty hours a week'.

The upper sixth pupils had experienced a more lenient system and they resented the changes:

> *Kim (non A leveller):* It's *our* common room — I don't think they've got the right to turn you out. I'd prefer to work in the comfort of me own home.

But the most acute resentment was expressed by the lower sixth form A-level pupils for whom the sixth form was very different from their expectations:

Jim: The sixth form's just the same. I think you should be able to play darts in your free periods — you're supposed to work even if you've got nothing to do, just sit and be bored. It's *your* lesson, a free lesson. I do more work at home anyway.

Pat: It's gettin' borin' here with everybody gettin' depressed. We can't go in the common room in our free lessons — I think that's terrible. I never do anything in me free lessons anyway. You should be allowed to do what you like.

Helen: Nobody likes the sixth form now. Everything's stricter. You're told it's better in the sixth but it's just the same. I think the sixth form should be quite separate.

Peter: It's depressin' in the sixth form. Borin'. I thought it would be more social and that the teachers would treat you different, but they don't.

The school not only attempted to 'claim' all the time during the school day for work purposes but also, through setting homework, impinged on the pupils' outside time. But the minimizing of the 'social' aspects of the day caused pupils to dichotomize 'work' and 'leisure' much more obviously than previously which resulted in over half of the sample of 20 A level pupils developing various kinds of negative attitudes towards homework which was seen as an imposition on their real 'free time'. Thompson (1982), in describing the move from task-oriented to timed labour which accompanies the move from peasant to industrial work, points out that those who are employed experience a distinction between their employers' time and their 'own' time as time becomes a currency which is spent, not passed. He concludes that one recurrent form of revolt within Western industrial capitalism has often taken the form of flouting the urgency of respectable time values. Similarly, pupils felt a dilemma in the allocation of their time to different aspects of their lives and they resolved the problem in different ways. That it was usually a *conscious* choice between alternative 'uses' of time is clear and the conflict between social life and school work is the most prominent theme. Four boys took the extreme path of doing virtually no work at all as they preferred to spend their own time on sport and did not consider that they could accomplish both as the amount of work given meant a choice between work and play:

Gordon: I seem to be sacrificing me work for sport. I can't be bothered with the work. Mr. T is chasing me up all the time, but I'd rather have done the sport than the homework.

Peter: Anne stops in every night to work, but socially she's just not with it. Roger works all the time as well. The only ones who do the work are those who never go out. I like to enjoy life — I value sporting achievement.

Four girls restricted the amount of work they did so that they could have some social life as well. They were defined as the 'brightest' pupils and the teachers had high aspirations for them. But the girls were prepared to settle for less, in terms of achievement, in order to maintain activities outside the school:

Sarah: I didn't work over Christmas, I went out. But I worked for the exams when I came back and I did all right. I go out twice a week and if I want to go out more I do.

Mandy: There's loads of work — I'm doing four A levels and an O level resit. I do about three hours homework on a couple of nights and about an hour and a half some other nights. I'm not prepared to do it all the time — I've got to go out sometimes.

Four pupils did most of the work, but with extreme resentment:

Jim: The work in school isn't hard, it's having to go home and do more — you're never up to date. I sometimes think 'what's it all for? What's after this?' ... If you do the work they want more, they want as much as you can do, and you've still got a chance of failing ... I've had enough.

Helen: I'm really fed up. Nobody likes it now in the sixth form. ...Lots of people not doing A levels go out and lots doing A levels go out, but they get behind, they're doing badly. I'd like to go out a bit. I think it's got to be work or social life.

Although the negative attitudes were expressed, initially, towards homework, after a while some teachers began to complain about the pupils approach to work in general. One such teacher, said a year later:

Mr. A: I don't think there's the drive or determination in the upper sixth there has been in previous years. I had a barney with them last year over homework — I found they were all copying Jim's answers. I had to get nasty with them, I've never had to treat a sixth form group like that. I've even kept some of them in after school to finish off their homework. There's no driving force. Teaching them has been a bit of a chore.

Carol Buswell

Differentiation

Whilst the A level pupils were expressing dissatisfaction and disappointment with the sixth form itself — feeling a disjunction between their expectations and reality — most of the non A level pupils found it a pleasant change:

> *Liz:* The sixth form's all right. You get free lessons and go in the library or something. The teachers are good, you can talk to them now. I never really knew what it would be like.
>
> *Sheila:* I like the sixth form, although you don't get what they say — all lounging around and that! No way can you do that, there's tons of work to do. But they don't treat you like kids any more. I'd rather be taught as a grown-up than as a child.
>
> *Roy:* It's different in the sixth — they treat you like they're supposed to treat you. They treat you more sensible.

The emphasis on the more adult treatment these pupils consider they receive compared with their fifth year is in sharp contrast to the A levellers' comments that this, for them, is the one feature that does not seem to be present although they expected it. Their differing fifth year experiences, though, are the base from which they start. The non A levellers, by and large, were in CSE groups in the fifth year, often with pupils who caused some problems for teachers and the non A levellers often remarked that it was 'better now the disruptive ones have left'. The A levellers, on the other hand, experienced O level fifth year groups and expected *more* adult treatment and autonomy to match the increased status they considered sixth formers should have.

There were, of course, non-A level pupils who did not like the sixth form and about a dozen left within the first four months of the lower sixth year in 1981. About one third of these had a job, government scheme or college course to go to, but the majority left to go on the dole rather than stay at school. Thus, the non A levellers who continued in the sixth form comprised a more contented group than the A levellers. Besides the higher level of contentment with the sixth form as a whole, the non A levellers also accepted the work given with more equanimity:

> *Liz:* I did all right in me typing test last week and shorthand's O.K. I do some work in the free periods in the library 'cos I

have to make the tea for me sister and dad coming in from work when I get home. But I work from about 7 onwards if I've got homework left to do.

Roy: When me English homework comes round I do it straightaway, and the drama. But with the lessons I don't like I don't do much.

Mary: Most nights I do two to three hours of homework, sometimes longer. But sometimes I can do it at school. At week-ends I've got essays and a lot of practice, like, for shorthand and things, and accounts takes a long time.

Some non A levellers sometimes 'forgot' or simply missed lessons in their least favourite subjects, but no more frequently than the A levellers, who simply tended to be a little more imaginative with their excuses.

The non A levellers might have found the work easier to encompass because, for them, it consisted largely of short essays or exercises which could be completed in relatively short periods of time, whereas for A level pupils each piece of work might take several hours which they often seemed to have difficulty in breaking up into smaller units that could be achieved in shorter spaces of time. This latter method of working was, in any case, discouraged by some teachers, one of whom said that he was attempting to get them out of the habit of working in 'small gobbits'. The result, however, was that pieces of work loomed large and seemed less manageable and the A levellers' reluctance to work during their non contact periods, compared with the non A levellers, might have been partly for this reason.

Not only were pupils from different courses beginning to diverge in their perceptions of school and work, but the curtailment of possibilities for socializing during the day meant that there were fewer occasions when social relations between them could be established and maintained. The following summer term saw some congregating in the common room during the exam period, but it was much more low-key than a year previously.

By the end of the research period most friendships did not, any longer, cross the course divides. There was a group of A levellers who used to go out together and a sporting group of boys, but the large social conglomerate with friendships waxing and waning across the whole group seemed to have disappeared. This appears to illustrate Crozier's (1964) contention that bureaucratic systems result in a lack of communication between groups and also supports Edwards' (1979) view that, under bureaucratic control, the workplace culture tends to express less of the workers and more of the firm.

Gender relations[1]

Within occupations the internal labour markets that prevail serve to locate women at the lower or at best the middle levels of the occupational hierarchy. This is particularly noticeable in 'female' professions such as teaching where men are over-represented in the higher positions.[2] Grimm and Stern (1975) maintain that when the 'administrative' component of a 'female' profession expands, the increased demand for administrators will enhance the tendency of males to dominate the field and their research indicates that most of the work in female semi-professions is planned, supervised and directed by men. This school reflected such a general pattern and sixth form pupils generally only had contact with female staff teaching vocational or lower level courses. This pattern of hierarchical and teaching responsibilities affects gender relations between teachers and pupils.

MacDonald (1981) points out that the category of gender — which is socially constructed — only has meaning when the concepts of masculinity and femininity are recognized as a pair which exist in a relationship of complementarity and antithesis. Davies (1983) also refers to the female role as a 'relational' one deriving from women's position *vis-à-vis* men. It is, therefore, necessary to consider the processes that are in operation for boys as well as girls and to consider them in relation to each other. In order to do this two processes — one of which was particular to boys and one to girls — will be considered with illustrations from the case studies of two individual pupils.

Sponsorship

There seems to have been a tendency, before O levels, for teachers to overestimate some boys' results but to be fairly accurate for all the girls. The tendency was most marked with a few boys who were expected to pass all their O levels and, in the event, passed between one and three subjects.

Peter was one of these boys and in the fifth year expressed his intention of staying on at school to take three A levels and go to college. He explained that he might well not have been allowed to stay on as he had been in some trouble in the fifth year but a teacher, Mr. T, who ran one of the football teams, and the P.E. teacher had 'spoken up' for him and advised him to 'change his ways'. Thus the informal male network of sports teams had some importance for him. Peter's reports before O level were glowing: 'a great lad', 'extrovert', 'articulate', and so on, and Mr. T thought that he would 'really blossom' in the sixth form.

Both Peter and the teachers were disappointed with his O level results but in the sixth form he started three A level and two new O level subjects. But the amount of work expected clashed with his desire to have an active social life and work was relegated to the bottom of his list of priorities. He had, however, only been in the sixth form three weeks when the 'chasing up' began; he was called in about his lack of work and encouraged to change his priorities, and this became a regular occurrence. His internal school report at the end of the first term said that he did insufficient work and his lack of progress was blamed on this.

Whatever his coursework and exam results no-one ever suggested that Peter was not able or capable and eventually Mr. T began to describe his parents as 'non-supportive' — a description not endorsed by Peter, who stressed that his parents wanted him to do well and were always 'on at him' to work. Half way through the lower sixth year Peter failed two of his three A level subjects in the school exams and was surprised because one of the subjects was considered to be his best one. But he had failed, he explained, 'because of the way that teacher marks. Everyone did badly except one girl'. His report at the end of that term stressed his lack of effort and waste of talents. The next year followed exactly the same pattern with Peter doing no work and the teachers attempting to encourage him to work. At the end of two years Peter failed two of his three A level subjects, having 'chosen' not to take the advice and opportunities offered to him.

Viaene (1979), in discussing the 'general expectancy model' with regard to success and failure in males and females, stresses that when performance is inconsistent with expectancy it is attributed to one or more temporary factors such as luck or effort rather than to a stable factor such as ability. This process was clearly in operation with marginal pupils like Peter. Peter's ability, for example, was never called into question even when his performance suggested it might be. Equally important is the fact that the pupil himself defined his own lack of achievement as due to boredom and lack of effort, which is consistent with Bisseret's (1979) findings with regard to male students who attributed their exam failures to similar reasons and even doubted the intelligence of those who actually passed exams. This system of sponsorship for some boys takes on crucial structural importance if one considers Parkin's (1974) view that, with regard to social closure in bourgeois society, forms of exclusion are based on the right to nominate successors through systems of sponsorship. Thus, the sponsoring of boys by male teachers, is one of the ways through which the exclusion of girls operates. The operation of such sponsorship within the classroom itself, affecting the actual teaching and the evaluations of both pupils and teachers, is also discussed by Stanworth (1983).

Nurturing

A process that applied only to girls is exemplified by the case of Judy who, like Peter, had been in some trouble in the fifth year and had left school to work in a shop. At the beginning of the sixth year, however, two of the A level girls with whom she was friendly had persuaded her to return to school to take some O levels. Soon after she had returned she said: 'Some people look down on me because I'm not all quiet and sweet. But I know that Mr. T and them are pleased I'm doing all right. As soon as someone gives us a bit of confidence I'm all right — but it just takes one dirty look from a teacher and it all goes away'. At this time she overheard herself being described by a (male) teacher as 'highly strung'.

During her lower sixth year there were complaints that she was too noisy in the common room and setting a bad example, and she was 'seen' about her behaviour. Her report at the end of the year stressed her 'lack of confidence' and 'fear of failure'. At the beginning of the upper sixth year Judy had a row with Mr. S and the next day was dominated by people trying to persuade her to go to him with the written apology he demanded, and one of the teachers (male) described her as 'neurotic'. When Mr. T was attempting persuasion in the matter of the apology, she shouted: 'You're trained to break my spirit' and rushed out of the room. She did, in the end, apologize and Mr. S described her as 'spoilt'.

During this year she decided she really liked Mr. C, whom she had previously 'hated': 'Mr. T and Mr. C are good because they tend to give us a bit of confidence because they know I lack it and Mr. W asks me to do little jobs'. A fairly typical exchange between Judy and a male teacher, during this year, is illustrated by this extract from a lesson:

Judy: Do I have to do this?
Mr. C: No. It's your decision.
Judy: Don't be horrible! (pouting)
Mr. C: I'm not being horrible, love. (Puts his arm round her shoulder in a friendly fashion.)

So, by playing the tentative, moody, unconfident female she elicits friendly and supportive responses. It is the aggressive, argumentative loud-mouth the teachers do not like. Her work does not figure much in her story at all, but this is not seen as a problem. Mr C said he had been through a bad patch with Judy. 'But we're over that now. I think chiefly because I handled it in a good-natured way.' It might be suggested that another reason for the improvement in their relationship was that she learned to manipulate him by using insecure, rather than aggressive, signals. He described her as 'manic-depressive'. Another male teacher recounted an occasion when she had stormed out of a lesson in response to something said to her. The teacher explained this as due to the fact that she 'lacked confidence' and was 'spoilt'.

So this girl, who had shouted at Mr. S, stormed out of a lesson and told a teacher he was trained to break her spirit and who might have been described as aggressive, rude and unpredictable was, in fact, variously described as 'spoilt', 'lacking in confidence', 'manic depress-ive' and 'neurotic': a fairly good sketch of a person who could only be female, according to traditional stereotypes. The labelling of her attributes in this way is important because it 'constructs' a person who needs nurturing. An aggressive loud-mouth requires quite different treatment.

Again, all the teachers involved in this case history are male and are playing out their own roles in interpersonal relations with the pupils. What Judy learned from these two years was to manipulate and control people (men) with an acceptable set of traits and behaviour patterns. The school felt it had succeeded with her because someone they had hardly been able to contain had 'grown up'. Boys, of course, present images as well, but the ones that girls such as this are learning will only be of benefit to them in interpersonal relations of an unequal kind. In Willis's 1977 terms they are going to 'locate' themselves in powerless and traditional positions, always dependent on the group they think they are controlling. Davies (1979), in studying 'oppositional girls' also points out that they close future avenues to themselves. But these girls are not members of counter-cultures — they are learning to behave in approved ways to become 'good pupils' and thereafter 'good women'.

This is not to suggest that girls, who were not nurtured, were given no encouragement at all. Some very able girls regarded themselves as being unduly 'pushed' by the teachers in order to achieve very high grades and, indeed, began to restrict the amount of work they did in order to have some social life as well. The important difference between encouragement for these girls and sponsorship of the marginal boys was that the girls were encouraged after they had *already* proved themselves. One such girl, Mandy, at the end of the fifth year said:

> I didn't like school for five years because they didn't know who I was. Then — all of a sudden — when I was doing O levels they all wanted to know what I was going to do. I know all the teachers can't know all the pupils, but I was a bit disillusioned that, all of a sudden, they wanted to know me.

This girl had moved from 'invisibility' to encouragement because of her high level of exam success but some girls remained invisible throughout the sixth form. Pat, in the fifth year, said: 'The subject teachers hardly know you — they take more notice of you if you do well in a subject — if you don't you're just background, sort of thing'. But, in the sixth form, things did not change much for her and she related it to being a girl:

> I just sit and listen in that subject because I don't think I'm very good at it. Mr. T has got his favourites. He doesn't like girls. He laughs at the boys' jokes and talks towards them all the time. Some of the lessons are just a conversation between him and Peter ... You can *really* tell he doesn't like us because, you know, he's just not bothered about us at all.

Anyon (1983) has noted that complete acceptance, or rejection, of sex role appropriate behaviour is actually rare. Instead, she suggests, there are processes of 'accommodation and resistance' which involve girls in a series of attempts to cope with contradictory social messages. Judy's behaviour can be seen partly as the 'use' of feminine behaviour to resist the demands of work and teachers. Mandy, who resented the teachers' sudden interest in her after five years resisted, in the sixth form, attempts to push her to very high levels of achievement — the school is obviously easier to resist if it shows little interest until late in the school career. The active processes of accommodation and resistance by the girls trap them in webs of dependency and may simply give the girls a measure of protection within the unchanging social structures. The bureaucratic school, in locating women teachers in the more subordinate positions, affects the gender relations between teachers and pupils particularly at the sixth form level where pupils more often come into contact with male rather than female teachers.

Conclusion

Hall (1981) suggests that it is worth considering the ways in which cultural factors within the school itself have the (perhaps unintended) consequences of reinforcing, rather than weakening, the mechanisms which bind the school to the social structure outside it. Some writers see the connection mainly in terms of educational qualifications and stratification. Although, as Hussein notes, credentials have a cultural — not an economic — worth in the sense that it is the status afforded them that allows people to enter the competition for jobs, they do not *guarantee* such jobs. The inflationary credential system affects cultural consciousness, according to Collins (1977), by mobilizing increasing proportions of the population in struggles for control of the stratification system. Such mobilization can become politically dangerous, he maintains 'to an authoritarian government which may react by cutting down the educational system ... or disillusion may set in among the purchasers of cultural credentials'. Boudon (1982), in explaining the results of perverse effects — one of which is qualification inflation — comes to a similarly wide conclusion:

> Educational expansion has not led to greater economic equality or reduced social mobility ... Perhaps these effects, at once unexpected and perverse, are at the root of the crisis in the educational systems of industrial societies. Because they were unexpected they have caused widespread disillusionment with the social and political virtues of education, and because they are perverse they have led people to doubt the ultimate purpose of educational systems and to fear that they will never be able to control them. (p. 29)

A connection between educational systems and other social institutions is also one of form. Bureaucratic activity is seen by Marxists as an essentially political, rather than a neutral, process and Gintis and Bowles (1981) maintain that it is the form rather than the content that is the most important feature of education. Weber (1978) also saw bureaucracies as expressions of the dominant and powerful social ideas. Thus, as Salaman (1978, p. 537) notes, 'For both Marx and Weber the major elements of the structure of modern large scale organizations stem from the efforts of those who own, manage or design the organization to achieve control over the members'. This control is surrounded by ideological activity which attempts to mask the political nature of organizations by referring to generally accepted values such as rationality and efficiency.

The development of hierarchical and bureaucratic control in industrial organizations was not developed, according to Marglin (1982), for reasons of technical efficiency but for capital accumulation. It allowed the entrepreneur to separate the efforts of workers and to substitute their own control over the work process. Thus, the resulting separation and differentiation that occurs among workers was not unintended. But such hierarchical forms in education also have the effect of separating and dividing — as has been shown — without the needs that give this form of organization a rationale in the industrial sphere. Although — if credentials come to be 'bought' with pupils' labour and 'cashed in' in the occupational market — schools are, in a sense, creating goods which are later sold.

Giddens (1982), in pointing out that pre-bureaucratic forms of organization allowed members less autonomy than is often romantically supposed, contends that bureaucracies can, in fact, be partially liberating. But the extent to which people can find some identification and meaning in bureaucratic organizations depends, if industrial studies are representative, on the ability and opportunity subordinate members have for creating voluntary informal networks within the larger framework. Bureaucracies, by creating profound inequalities of power, often leave the weaker and less autonomous members more open to direct control and sometimes less able to use the informal group as a 'buffer' between themselves and the larger institutions. The pupils in this study, because of the nature of the rules enforced, found themselves unable to develop the widespread networks of informal relations that might have given them greater control over the work process. Kumar (1979) makes a pessimistic assessment of this trend: 'There is no longer any place for the young in this society other than school. Serving to fill a vacuum, schools have themselves become that vacuum, increasingly emptied of content and reduced to little more than their own form' (p. 257).

But if alienation towards institutions is the obverse of the culture of individualism in modern society, as Berger *et al.* (1974) suggest, then schools — in adopting bureaucratic processes which separate and divide — are contributing to the very cultural form that will ensure their own ineffectiveness. It must be time to consider the extent to which more egalitarian and cooperative forms of organization would enhance other cultural traits that would ultimately reinforce the educational, rather than the procedural, goals in education.

Notes

1 An extended version of gender relations in this study appears in ACKER, S. and MEGARRY, J. (Eds) *World Yearbook of Education 1983/4: Women and Education*, London, Kogan Page.
2 For a discussion of this see ACKER, S. (1983).

Reference

ACKER, S. (1983) 'Women and teaching: a semi-detached sociology of a semi-profession', in WALKER, S. and L. BARTON, (Eds) *Gender, Class and Education*, Lewes, Falmer Press, pp. 123–139.

ANYON, J. (1983) 'Intersections of gender and class: accommodation and resistance by working-class and affluent females to contradictory sex-role ideologies', in WALKER, S. and L. BARTON (Eds), *op. cit.*, pp. 19–37.

BERGER, P., BERGER, B. and KELLNER, H. (1974) *The Homeless Mind*, Harmondsworth, Penguin.

BISSERET, N. (1979) *Education, Class, Language and Ideology*, London, Routledge and Kegan Paul.

BOUDON, R. (1982) *The Unintended Consequences of Social Action*, London, Macmillan.

BRAVERMAN, H. (1974) *Labor and Monopoly Capital*, New York, Monthly Review Press.

COLLINS, R. (1975) *Conflict Sociology*, London, Academic Press.

COLLINS, R. (1977) 'Some comparative principles of educational stratification', *Harvard Educational Review*, 27, 1, pp. 1–27.

COLLINS, R. (1979) *The Credential Society*, London, Academic Press.

CROZIER, M. (1964) *The Bureaucratic Phenomenon*, London, Tavistock.

DAVIES, L. (1979) 'Deadlier than the male? Girls conformity and deviance in schools', in BARTON, L. and R. MEIGHAN, (Eds) *Schools, Pupils and Deviance*, Driffield, Nafferton, pp. 59–73.

DAVIES, L. (1983) 'Gender, resistance and power' in WALKER, S. and L. BARTON (Eds), *op. cit.*, pp. 39–52.

DEAN, J. and STEEDS, A. (1981) *17 Plus: the new sixth form in schools and further education*, Windsor, NFER-Nelson.

DORE, R. (1976) *The Diploma Disease*, London, Allen and Unwin.

EDWARDS, A.D. (1983) 'An elite transformed: continuity and change in 16–19 educational policy', in AHIER, J. and M. FLUDE (Eds), *Contemporary Education Policy*, London, Croom Helm, pp. 59–79.

EDWARDS, R.C. (1979) *Contested Terrain*, London, Heinemann.

GIDDENS, A. (1982) 'Power, the dialectic of control and class structuration', in GIDDENS, A. and D. HELD (Eds), *Social Class and the Division of Labour*, Cambridge, Cambridge University Press, pp. 29–45.

GINTIS, H. and BOWLES, S. (1981) 'Contradiction and reproduction in educational theory', in DALE, R. *et al.* (Eds) *Schooling and the National Interest*, Lewes, Falmer Press, pp. 45–59.

GRIMM, J. and STERN, R. (1975) 'Sex roles and internal labor market structures: the 'female' semi-professions' *Social Problems* 21, 5, pp. 690–705.

HALL, S. (1981) 'Schooling, state and society', in DALE, R. *et al.* (Eds), *op. cit.*, pp. 3–29.

HUSSAIN, A. (1981) 'The economy and the educational system in capitalist societies', in DALE, R. *et al.* (Eds), *op. cit.*, pp. 159–79.

KEOHANE COMMITTEE (1979) *Proposals for a Certificate of Extended Education*, London, HMSO.

KUMAR, K. (1979) *Prophecy and Progress*, Harmondsworth, Penguin.

MACDONALD, M. (1981) 'Schooling and the reproduction of class and gender relations', in DALE, R. *et al.* (Eds) *Politics, Patriarchy and Practice*, Lewes, Falmer Press, pp. 159–177.

MARGLIN, S.A. (1982) 'What do the bosses do? The origins and functions of hierarchy in capitalist production', in GIDDENS, A. and D. HELD (Eds), *Classes, Power and Conflict*, London, Macmillan, pp. 285–298.

NISBET, R. (1967) *The Sociological Tradition*, London, Heinemann.

PARKIN, F. (1974) 'Strategies of social closure in class formation', in PARKIN, F. (Ed), *The Social Analysis of Class Structure*, London, Tavistock, pp. 1–18.

SALAMAN, G. (1978) 'Towards a sociology of organisational structure', *The Sociological Review* 26, 3, pp. 519–554.

SARUP, M. (1982) *Education, State and Crisis*, London, Routledge and Kegan Paul.

SQUIRES, G.D. (1979) *Education and Jobs*, New Jersey, Transaction Books.

STANWORTH, M. (1983) *Gender and Schooling*, London, Hutchinson.

STATISTICS OF EDUCATION 1979 (1981) Vol. I, London, HMSO.

THOMPSON, E.P. (1982) 'Time, work-discipline and industrial capitalism', in GIDDENS, A. and D. HELD (Eds), 1982 *op. cit.*, pp. 299–309.

TYLER, W. (1977) *The Sociology of Educational Inequality*, London, Methuen.

VIAENE, N. (1977) 'Sex differences in explanations of success and failure', in HARTNETT, O., G. BODEN and N. FULLER (Eds), *Sex-role Stereotyping*, London, Tavistock, pp. 117–139.

WEBER, M. (1978) *Economy and Society*, edited by ROTH, G. and C. WITTICH, London, University of California Press.

WILLIS, P. (1977) *Learning to Labour*, Farnborough, Saxon House.

Asian Girls and the Transition from School to . . .?

Sheila Miles

Author: Would you like to do the same sort of work as your mother when you leave school?

Pushpinder: Not at the laundry! I'm sort of educated and she isn't . . . so I might as well become something when I can.

Much of the literature on white working class girls emphasizes the importance and priority they place on getting married and having a family; their attitude to work is seen as 'little more than a stop-gap between school, marriage and children' (Moor, 1976).[1] Explanations for this suggest that certain ideas about femininity are transmitted within the family and at school, by codes which are based on class and gender (Bernstein, 1977; MacDonald, 1980). These lead to the construction of identities and roles which are reproduced in the home, at school and in the workplace. School is the mediating space between the family and the labour market. Wolpe (1974) stresses its role in generating 'a common code' of gender differentiation; the research by Stanworth (1981) and Deem (1980) supports this view. They see the differential achievement of girls as a result of curricular limitations and careers advice. Stanworth blames schools for 'habituating' girls to their subordinate roles. McRobbie's study (1978) of white working class girls suggests that their attitude to work is due to an acceptance of the 'traditional' female role. This is generated by families through a 'pre-existent culture of femininity which they as females in a patriarchal society' accept as perfectly natural. They are aware of the limitations of schooling for girls and therefore reject it as irrelevant. Their response is to 'assert their femaleness' via an anti-school culture dominated by marriage, family life, beauty and fashion. McRobbie argues that

> It is their own culture which itself is the most effective agent of social control for girls, pushing them into compliance with that

role which a whole range of institutions in capitalist society also, but less effectively directs them toward. (p. 104)

Studies of black girls, however, show that their response to work is quite different from white girls. They see work as an important and meaningful part of their lives. The West Indian girls in Fuller's (1980) study saw educational qualifications as a way of gaining entry to the labour market and responded to school instrumentally. They found it boring but not irrelevant, and adopted a role of semi-conformity in school. Both Sharpe (1976) and Fuller (1980) found that the Asian girls in their studies viewed marriage as 'a fact of life' and saw both school and work as a means of achieving a better, more fulfilling life than their parents. Given that Asian girls are subject to the transmission not only of class and gender codes, but also of what Mullard (1983) calls a racial code, one might expect them to have similar attitudes to work and marriage as white working class girls, particularly as they are expected to have arranged marriages. It could be argued however, that if class and gender are held constant, it is the racial dimension that influences their aspirations for the future, and it is this aspect that I will explore in this paper. It will look at the experience of immigration, the girls' perceptions of their mothers' working lives, attitudes to marriage, work and education. It examines some of the constraints and limitations that constitute their lives at home and school and the structure of the labour market they hope to enter. It suggests that despite the problems they face, they see work as of crucial importance; getting an interesting job is seen as the key to more freedom. Finally, it looks at some of the issues this raises for teachers working in schools with diverse ethnic pupil populations, often with little or no preparation for the complex and demanding tasks they face, particularly in helping their pupils at the sensitive stage of the transition from school to adult life.

The Data

This paper draws on a variety of data including observation in four London and Greater London comprehensive schools, three of which were mixed, and one an all girls' school. Three of the schools were used for pilot work and involved observations of classes and interviews with groups of pupils and careers teachers. One large mixed comprehensive school was used for the main case study, and the pupils selected were those doing work experience. Two groups were involved — some fifth year pupils selected to do work experience as part of their general curriculum, and the second group were those taking a City and Guilds Foundation Course in the sixth year, the 'non-academic' pupils. The fieldwork was conducted over the three year period 1980–82. I carried out a survey of the whole of the fifth year group in the case study school, which provided background information on the students, including family composition, job aspirations, attitudes to leaving school and starting work, option choices and examinations to be taken that year. Using semi-structured interviews, I spoke to Asian boys and girls doing work experience one day a week. I observed these pupils on their placements and was present during the follow-up work in school including observation of careers lessons. During this period I interviewed headteachers, teachers, careers officers, parents and school counsellors. Follow-up work was carried out in the homes in 1982. Documentary information included the folders kept by the pupils on their work experience placements (a different one each term), and further written work included some essays they did for me: first, 'My Life as a Journey'[2] and, a week before leaving school, a continuation of the metaphor, 'One week to go ... all change!' The written work was an attempt to tap their perceptions of important moments of their lives, particularly the one they were just about to face. It is here that I will start because I think that the hardship and upheaval experienced by Asian families on coming to Britain has played a significant role in influencing the aspirations they have for their children, and the determination boys and girls have to get decent jobs as an access to better living conditions. For the purposes of this paper I have restricted my discussion in the main to girls.

My life as a journey: the experience of immigration

The pattern of immigration from the Indian sub-continent in the 1950s and 1960s was mainly of the male members of the family coming here to find work, filling jobs vacated by indigenous workers. Many were directly recruited by textile manufacturers who went to India, Pakistan and Bangladesh in search of workers (Sivanandan, 1976; Brah, 1982). Their families followed often with a gap of many years in between. For the children this often entailed leaving close kin who had cared for them. Rupinder's parents left her in India with her grandparents whilst they established themselves in England. She said, 'When my mum came back to India after five years, I wouldn't believe that she was my mother and this was a very big problem for me'.

Nasreen's life had been a journey and a difficult one:

> I was born in 1964 in Uganda in Africa. I lived there for eight years. Then we went to Pakistan and my dad came to England. The life without my dad was not very good. I went to school in Pakistan. I learned how to speak and write and read. I loved Pakistan. Then suddenly my dad decided to bring us to England. I thought life in England was easy and that it was easy to learn English. We came to England in 1977. Oh, how I wish I had never set foot in England. I never thought life was so hard. It's hard to speak and write.

By the time Nasreen's father came to England, the country was experiencing an increasing economic recession; immigrant labour was no longer required and immigration control was tightening. The Act of 1971 placed restrictions of entry on certain types of workers; also rights of abode were confined to 'patrials' (those born, adopted, registered or naturalized in the UK and not in a colony, or whose parents or grandparents satisfied this requirement). Nasreen's father had been an engineer in Uganda, a category B worker under the 1962 legislation — those with skills or qualifications likely to be of use in this country. He came to Britain in 1972 when the Asians in Uganda were expelled by Idi Amin.

Coming to Britain is described by many of the girls as an important moment in their lives, often because it meant a reunion with their parents. Jaswinder described it graphically:

> The major turning point in my life was when I came to this country. It was sort of strange looking at people to see if one of them was my dad and the sheer delight finding him standing there waiting to pick me up.

The plane was exciting:

> I wanted to sit near the window and look down at the clouds. The place where I came from is Nairobi in East Africa where it is very hot. It was a drastic change when we came to England to find it snowing. We didn't know many people, the only relatives living in England at that time were dad's brother and his family. He had found a room for us to stay in. I remember feeling very excited about where I was going to sleep. It was one of those folding beds.

Many families found considerable difficulty with housing. Often large families were forced to live in a few rooms, moving when something between was available. Surinder described the problems her family had:

> We moved from house to house about five times. It was really difficult for mum because she had a lot to do. I moved from school to school about two or three times. I was scared to go to school. I didn't know any English at all when I first came here and when somebody asked me a question I turned my face away.

Tabisan said that her family had only two small rooms for six of them to live in, and they were damp. She said, 'I really didn't enjoy going to school because of all these problems we had.'

Often the only way to find decent accommodation was to buy a house and mortgage repayments made it essential for the wife to work, often long unsocial hours in poorly paid menial jobs. This put an additional strain on the teenage girls who took over most of the housework and care of younger children as well as trying to settle down at school and keep up with their work. Parveen explained why she had trouble getting to school on time:

> Before I come to school, that's why I'm always late you see, I try to explain to the teachers but they don't believe me you know, they say it can't be possible, but it's true. I do everything, I do the beds, I do the broom, do the washing up, do the bathroom before I come.

Her mother was a domestic cleaner in a hospital, working from 6 in the morning until 4 p.m.

It is essential that teachers are aware of the difficulties faced by their pupils in their home life as well as their school life, and realise the implications of moving to a strange country. One counsellor in a school I visited talked about housing for immigrants in this way: 'A family arrives and they're put in temporary accommodation — then they are immediately rehoused — can you imagine what that costs?'

In fact, nationally, a very small proportion of Asian families occupy council housing (see Figure 1). A surprisingly high percentage of semi-skilled and unskilled manual workers are owner occupiers compared with the general population. Smith (1977) explains this paradox:

> for a substantial proportion of Asians, buying their own home
> is not a way of getting superior housing at a premium price, but

Sheila Miles

Figure 1   Tenure by ethnic group and job type of head of household.

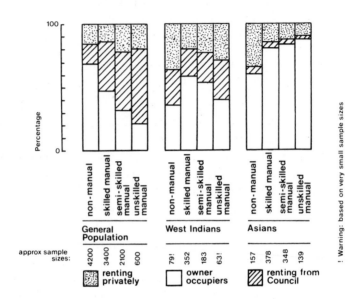

Source: Runnymede Trust and Radical Statistics Race Group, 1980, p. 78.

a way of getting poor housing cheaply. Equally important, it is a way of getting housing which, in terms of size, arrangement and location, is more suited to the family's needs. (p. 19)

The experience of immigration was not an easy one for many of the girls in my study, and some regretted coming here:

I now wish my parents did not come to this country and took us where we would not know about such things we do now and only did what they did when they were young. Since being in the fifth form, my worries have been rolling in one by one. I want to try to get somewhere in my life, but no matter how hard I try I'm just let down. I want to be happy all my life with a good *career* [emphasis added], a good husband and a good family. (Rupan)

It is important to note that Rupan placed career first in her order of importance. She was in the sixth form at the time of the interview and wanted to be a typist. She wanted to stay on at school because she felt it would help her to achieve this. She added realistically: 'I don't want to start work yet, you have to work all your life if I want to stay in this country, so I prefer to go to college, learn typing a bit more and then get a good job in the end'.

I have suggested in this section that the experience of immigration has played a significant part in structuring the aspirations of the girls in relation to their working lives. I have stressed the need for teachers to have an awareness of these issues in order to be able to deal sensitively with the range of problems they face. What I want to consider now is how far the assumptions and stereotypes about Asian family life and culture which are pervasive in society influence them in the way they respond to the girls. By unquestioningly applying the view (expressed to me by several teachers) that Asian girls 'will get married anyway' because of arranged marriages, teachers could be generating 'the everyday and institutional racisms which permeate British society' (Parmar, 1982, p. 238).

Does the inevitability of marriage and having a family exclude these girls from labour market participation? As Rupan noted, it is likely that most will work for a large part of their lives. Teachers have an important role to play in the advice they give on curricula choice, careers and generally in the expectations they hold about the girls' future lives. The University of Bradford study (1982) criticized teachers and careers officers for often operating on the basis of stereotypes, unproved assumptions and self-fulfilling prophecies. Teachers must ensure that they do not, albeit unwittingly, channel Asian girls into low-paid secondary sector jobs, those held to be "womens' work" and thus contribute to the reproduction of class, race and gender roles in the labour market. I will discuss labour market segmentation later in the paper.

Womens' working lives

Much of the literature on Asian women supports the view that due to cultural barriers and patriarchal domination, women are forced into a dependent role within the family and are not allowed to work outside the home (Khan, 1974; Wilson, 1978). Home-work, usually very badly paid, is seen as an alternative for women with language difficulties and cultural constraints (Runnymede Trust, 1980). Nevertheless a substantial proportion from India and Pakistan are in waged work, as can be seen from Table 1.

The 1971 census showed that 40.8 per cent of women from India and 20 per cent from Pakistan were engaged in waged labour, the majority of whom worked full-time. Lomas and Monck (1977) show that married women aged 35–49 from India and Pakistan work long hours: 67 per cent and 60.6 per cent respectively work more than 30 hours a week (Table 2).

The conceptualization of Asian women as 'submissive, economically and socially dependent, allowed outside the house only under the control of the husband or his relatives and unlikely to work in paid employment' is questionned by Sheila Allen (1982 p. 31) who says there is a disjunction between cultural norms and actual practice. She quotes the research of the National Committee on the Status of Women in India which dispels the myth that women from India have been confined to 'domestic activities in any narrow sense'. This document states that women were employed in large numbers in agriculture as labourers and cultivators. In 1971 there were 4 million women working in construction, and in 'sweated industries' as sweepers, domestics, and

Table 1   *Women of childbearing ages at work, by region and place of birth 1971*

Region	Percentage of working women of total female population of same place of birth aged 15–45		
	All places of birth	India	Pakistan*
North	50	34	10
Yorkshire and Humberside	51	32	7
North West	53	32	10
East Midlands	52	39	15
West Midlands	52	23	7
East Anglia	48	42	18
South East	53	50	27
South West	48	41	27
All regions	52	40	16

* Includes Bangladeshis
Source: Community Relations Council (1975) p. 8

Table 2   *Married women, hours of work*

Age group	Hours worked	India	Place of birth Pakistan	U.K.
20–34	Less than 30	18.4	25.3	40.5
	30+	17.5	70.0	56.9
35–39	Less than 30	29.6	29.6	52.4
	30+	67.0	60.6	44.5

Source: Lomas and Monck (1977) Table 4.3, p. 59.

garment workers, as well as in manufacturing and service industries. Allen therefore concludes that women working outside the home as well as in it is no new phenomenon.

In the research, the questionnaire of the fifth year pupils as a whole, of which just under one third were indigenous showed that 54 per cent of all mothers worked full-time, 10 per cent part-time, while 29 per cent were housewives (this may have included home-workers). In 12 per cent of the homes, women were the main wage earners. Of the fifth form Asian girls I interviewed, 10 of the mothers worked full-time, 1 could not work because of ill-health and the other 5 were housewives. One mother was away in Pakistan. Of the 10 who worked, 1 was a machine operator in a factory, putting labels on jars, 3 worked in a hospital laundry, 2 at the airport clearing tables in the cafeteria, 3 were domestics, and 1 a dietician for an airline. For those who worked as domestics in hospitals or at the airport, work started early in the morning; some worked through the night, from 10 in the evening until 7 in the morning. Of the 15 girls in the sixth year group, 11 mothers worked full-time as cleaners, and in factories. Pushpinder described her view of women's lives thus: 'They go to work and they look after the children, they have to do the housework as well'. Manminder said that the girls in her family did all the cooking: 'My mum don't do anything because she comes late at night you know. And we do the cooking at home for my dad ... the boys, they just sit around'. Tarnjit said, 'I do the cooking, cleaning and ironing, everything. And I look after my sister because my mum is asleep. She sleeps in the day and she works at night'.

The girls in my study had a clear understanding of the realities of their mothers' lives; housing problems and the high cost of living made it essential for them to accept shift work and long hours. One mother I interviewed said,

> I work in a laundry — we're doing a dirty job you know, sorting out the clothes — a dirty job. It's hard work and a hot job. I see my life — you know my life is no good, but my girls, they will do office work. It's a good job, easy.

It is an awareness by the girls of the problems of women's domestic and waged work that appears to influence them in their desires for better jobs than those their mothers are forced to take. White working class girls are undoubtedly similarly aware of the hardship involved in the double role, but their response to the constraints is to seek status in marriage and the family. The girls in Davies and Meighan's (1975) study envisaged returning to work later but had not given any real thought to a job 'with a definite career path that would occupy the remaining 20 years of their working life: their vision of the future came to a halt at the wedding' (p. 174).

Both Asian and white working class girls share a future of work after marriage, but there seems to be a difference in the way they perceive it. Asian girls do not place the same emphasis on the romance of marriage or on the 'cult of femininity'. Marriage in Asian culture is seen as a union of families rather than of individuals, and girls see it as part of their responsibility towards their families to make an acceptable liaison. As one girl told me, with arrangements for a suitable match being taken care of by her family, she didn't have 'to waste time going on the hunt'.

Perceptions of marriage and work

The girls in my study saw marriage as an inevitable part of their future lives and therefore seemed to take it for granted. When they talked about it, few expressed any great reservations about it. One has to remember however, that I was a white researcher and this may have influenced what they said to me. There may have been a sense of 'keep it in the family', an unwillingness to be critical of one's traditions to an outsider. The school counsellor mentioned a few incidents of unhappiness caused by arranged marriages she had encountered, but I did not find any strong feelings against it, more a feeling of wistfulness about white girls who could have 'love marriages'. In reply to my question, 'Do you want to get married?', Parveen replied, 'Yes, I suppose I have to [laughing], well even if I don't want to, I'd have to go along with my parents' rule wouldn't I? And I suppose I do want to get married, that's a fact of life isn't it?'

Although marriage is arranged by families, the girls felt that they would have some choice, even if it was only the right to refuse. Many felt their parents would not force them. Asha told me that her sister had had twenty-four 'possibilities' of marriage and had only recently agreed to the match her parents had arranged, because 'this man was worldly'. Rupinder said, 'parents think best for the children, what job you do and they always think best for you; they find a nice man, and they, the mother feels that, you know, they will be good'. The girls were concerned to please their parents and did not want to 'let them down'. Bharti said that her parents would not mind if she had a 'love marriage', but 'I know, deep inside, it wouldn't work for them and I don't want to take a risk, whereas if I had an arranged marriage, my mum and dad would be pleased, and I would always have someone to rely on'.

Brah (1982) suggests that the notion of 'culture clash' projected by the media and in general currency, is not supported by evidence, and that young Asians, rather than experiencing stress and identity conflicts, draw upon the culture both of the home and of the school. This was certainly the impression I gained from my discussions with the girls. Many expressed the view that they would sooner marry a boy who had been brought up in this country than in India because they felt that they would be allowed more freedom and be able to work if they wanted to. Gurgeet said, 'a boy from India would want me to stay at home and look after my children and just do boring work. ... I want to be able to go out and look for a job and enjoy myself'.

Most of the girls realized the limitations being married would impose on their work aspirations. When asked what they felt was a suitable age for marriage, most opted for between 20 and 25. Only three thought 18 to be 'a good age'. I asked them why they wanted to wait before getting married. Vanita said she felt too young to get married for a few more years and wanted to go to college first to do a business studies course. Most of the girls expected what Hakim (1979) calls a 'bi-modal' career pattern — in two stages, working until marriage and children and then returning to work when the children start school. Satminder, who wanted to be a ground hostess was aware that having children would affect her career: 'I want to become something. I'm really ambitious, but probably children will affect my career. You have to go into training and then everything. And then, if I have kids, it kind of stops me having training'. Similarly, Jawsinder said, 'Well, if I want to go into nursing, then I will have to spend most of my time in the hospital. I won't get much time to go home'. She said that if she had children, she hoped to leave them with her mother who at that time worked in a canteen. Pushpinder who already had a marriage arranged said she didn't know how it would affect her career: 'It depends on my husband. His parents said I could do one year course secretarial or something, if I wanted to, and they might not like me going out to work or something like that. I tell my mum that I really want to go to work'.

It was the husband's family who would make the decision; after marriage, the responsibility for the girls shifted to the in-laws. Several girls expressed worries about being influenced by their husbands. Nasreen said, 'It depends on what my husband's like ... I won't like it if he says to me "stay home"'. Some realized that only part-time work would be possible when they had families and this might make it impossible for them to return to their original jobs. They anticipated returning to work and doing a double day, waged and domestic work, when their children were old enough. A few felt they would want to stay at home and be housewives if they could afford to, but most did not see working life ending with marriage; marriage was an interruption, necessary and inevitable. For most of the girls I talked to, acceptance of marriage was not a problem; what was important to them was that they could control, to some extent, the timing of it, and that they should be able to create some space for themselves. This could be achieved through work but equally importantly through education. Time to gain additional qualifications was a legitimate means to gain the space they needed, perceived as legitimate by their parents who saw education as giving their daughters access to better careers but also as enhancing their chances of a good marriage, 'a route round the dowry system' (Sharpe, 1976).

Being educated

Staying on at school was therefore one way in which the girls felt they could control the timing in their lives, a space for them to have freedom to mix with other pupils (Giddens, 1979). Their parents supported them in this for the reasons I have mentioned above, but also because of the esteem they held for the British education system (Brah, 1982), a legacy of colonial attitudes whereby a western education was seen as a means of social mobility. The girls frequently expressed the view that their parents wanted them to have a good education. Manminder said her parents wanted her to stay on at school for another year: 'They think the more you educate, the better paid job you get'. She herself had reservations about this because, she said, 'there are getting less and less jobs, and hardly any people get any jobs so education is alright, but it is hard even with CSE and O levels'. Most felt that staying on at school would give them a chance of better jobs than those their mothers were doing. Such jobs were 'not for educated people, not the sort of work people from my school go to'. Lakbir said, 'I don't want to work in the airport like my mother does, she doesn't speak English at all, and she can do it. I want to do something I can with my education'. One girl, whose mother was a machinist in a factory explained, 'I don't want to work in a factory; people who aren't educated work in a factory, I want a more suitable job'. Factory work was only seen as suitable for those handicapped by lack of alternatives, due to being unable to speak English. Gurdeep expressed her parent's view, 'They goes, look we got no education, and we can do that sort of work, but you have got education, why should you want to do a factory job?'

Being educated seemed to mean being able to read, write and take examinations. Most of the girls doing work experience on the City and Guilds Course had gained CSEs at grade 3 and 4, with a few getting an odd O level pass. These sixth formers had stayed on not to take re-sits but to do a course which would give them a certificate on completion which would not have much of an 'exchange value' on the job market according to the careers teachers. Most of the pupils and parents I spoke to however saw it as a valid credential although they realised that O levels were what was needed to secure a good job or entry to a college course. School was seen as the means whereby qualifications could be sought, yet the organization of the school placed limitations on those pupils who had not fared well in their fifth year exams by not giving them opportunities to re-sit the following year. Nevertheless the girls were very enthusiastic about school, and were very reluctant to leave. Many said they loved it, and would miss their friends. Tabisan said, 'In school, you are busy all day, at home all you have to do is just the housework and that's it, you sit down quiet'. Bharti felt that she had wasted the last few years at school because she had not worked hard enough:

> I really like school ... I want to make something of my life, and you see I have realised this too late, that all the years I have just wasted, and now when I really want to do something about it, I can't. My mates in the fourth year ... they can't understand why I have suddenly changed, but what I try to tell them is don't make the same mistakes as I have, work while you have got the chance.

She was in the fifth year and hoped to do a business studies course when she went to college. Failure to gain the necessary passes might make this impossible and she would then find it difficult to find 'a nice job in an office'.

'A nice job for a girl'

Working in offices and banks was seen by many of the girls as 'a nice job for a girl'. In the questionnaire, a large number of girls chose it for themselves, and boys thought it a suitable job for a girl. A substantial number wanted to do nursery nursing and nursery teaching. In the fifth year as a whole, girls chose from a far narrower range of jobs than the boys. Girls selected a total of 24[3] types of jobs, whereas boys chose 49. Eighteen of the jobs were chosen by both sexes. These were:

actor/actress	economist*
artist	engineer
banking	electrical engineer*
biologist*	lawyer
catering and hotel management	manager*
clerical	police*
computer programmer	scientist*
designer	teacher
doctor*	travel agent

*choice of only one girl.

Only 6 boys and 1 girl chose to be a doctor, whereas 16 of the boys said their parents would like them to do this job and 12 of the girls. Most of the boys chose some form of engineering. Only 1 girl chose hairdressing, 3 social work and 6 wanted to be air-hostesses. Very few chose professional jobs: 3 chose the law and 9 teaching. No-one mentioned factory work. Only 2 said they wanted to work in a shop. As a whole, the pupils said their parents were doing semi-skilled or un-skilled manual jobs; the jobs they themselves chose were, in the main, skilled.

What sort of the jobs did the girls doing work experience choose? At least one third wanted to do secretarial or clerical work and several wanted to work in a bank. Only 2 wanted to be air-hostesses, 2 to work in a shop (the only two in the fifth year survey), and the rest were interested in work with children, nursery nursing, nursery teaching or nursing. None of them opted for professions except one who was good at art and wanted to be a designer. It has been suggested that many Asian pupils have unrealistic job aspirations (Brooks and Singh, n.d.). There is a joke amongst careers officers that I heard several times, that all Asian pupils want to become brain surgeons. In my interviews with both boys and girls and in the fifth year questionnaire, this did not appear to be the case. I detected a great deal of realism about the job market and also some flexibility about job choice such as in the case of Parminder who said, 'I want to work in a bank when I leave school. If I don't get that job I will go into college. If I can't do banking, a job in a shop will be open'. Another girl said, 'I'd like to do a nursing course but realistically I'll try to be a nursery nurse. That's the nearest to it I might get'. One said her parents had unrealistic hopes for her: 'They wanted me to go into medicine, get a degree. I don't think I can do that, but they want me to carry on no matter what, to do more'. Rarinder wanted to be a ground hostess. She said, 'If I can't, I'll become a secretary'. I asked her why she chose that job. She said, 'Well, I seem to think it's a nice job. You meet people, get along with them and I like meeting people enormously'.

Many wanted to do a job that involved caring for people, (an extension of the maternal role?). Tabbissan wanted to work in a hospital because 'You can help everybody . . . like old people, they need special care, children, little babies, they need care'. Asha wanted to do nursery nursing because, she said, 'I love children, I'm interested in people you meet and patients and I just love it'. Clearly the girls in my study were still choosing jobs within the areas of traditional women's work. However they were very different jobs from those their mothers were doing.

What are the important things about a job?

One of the questions in the survey asked the fifth year why they had chosen the jobs they had. Just over 25 per cent mentioned something to do with the quality of the job itself, such as being interesting, varied, exciting and enjoyable. Another 25 per cent felt that it was to do with personal competence, with comments such as, 'I'm good at . . . repairing things, working with cars, hands', and so on. And 20 per cent chose the job because it involved people; they mentioned helping, caring, meeting and organizing aspects. Another question asked the pupils to rank certain characteristics of jobs they thought important. Learning a trade was ranked first by 39.9 per cent and pay by 26 per cent as was a job with training. One fifth chose 'fits in with family life.'

One of the questions I asked the work experience girls was what was important to them about a job. They stressed getting on with and working with people: 'The people who work there must be friendly, and the job should be nice. There should be good hours and work that isn't too difficult'. Interest was another important criterion. The job should not be boring. Most of the girls doing work experience in shops found standing around extremely boring: 'It's just that it's boring and you are standing on your feet a lot of the time'. Time goes very slowly for some: 'I wait two hours for two minutes to go past'.

The girls in my study wanted jobs that would provide them with a reasonable income, interesting work and social contact. Freedom to mix with their friends was a very important aspect of their lives but this was restricted by the cultural norms for Asian girls. Those I spoke to after leaving school regretted that they had lost contact with their friends and were living a fairly isolated existence. Both school and work were seen by their parents as legimitate areas for social contacts, within limits, and the girls responses to both these institutional situations were to utilise the space they offered. Their preparation for the labour market involved a complex interplay between their familial and cultural role, and their educational experiences. In addition to this were factors such as the structure of the labour market and high youth unemployment, as perceived by parents, pupils and teachers.

Labour Market Segmentation

What is the nature of the labour market that the girls in my study hope to enter? Is it the labour market itself which produces constraints of race, class and gender or is it the characteristics of the girls themselves who choose secondary-type jobs? I will look at some of the work on segmentation and relate it to the perceptions of the girls in order to locate their choices within a wider setting.

Several writers on labour market segmentation have looked at the concentration of women in 'traditional', low-paid jobs. They explain it in terms of the complex interaction between patriarchy and capitalism (Hartmann, 1979; Beechey, 1979; and Anthias, 1980). Women's primary role is one of domestic labour within the home, not wage earners in their own right but a 'reserve army of labour' brought into the economy or dispensed with to fit in with the requirements of capitalism. Garnsey (1978) says that it is the recognition of the limited job opportunities open to women in the labour market that lowers their expectations and incentives to gain qualifications and skills, thus reinforcing their commitment to their domestic role in the family. Dual labour market theory seeks to explain why it is that certain types of workers are concentrated in the secondary sector of the labour market (Barron and Norris, 1976).[4] Women and black workers are said to be largely confined to this sector, characterized by low pay, unsocial hours, jobs with little or no training, high turnover rate and insecurity. Barron and Norris state: 'Jobs confer upon individuals a biography . . . which reinforces the attitudes of employers and of agencies which serve the employment market' (1976, p. 50).

The secondary workforce is said to have certain attributes. These are: dispensability; clearly visible social differences (gender and race would constitute these); little interest in training; low economism (not interested in pay); and lack of solidarity (not unionized or organized as a group). These attributes, it is said,

> are to some extent shaped elsewhere in the social structure and brought to the employment market. Thus they are not charac-teristics which an individual possesses solely by virtue of his market situation, but they help to determine an individual's market situation in conjunction with the interests and require-ments of employers. (p. 53)

Did the girls in my sample possess the particular attributes that would limit the range of their choices? Was it the acknowledgement of the sexual division of labour in the home which meant the major responsi-bility for domestic chores would be theirs, or is the cause the fact that the labour market structures their possibilities, particularly when racism, sexism and agism[5] are in operation? (Smith, 1976; Runnymede Trust, 1980; Troyna, 1983) Is it possible to determine the answer, given the subtleties and complexities involved in this process? The girls in my study were determined to work but were undoubtedly influenced by ideologies of women's work, in the family, at school and in the labour market. How could it be otherwise when these are so pervasive?

Let us look at the five characteristics of the secondary workforce in relation to the girls in my study.

Dispensability: leaving work for marriage and a family was the main reason these girls gave for interrupting their working lives. It was not part of their plans to stay out longer than necessary.

Clearly visible social differences: The fact that they were black and female could constitute them in this way. When I asked them whether they thought this would make it difficult for them to find a job many thought it would in terms of colour but not of gender. Gender was not a category suggested, and as their choices were all within the range of womens' work, this was not surprising.

Training was seen by all the girls without exception to be important. It was seen as a means of being able to cope with the job, a worry expressed by many of the fifth year pupils on the questionnaire. Amrit said, 'I think training is very important because if you don't know how to do the job, you get messed up'.

Stereotypical notions of Asian women have given support to the view that there is no point in training the girls when they will have their 'arranged marriages' and be dependent on their husbands.

Pay was considered important by most of the girls but not as important as the job itself. Peaki said, 'I don't just want to go for a job for the pay — it's just something I want to do — if I have a chance of going for nursing and not getting paid for it, I'd do it — I don't know, I like it so much'. This girl could not do the job of her choice as she did not have the necessary qualification, and in this situation, pay seemed less important to her. Many agreed with this view but stressed the need for money to buy a house. They expressed a combination of realism and idealism.

Lack of solidarity is the other characteristic that relegates women to low-paid jobs. Parmar (1983) has challenged this in relation to Asian women workers, demonstrating their participation in disputes such as that at Grunwick and in the nursing profession for better working conditions.

In looking at the girls' views of jobs, it is clear that they do not possess intrinsic characteristics that inhibit the range of job opportunities open to them; rather it is the labour market itself which, as Hakim (1979) shows, 'has remained relatively unchanged over seven decades'. An important point to note here is that the sort of jobs aspired to by these girls are those which are most susceptible to redundancy, either in the service industries or the clerical sector with the impact of new technology. Table 3 shows the structure of employment for ethnic groups by socio-economic group and sex, 1981. Asian women work in the intermediate and junior non-manual sector, in semi-skilled manual and personal services as well as unskilled manual work.

Finally, I would like to look at the statistics for unemployment among Asian girls in relation to other groups. Table 4 shows that within the 16–24 age group, 30 per cent of Asian girls are unemployed compared with 16 per cent of white girls. In fact they have the highest unemployment rate of all age groups for females. Figure 2 shows the rise in unemployment over the past ten years.

Paradoxically, despite the aspirations of the girls in my study to find suitable jobs, the reality is that the opportunities are rapidly shrinking. Unemployment is far higher for their age group than for their mothers'; it would appear that the type of jobs they seek are diminishing in relation to the menial jobs still available for older women workers. Their quest for qualifications becomes meaningless

Table 3   Employment by ethnic group and sex in Great Britain 1981

	White	West Indian or Guyanese	Indian/ Pakistani/ Bangladeshi	Other[1]	All ethnic groups
			Ethnic group		
Males (percentages)					
Professional	6	2	8	10	6
Employers and managers	16	4	12	14	16
Intermediate and junior non-manual	18	7	14	23	18
Skilled manual and own account non-professional	38	49	35	27	38
Semi-skilled manual and personal service	16	27	25	20	16
Unskilled manual	5	11	6	4	5
Armed forces and inadequately described	1	1	—	2	2
All males aged 16 and over in employment (= 100%) (thousands)	13,325	120	243	114	13,962
Females (percentages)					
Professional	1	—	3	2	1
Employers and managers	7	2	4	3	6
Intermediate and junior non-manual	53	50	41	52	52
Skilled manual and own account non-professional	7	4	13	8	7
Semi-skilled manual and personal service	23	34	35	29	24
Unskilled manual	8	8	3	5	8
Armed forces and inadequately described	—	1	—	1	1
All females aged 16 and over in employment (= 100%) (thousands)	8,945	107	104	70	9,328

[1] African, Arab, Chinese, other stated, and mixed.
Source: *Social Trends*, 1982, Table 13.7 (p. 184) CSO.

particularly when racism in employment practices is operating (Anwar, 1982). This must have important implications for the comprehensive school; how long will it be before the credibility of what they have to offer is questionned by Asian youth too?

The Comprehensive Response

The modern comprehensive school faces the problem of insufficient resources, both financial and human, as outlined by Ball in the Introduction to this book. It needs to take into account the diverse pupil

Sheila Miles

Table 4   *Unemployment by ethnic group, age and sex in Great Britain 1981*

		Ethnic group			
	White	West Indian or Guyanese	Indian/ Pakistani/ Bangladeshi	Other[1]	All ethnic groups
Unemployment among males aged (percentages)					
16–24	19	38	25	34	19
25–44	8	13	13	7	8
45–64	7	17	19	10	8
All aged 16–64	10	21	17	14	10
Total unemployed aged 16–64 (thousands)	1,423	31	49	18	1,528
Unemployment among females aged (percentages)					
16–24	16	28	30	25	17
25–44	8	10	14	10	8
45–59	5	7	10	12	5
All aged 16–59	9	15	18	15	9
Total unemployed aged 16–59 (thousands)	839	18	23	12	894

[1] African, Arab, Chinese, other stated and mixed.
Source: *Social Trends*, 1982, Table 13.8 (p. 184) CSO.

Figure 2   *Estimated change in unemployment rates by ethnic group Great Britain 1973–81*

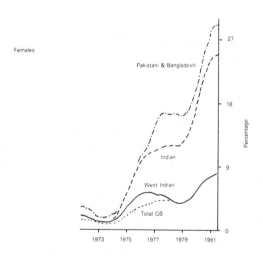

Source: *Ethnic Minorities in Britain*, Home Office Research Study No 68

population it serves, particularly the needs of its black pupils. This raises important questions about how well prepared teachers are to do the job, both by initial and in-service training. The recent White Paper on *Teaching Quality* (DES, 1983) states that initial training cannot prepare teachers for every kind of teaching they may encounter:

> Qualifications and training alone do not make a teacher … Good teachers need to have a mastery of the subject matter they teach and the professional skills needed to teach it to children of different ages, abilities, aptitudes and backgrounds. (p. 8)

Yet one of the areas neglected in initial training in many institutions is not mentioned, an area which remains highly controversial, that is the preparation of teachers for work in a multicultural society (Carby, 1980, 1982; Hall, 1981; Troyna, 1983), and crucially, an examination of practices within education which could be examples of overt or inadvertent racism. Educational underachievement on the part of West Indian pupils has been widely documented (Coard, 1971; Tomlinson, 1981; Stone, 1981; DES, 1981). The Rampton Report (DES 1981) showed, however, that Asian pupils have been increasingly successful in gaining GCE O level passes. Occupational mobility for all black pupils is low, even where their qualifications are equal or better than their white peers (CRE, 1978; Troyna, 1983). Nevertheless there is no statutory commitment by LEAs to address these issues, although some have produced their own guidelines for schools.

The school in which I carried out my case study had a fifth year of which only one third of the pupils' main language was English, whose religion was Christian and whose family structure conformed to the 'nuclear family', though it is questionable whether the latter is really typical in the indigenous population.[6] Hindi and Punjabi, the main languages spoken at home for the majority of the pupils were not subjects on the curriculum, although several pupils expressed the wish to take them (Craft and Atkins, 1983). There were few Asian members of staff; they were not in positions of responsibility and few were permanent members of staff. I saw no evidence to suggest that the curriculum took into account the cultural specificity and special needs of its pupils other than remedial work and additional English, there was no 'mother tongue' teaching.

The careers lessons I observed did not discuss the constraints of high youth unemployment or the structure of the local labour market, but concentrated on life and social skills, and an examination of personal adequacy in relation to different types of jobs. Work experience was in the main 'selected' by the less academic pupils, although the school rhetoric was that it was open to all pupils. The survey in fact showed that there was some discouragement of O level pupils whose teachers felt that they could not miss a whole day's school. The work experience confirmed the usual sexual divisions: girls were sent to shops, offices, and nurseries; boys to workshops and engineering firms. I am using this school as an illustration of some of the issues that need to be addressed by comprehensive schools. What is needed is a critical examination of practices to ensure that inequalities of race, class and gender are not reproduced. The inclusion of multi-cultural education as part of the curriculum will not serve to alleviate these inequalities. A curriculum both overt and hidden that is geared to mainstream white middle-class culture is inappropriate; *token* gestures to incorporate other cultures, inadequate. It is essential that teachers have an understanding of their pupils' lives and cultural practices. There should be close liaison with the local community. Opportunities for mother tongue teaching should be available and the inclusion of a range of languages on the curriculum at all levels is crucial.

Conclusion

In this paper I have explored the attitudes of a group of girls to important issues that face them on the point of transition from school to adult life. The title of the paper suggests that it may not be a transition to work. As it turned out for Peaki:

> I have been to the Careers Office at least about fifteen times, but they just couldn't find me anything suitable, so they told me to go on a course. At the moment I am desperate to get a job, and we have financial problems at home. It is very boring and I am so depressed.

Sadly, unemployment is the reality for many who leave school, negating their cherished hopes.

What comes through very clearly from the girls is their persistence, despite the enormous constraints they face at every level. In the main, the fifth year girls who could not find jobs opted to return to school to try for the City and Guilds qualification, or managed to find places at the local technical colleges. The sixth year girls had to leave since the school would not allow them to stay on to re-sit exams and they had the choice of taking places on YOPs schemes, mostly short term, or of continuing their quest for jobs with the weekly trek to the Careers Office. Certainly schools cannot solve the problems these pupils face. They cannot create jobs — the responsibility for that lies elsewhere in the social system. But schools can have a powerful impact, given an awareness of the inequalities generated by class, race and gender.

Notes

1 See also DAVIES and MEIGHAN (1975), WOLPE (1974), McROBBIE (1978), SHARPE (1978), GASKELL (1983), RAUTA and HUNT (1975). The girls in this study saw marriage as an interruption but this is the only research on white working class girls that supports this view.
2 This came from a discussion with PHIL COHN. Other writers have used the theme, 'My life in ten years' time'. In these studies, most girls mentioned marriage and the family, whereas boys talked about work.
3 Sharpe's girls covered 30 jobs. She found that 4 out of 10 girls chose some sort of office work (p. 161).
4 There is a growing literature on segmentation which includes DOERINGER and PIORE (1972), REICH, GORDON and EDWARDS (1973), RUBERY (1978) and HAKIM (1979).
5 ASHTON and MAGUIRE (1980 p. 119) discuss the bias against young school leavers by employers who see married women as more stable.
6 See BARRETT and McINTOSH (1982) on the concept of the nuclear family.

References

ALLEN, S. (1982) 'Perhaps the Seventh Person?' in HUSBANDS, C. (Ed) *Race in Britain* London, Hutchinson.
ANTHIAS, F. (1980) 'Women and the reserve army of labour: a critique of Veronica Beechey', *Capital and Class* special issue 10, Spring, pp. 50–63.
ANWAR, M. (1982) *Young People and the Job Market-A Survey*, London, CRE.
ASHTON, D. and MAGUIRE, M. (1980) 'Young women in the Labour market: stability and change' in DEEM, R. (Ed) *Schooling for Womens' Work*, London, Routledge and Kegan Paul.
BARRETT, M. and McINTOSH, A. (1982) *The Anti-Social Family*, London, Verso.
BARRON, R.D. and NORRIS, G.M. (1976) 'Sexual divisions and the dual labour market' in BARKER, D.L. and ALLAN, S. (Eds) *Dependence and Exploitation in Work and Marriage*, London, Longman with the BSA.
BEECHEY, V. (1979) 'Some notes on female wage labour in capitalist production', *Capital and Class*, 3, Autumn.
BERNSTEIN, B. (1977) *Class, Codes and Control, Vol. 3*, London, Routledge and Kegan Paul.
BRAH, A. (1982) *Minority Experience: The South Asians*, E354, Block 3, Unit 8, Milton Keynes, The Open University Press.

Sheila Miles

BROOKS, D. and SINGH, K. (n.d.) *Aspirations versus Opportunities: Asian and White School Leavers in the Midlands*, London, CRE.
CARBY, H. (1980) 'Multi-culturalism', *Screen Education*, 34, Spring.
CARBY, H. (1982) 'Schooling in Babylon' in *The Empire Strikes Back: race and racism in Britain*, London, Hutchinson in association with CCCS.
COARD, B. (1971) *How the West Indian Child is Made Educationally Sub-Normal in the British School System*, London, New Beacon Books.
COMMISSION FOR RACIAL EQUALITY (1978) *Looking for Work: Black and White School Leavers In Lewisham*, London, CRE.
COMMUNITY RELATIONS COUNCIL (1975) *Who Minds: A Study of Working Mothers and Child Minding in Ethnic Minority Communities*, London, CRC.
CRAFT, M. and ATKINS, M. (1983) 'Training teachers of ethnic community languages', Nottingham University, Faculty of Education.
DAVIES, L. and MEIGHAN, R. (1975) 'A review of schooling and sex roles with particular reference to the experience of girls in secondary schools', *Educational Review* 27, 3, June.
DEEM, R. (1980) (Ed) *Schooling for Women's Work*, London, Routledge and Kegan Paul.
DES (1981) *West Indian Children in our Schools (The Rampton Report)*, London. HMSO.
DES (1983) *Teaching Quality* London, HMSO.
DOERINGER, P.B. and PIORE, M.J. (1972) *Internal Labour Markets and Manpower Analysis* Mass, Lexington.
FULLER, M. (1980) 'Black girls in a London comprehensive school' in DEEM, *op. cit.*
GASKELL, J. (1983) 'The reproduction of family life', *British Journal of Sociology of Education*, 4, 1.
GARNSEY, E. (1978) 'Women's work and theories of class stratification', *Sociology*, 12, 2.
GIDDENS, A. (1979) *Central Problems in Social Theory*, London, Macmillan.
HAKIM, C. (1979) *Occupational Segregation*, Research Paper 9, Department of Employment, London, HMSO.
HALL, S. (1981) 'Teaching Race' in JAMES, A. and JEFFCOATE, R. (Eds) *The School in the Multicultural Society*, London, Harper and Row.
HARTMANN, H. (1979) 'Capitalism, patriarchy and job segregation by sex' in EISENSTEIN, Z.P. (Ed) *Capitalist Patriarchy and the Case for Socialist Feminism*, New York, Monthly Review Press.
KHAN, V.S. (1974) 'South Asian women in south London' in WALLMAN, S. (Ed) *Ethnicity at Work*, London, Macmillan.
LOMAS, G. and MONCK, E. (1977) *Employment and Economic Activity 1971*, London, Runnymede Trust.
MACDONALD, M. (1980) 'Socio-cultural reproduction and women's education' in DEEM, *op. cit.*
McROBBIE, A. (1978) 'Working class girls and the culture of feminity' in WOMEN'S STUDIES GROUP, CCCS, *Women Take Issue*, London, Hutchonson in association with CCCS.
MOOR, C. (1976) *From School to Work*, London, Sage.
MULLARD, C. (1983) 'The Racial Code: Its features, rules and change', in

BARTON, L. and WALKER, S. (Eds) *Race, Class and Education*, London, Croom Helm.

PARMAR, P. (1982) 'Gender, race and class: Asian women in resistance' in *The Empire Strikes Back, op. cit.*

RAUTA, I. and HUNT, A. (1975) *Fifth Form Girls: Their Hopes for the Future*, London, HMSO.

REICH, C. GORDON A. and EDWARDS, P. (1973) 'A theory of labour markets, worker organisation and low pay', *Cambridge Journal of Economics*, 2, pp. 17–36.

RUNNYMEDE TRUST and RADICAL STATISTICS GROUP (1980) *Britain's Black Population*, Heinemann Educational.

SHARPE, S. (1976) *Just Like a Girl*, Harmondsworth, Penguin Books.

SIVANANDAN, A. (1976) *Race, class and the state: the black experience in Britain*, Race and Class pamphlet No. 1, Institute of Race Relations, London.

SMITH, D.J. (1977) *Racial Disadvantage in Britain*, Pelican Books.

SMITH, D.J. (1981) *Unemployment and Racial Minorities*, No. 594, London Policy Studies Institute.

STANWORTH, M. (1981) *Gender and Schooling*, London, WRRC.

STONE, M. (1981) *The Education of the Black Child in Britain*, London, Fontana.

TOMLINSON, S. (1981) 'The Educational Performance of Ethnic Minority Children', in JAMES, A. and JEFFCOATE, R. (Eds) *op cit.*

TROYNA, B. (1983) *Multicultural Education: Emancipation or Containment*, paper presented to the Sociology of Education Conference, Westhill College, January.

UNIVERSITY OF BRADFORD (1982) *Problems of Vocational Adaptation of South Asian Adolescents in Britain, with Special Reference to the Role of the School*, Postgraduate School of Studies in Research in Education, University of Bradford.

WILSON, A. (1978) *Finding a Voice: Asian Women in Britain*, London. Virago.

WOLPE, A.M. (1974) 'The Official ideology of education for girls' in FLUDE, M. and AHIER, J. (Eds) *Educability, Schools and Ideology*, London, Croom Helm.

131

Control, Controversy and the Comprehensive School

Martyn Denscombe

The gradual reorganization of secondary education along comprehensive lines that followed the issue of DES Circular 10/65 has taken place in the context of a long standing debate about the relative merits of selective and non-selective secondary education. Opponents have argued that the comprehensive school fails to provide the kind of education suited to the gifted pupil and therefore fails to maintain the standards of excellence associated with the grammar schools in the tripartite system. They also allege that comprehensives fail to provide the basics of education — the 3Rs — and that standards of numeracy and literacy are consequently falling[1].

Parallel with the discussion on academic standards there have been persistent allegations that standards of discipline and control in the comprehensives have declined. These allegations have come mainly from the more right wing press, politicians and teachers, for whom the levels of violence, vandalism and indiscipline in the comprehensives bear testimony not only to a more general problem caused by social decay but also to a specific malaise associated with comprehensives. This line of thinking was clearly evident in the series of Black Papers (Cox and Dyson, 1969; Cox and Boyson 1975, 1977) in which comprehensive organization, progressive teaching methods and poor quality teaching — three features of the reforms of the 1960s — were 'held responsible for an alleged decline in general standards and basic skills, for a lack of social discipline and the incongruence between the worlds of school and of work' (CCCS, 1981, p. 212).

Time and again the tabloids and right wing press have fanned the flames of the controversy with alarmist reports of violence, vandalism and truancy of crisis proportions and, as the contributors to *Unpopular Education* discovered when analyzing the coverage of educational matters by the *Daily Mirror* and the *Daily Mail* between 1975 and 1977,

Martyn Denscombe

> What was presented as 'debate' was in effect a monologue concentrating on items concerning teachers' lack of professional competence or the negative aspects of pupil behaviour. Central to the reporting were pictures of the current state of British schooling. Images of incompetence, slovenly, subversive or just trendy teachers who had failed to teach or control the undisciplined pupils in their charge became too familiar to need elaboration. (CCCS 1981 pp. 210–211)

Recent reporting by the *Daily Mail* would suggest that things are much the same in 1983, with violence, vandalism and arson continuing to capture the headlines (see Figure 1)

Sections of the press have not been alone in their concern about declining standards of behaviour in schools, because — whether as a cause or a consequence — the image of schools as 'blackboard jungles' is widespread amongst the public. There is considerable anxiety about standards of discipline and control exercised by teachers and, as Wilson (1981) found recently, 99 per cent of the parents he interviewed felt that discipline was not adequately enforced in schools. Even amongst the teaching profession itself there are those who share this view. Part of the policy of the National Association of Schoolmasters and Union of Women Teachers (NAS/UWT) over the last decade, for instance, has been to expose what it regards as the very real crisis of control in schools and to draw attention to 'the facts' about violence, vandalism and truancy in schools (see Lowenstein, 1972, 1975; Comber and Whitfield 1979). And consistent with this, the problem of control was one that received considerable airing amongst delegates to the national conference of the NAS/UWT in 1983.

There are, however, question marks that need to be placed against this idea of a current crisis of control because a notable feature of the allegations and anxieties about falling standards of behaviour has been their tendency to resort to rhetoric rather than research to substantiate their claims. The facts of the matter — the decline in control and discipline and the rise in school violence — tend to be taken as self evident truths obvious to everyone. The basis for this truth, however, owes much to a 'sturdy common-sense' and a 'process of circular validation' amongst press and politicians in which individual instances and personal anecdotes come to feed on themselves as evidence of a real, and much more widespread, problem of control (CCCS, 1981, pp. 212, 214). Clearly, this is a shaky foundation on which to build a picture of the situation in today's schools and, before accepting the idea

Daily Mail, Friday, April 8, 1983

Rough schools 'may need class guards'

By CHRISTOPHER ROWLANDS, Education Correspondent

WEAKNESS by head teachers could create a situation where American-style classroom policing will be needed to control growing violence in British schools, a teachers conference was warned yesterday.

The growing menace of petrol bomb pupils

A GROWING number of pupils are hitting back at authority by trying to burn down their schools, according to a new report.

Lack of achievement in the classroom is thought to be one of the reasons behind an alarming increase in the number of school fires.

In its annual report the Fire Protection Association reports more than 2,000 blazes, of which a third were probably started deliberately. The 34 biggest caused £13.8 million worth of damage.

According to Municipal Mutual Insurance, which specialises in local authority insurance, children as young as four have started serious fires deliberately.

'Youngsters use diabolical devices to ensure fire takes a firm hold,' a spokesman said. These included petrol bombs made from bottles or washing up liquid containers.

School fires have now taken over from warehouse blazes at the top of Britain's fire damage league.

Inner London Education Authority had 40 fires in 1981-82, of which 34 were started deliberately, at a cost to the authority of £386,000. The previous year there were 19 blazes (ten arson) costing the authority about £500,000.

Although the number of fires doubled, the cost in damage was due, in part, to increased linkage of school alarm systems to police and fire stations.

Daily Mail, Monday, November 22, 1982

AS CITY PLANS TO BAN CANE...

77 attacks on teachers in a year

TEACHERS in a city which plans to outlaw the cane, today reveal frightening details of violence in their classrooms.

In a single year a group of staff in schools in Leeds have been physically attacked 73 times by pupils — and four times by parents.

They also recorded 17 incidents of abusive child behaviour and say that in a frightening proportion of schools they have to withstand 'a daily diet of abuse from rude, insolent and unruly pupils.'

The survey was carried out by the Leeds branch of the National Association of Schoolmasters and Union of Women Teachers because of worries over the increase in classroom disruption and violence. Members of the National Union of Teachers were not involved in the survey.

By CHRISTOPHER ROWLANDS and RICHARD CLARK

received from 90 per cent. of the city's 51 high schools ; 75 per cent. of the 66 middle schools and 40 per cent. of the primary schools.

In addition to the four attacks on staff by parents another 12 cases of abusive behaviour by parents were recorded ; and 124 teachers said verbal [abuse] included [school] in an 11-[number] teachers ce by [pun]iched lesson. ary of 'This s that good ening many [dur]ation well-y the

enda-should with ---l-

Daily Mail, Monday, May 30, 1983

Teacher quits after pupils rampage

CHANTING, swearing children on the rampage have driven a teacher from his job.

Staff returning to a school after lunch on Friday had to run a gauntlet of about 60 senior pupils, who were hissing, jeering, chanting obscenities, and some of whom tried to spray teachers with lacquer.

The pupils' siege was the last straw for Mr Allan Steven, £9,000-a-year head of the drama department at Malbank comprehensive school in Mantwich, Cheshire.

He says he will never teach in a State school again.

And he claims he has seen other teachers forced to turn to tranquillisers because of the stress of coping with school 'bullies'.

In his letter of resignation, Mr Steven, a 31-year-old bachelor says: 'Distasteful verbal abuse in and out of school is well established. How soon before it turns to a case of serious physical assault?'

Trouble began on Friday when some senior children gathered in the town square a few hundred yards from the school.

The headmaster, Mr Herbert Rowsell, had told senior pupils not to attend school on Friday, the last day of term.

But shortly before one o'clock on the day the children moved from the town centre to the school.

'It was obvious their actions were orchestrated,' said Mr Steven at his home in Lansdowne Road, Crewe, yesterday. 'Girls appeared to be playing a major part and the behaviour around the school grounds got out of hand.

'The pupils were chanting insults at staff as they returned from lunch to teach the first, second, third and fourth forms.

'There were attempts to spray teachers with lacquer and although none was physically assaulted there was a great deal of intimidation.

The headmaster of the 1,100-pupil school was not available for comment yesterday.

Daily Mail, Thursday, June 2, 1983

Detention rebel 'attacked his teacher with a brick'

A YOUNG teacher was savagely beaten in a revenge attack by a 13-year-old boy he kept in detention, a court heard yesterday.

The boy, who found the punishment 'humiliating,' lay in wait for Mr Allstair Phillip with his 21-year-old brother, it was alleged.

As the teacher arrived at his aunt's grocery shop, the older brother attacked Mr Phillip with a rice flail and the 13-year-old boy smashed a brick and then a yam into his face, Inner London Crown Court was told.

The chilling side is that as the brothers left they shook hands and the older man congratulated the younger boy on his fighting,' said Mr James Curtis, prosecuting.

Mr Phillip, 28, suffered cuts and bruises needing stitches.

The jury heard that Mr Phillip had tried to control the 'unruly' 13-year-old who refused to work or behave in the classroom.

The 'wild' boy would not even sit down and read while the newly-qualified maths teacher taught the rest of the class at Hatcham Wood High School, in Brockley, South London, said Mr Curtis.

Things came to a head in January when Mr Phillip, as a last resort, ordered the youth to remain behind for detention.

The youth went berserk and 'it took other boys and members of the staff to control him when he went wild', said Mr Curtis.

'Detention was a humiliating and thoroughly unpleasant punishment for this youth and he clearly couldn't stand it.

'He seemed to want to pick a fight and provoke a confrontation.

'The boy told his older brother that he had been hit by Mr Phillip and 'the brother took the law into his own hands,' said Counsel.

Both defendants deny wounding Mr Phillip with intent, assaulting him and damaging property. The trial continues.

of an impending Armageddon in the classroom, we need to consider the available *research* findings to see what support, if any, they lend to the belief that there is a crisis of control facing teachers in comprehensive schools.

A Crisis of Control? The Facts

The studies of control and discipline in schools, though they are relatively few in number, tend to agree that it is amongst 13–15 year olds in urban, secondary schools suffering from social deprivation (of whatever kind) that violence, vandalism and truancy are most prevalent — i.e. amongst pupils in the maintained sector, urban *comprehensive* schools[2]. To this extent, the popular impression that control is a problem associated with comprehensives is borne out. Yet at the same time, there is also a large agreement that, as a problem, it is one whose reputation exceeds its reality (Docking 1980; Galloway *et al* 1982, Jones-Davies and Cave 1976, Laslett 1977a) and, on this point, the research evidence would seem to be in marked disagreement with 'sturdy common sense'. Rather than support the idea that standards of discipline are declining or that control problems are reaching epidemic, crisis proportions, it suggests that a far more cautious and qualified position is warranted.

First it is important to recognize that historical evidence casts doubt on the idea that the control problem is anything new to schools (Grace, 1978; Humphries, 1981; Swift 1971) and, as Galloway *et al* conclude:

> the evidence does not suggest that schools today are any closer to anarchy than they were in the 1920s and 1930s (...) The limited available evidence lends no support to the notion of a large increase in the number of pupils presenting problems, or in the severity of the problems they present. (Galloway *et al*, 1982, p. 11, ix)

Humphries, emphasizing the point, produces evidence of severe disruption in schools during the period 1889–1939, specifically to:

> challenge the popular stereotype and academic orthodoxy that portrays pupils in the pre-1939 period as disciplined, conformist and submissive to school authority (... and to ...) expose this misleading stereotype by tracing the extensive nature of pupil opposition to provided schools. (Humphries 1981, p. 28)

And Swift (1971) points out that, in the United States, control difficulties have an even longer history. As far back as 1837 the records show that 10 per cent of Massachusetts' schools were broken up by rebellious pupils. This kind of information should make us wary about getting caught up in any hysterical response to a 'new crisis' of classroom control. It does not prove that things have always been the same but it does warn us against a blind acceptance of the common sense truth that control problems are worse than they used to be.

The second reason for caution concerns the evidence of violence. If, for the purposes of the present discussion, we turn a blind eye to corporal punishment as a form of institutionalized violence administered by teachers on pupils (and since 111 of Britain's 125 LEAs still permit corporal punishment, this is quite a significant narrowing of the whole issue) then it seems that violence in schools is actually quite rare. Mills (1976), for example, on the basis of extensive research on 13–16 year old pupils in a midlands local education authority, found that the chances of a teacher being assaulted were very low,[3] and that within the area there appeared to be a hard core of only about 3 per cent of this age-range who could be identified as 'seriously disruptive children'. Even Lowenstein's (1972) inquiry for the NAS in which it was claimed that 'the amount of varied violence occurring both in secondary and primary schools is much larger than might have been anticipated from the occasional press report' (p. 25), did not actually uncover a picture of extensive violence in schools. Of the 1065 questionnaires returned by NAS representatives in secondary schools (from 4800 sent out) 443 reported 'no real problem of violence' in their schools. Of the 622 who reported the existence of violence in their schools, only 66 said it was frequent. Furthermore, the *kinds* of violence reported were not always matters as serious as assaults on teachers or other pupils. There were many more reports of violence against property than of violence against the person.

Attacks on teachers, of course, are only one facet of the control issue. There are other, less extreme, kinds of pupil activity that can pose control problems and, in fact, the evidence indicates quite clearly that it is actually 'disruptive behaviour' by pupils rather than violence as such that is regarded by teachers as the major control problem.[4] The reason for this, it seems, is not that physical assault, arson and vandalism are regarded in their own right as trivial but that they occur quite rarely in comparison with the less extreme forms of disruption. This point emerged from the research of Lawrence *et al* (1977) in a London comprehensive school where they tried to gauge the extent of, and nature of, disruptive behaviour during two one-week periods; the first in November 1976, the second in February 1977. Thirty-six of the teachers were asked to write reports on disruptive incidents and these reports were subsequently followed up by interviews to clarify the nature of the event. During the two weeks, 101 incidents were reported by teachers of which only nine could be categorized as 'very serious'. Lawrence *et al* admit to some surprise about this since in their definition of 'disruptive behaviour' as 'behaviour which seriously interferes with the running of the school (pp. 6, 11) they originally had in mind the more extreme cases of disruption such as 'physical attacks' and the 'malicious destruction of property'. As became evident, the teachers were anxious to include boisterousness and minor infringements of rules since these were the prevalent form of control problems they experienced as teachers.

This feature of teachers' understanding of classroom control is worth emphasizing. From their point of view, control problems are not restricted to the explosive instances that occur occasionally — the serious incidents involving violence or extreme verbal abuse. What troubles teachers more are the less extreme challenges to their authority — indiscipline, such as lack of cooperation or attention during lessons, dumb insolence, noisiness in class, cheeky comments to teachers, larking about and 'having a laugh'. Even on this score, though, it does not appear that teachers are facing an acute problem. Indiscipline is certainly a *common* problem facing teachers (and one that clearly becomes worse depending on the motivation of the pupils in the school or class, the time of day, week or term, the weather, and the subject of the lesson) but the great majority of teachers work in schools where it would not appear to be a *desperate* problem. As HMI (1979) conclude, having investigated 384 secondary schools, it was only in 6 per cent of cases that indiscipline could be seen as a 'considerable problem' and in less than 1 per cent of the schools was it a 'serious problem'. Similarly, Dierenfield (1982), surveying the opinions of 465 comprehensive school teachers in 41 LEAs found that none felt disruption in their school to be 'totally out of hand' and only 3.6 per cent regarded it as a 'severe situation'. The majority (67.8 per cent) felt it to be a 'problem but one with which it is possible to cope'.[5] Indeed, Dierenfield argues from his research that:

> The most important conclusion to be drawn from the data . . .
> is that the people most directly concerned with disruptive
> behaviour in comprehensive schools, the teachers and heads, are
> convinced that classroom discipline is a serious, but not critical

problem ... Teachers and heads in comprehensive schools look upon classroom disruption as a serious problem but believe it can be handled by emphasizing several standard procedures available to every school.

The Need for Ethnographic Fieldwork

The picture that emerges from existing surveys on violence and disruptive behaviour on the part of pupils is quite different in some respects from the popular myth. As we have seen, research would suggest that violence against teachers is relatively uncommon and that, so far as the teachers themselves are concerned, it is the more mundane kinds of disruptive behaviour by pupils which are of greater importance. These, in turn, are seen as a 'serious, but not critical problem' and teachers seem both willing and able to cope with it using 'standard procedures available to every school'.

This version of the situation, of course, can claim to be more valid than the one based on 'sturdy common sense' because it is based on research rather than impression. However, a cautionary note is needed on this point. Research on control is particularly difficult in view of the nature of the event(s) being studied and it would be naïve to treat the research evidence as conclusive or to ignore the fact that it often faces methodological problems which limit the reliability of its findings. We need to recognize that the measurement of control problems in schools is very much affected by the ways in which incidents are defined, identified and recorded, and that events connected with control do not readily lend themselves to objective or unequivocal analysis because they generally involve subjective interpretation and personal discretion rather than precise, absolute matters of fact (Hargreaves *et al*, 1975; Stebbins, 1970). In the case of assaults on teachers, for instance, whilst teachers might claim to have been the victim of an assault they might not be prepared to make a formal complaint or prosecute the pupil(s) involved. The degree of the assault will obviously have a bearing on this and the matter is further complicated because the term 'assault' itself covers the whole range of violence from vicious attacks that cause serious injury to milder forms of physical contact that leave no real damage. The crucial point is, though, that where statistics on assault are restricted to those that teachers are prepared to follow up in such a way (ILEA figures, for example) then clearly the official figures will understate the situation.

Equally, if not more important, are the limitations inherent in the use of questionnaires as the means for gathering data on control problems in schools. Questionnaire surveys[6] depend either on reports by local authorities or on reports from teachers about their own experiences of the problem, and such 'self-reporting' causes two kinds of difficulty. First, as Docking (1980, p. 8) indicates, surveys of this kind cannot control for variations in teacher perceptions of, and attitudes towards, violent or disruptive behaviour and cannot, therefore, provide any objective index of trends in the incidence of such behaviour. And second, 'self reporting' assumes that teachers are *willing* to reveal the extent of control problems they face. Yet, as Comber and Whitfield conclude from their survey: 'Perhaps the most significant impression of all is that of most teachers to admitting any disciplinary problems and the stigma attached to not being able to keep order' (1979, p. 10). Understandably those who believe that comprehensives are facing a crisis of control are quick to point to the implications of this — namely that estimates based on teachers' reports will be prone to *under*-estimating the extent of the actual control problems in schools because teachers themselves might not wish to admit to such problems.

Complications such as these, whilst they do not entirely invalidate the survey estimates of control problems, suggest the need for a method of enquiry about control in the comprehensive school which does not rely just on teachers' self reports. In particular, it suggests the need for some in depth fieldwork to complement the survey/self report type of research and to check just how far the survey/self report conclusions can be substantiated *in the practice* of control in comprehensives.

What follows is an investigation of control in comprehensives which moves in this direction in the sense that it is based on ethnographic fieldwork in two London comprehensives. Classroom observation, lengthy tape-recorded interviews with teachers and documentary information, combined with many less formal sources of data, were used over a period of four years to compile a detailed picture of the situation in the schools.

Violence and Disruptive Behaviour at Ashton and Beechgrove: Some Fieldwork Observations.

The schools, 'Ashton' in Brent and 'Beechgrove' in Camden, were both reasonably large, urban comprehensives. Ashton had about 1500 pupils and 88 staff, Beechgrove had 1250 pupils and 78 staff (its school roll had fallen from a peak of 1900 as a result of redevelopment in its catchment area).[7] Both were in predominantly working class areas with markedly higher proportions of 'immigrant' pupils than for the rest of London or the rest of the country, and both received an intake that was lower than average in terms of measured ability. Because they were 'urban', because they were quite large, they were the kind of schools identified both by research findings and by the critics of comprehensives using 'sturdy common-sense' as the kind of schools most vulnerable to control problems. We might predict, indeed, that if there was a crisis of control to be found anywhere in comprehensives, it would be found at Ashton and Beechgrove.

Certainly, there were some incidents that matched the atrocity stories to be found in sections of the press. One, in particular, was horrific. During fieldwork at Beechgrove a teacher was stabbed in the back with a chisel. She suffered a punctured lung and did not return to teaching when she eventually recovered. Fortunately, this incident was the only serious piece of violence against a teacher or pupil that occurred at either school during the four years. There were a number of milder assaults on teachers during the period of research and certainly at Beechgrove a male chemistry teacher, quite small in stature, even developed something of a reputation for getting assaulted by pupils. On two occasions actually witnessed during fieldwork he was punched repeatedly on the chest and had abuse shouted at him by a boy who appeared to have completely lost his temper. Interestingly, on neither occasion did the boy (a different one each time) hit the teacher in the face, stomach or elsewhere that would have caused real injury and the attacks actually seemed, consciously or otherwise, controlled and limited in their viciousness. The teacher was left standing and, before the pupils could be restrained by other teachers, was warning the boys 'You're in a lot of trouble already doing this. I'd stop now if I were you before you go too far'. These incidents led to the boys being reported to their heads of house but did not lead to any kind of official complaints against either boy for assault. In consequence, the two 'assaults' would not have appeared in the official statistics for attacks on teachers because neither the teacher himself nor the other teachers immediately involved chose to pursue the matter any further. In effect, the incidents were treated as cases of particularly disruptive behaviour but not as assault.

These incidents pose an intriguing question: 'how often do such minor assaults occur behind the closed doors of the classroom, never to be brought to light to those outside?' It has to be said on this point that not even protracted fieldwork in a school can give an accurate answer because classrooms are 'private' settings that normally prevent non-participants from witnessing the teacher-pupil interaction that goes on within (Denscombe, 1980b). So far as could be gauged from fieldwork, though, assaults even of the milder variety were not common events and it became quite clear at least from interviews with the staff that violence, or the threat of violence, was not a major source of anxiety for them. Approximately a third of the staff at Ashton and a third of the staff at Beechgrove were formally interviewed, in each case after their lessons had been observed on a number of occasions. Apart from the incidents involving the chemistry teacher at Beechgrove who was in an adjacent room, at no time during classroom observation was a teacher molested, assaulted or threatened with violence and in none of the 67 formal interviews did a teacher suggest that the threat of violence affected his or her routine work. When the subject of violence in classrooms was broached during interviews the general theme of the responses was that violence certainly *might* happen but it could generally be avoided unless the pupil concerned was 'psychopathic'. In fact the spirit of the responses was captured by the comments of the language teacher at Beechgrove whose lessons were interrupted by the attacks on the chemistry teacher next door:

> You see, there are some kids who really ought not to be here because they're emotionally unbalanced. There's not a lot you can do about them is there? I mean if they're in the school and you're stuck with them, if they're going to do something dreadful like with [Miss ...] who got stabbed, well ... you can't do much to prevent it. But I think you'll find most of the teachers here would argue that when there's trouble it's usually the case that the teacher can sense when something's brewing and can usually manage to calm the situation before the kid goes over the top — you know, get them out of the room or something. But then there are some teachers who just seem to aggravate the stroppy kids and then don't know how to ... kind of back down or defuse the situation.

Naturally, the stabbing at Beechgrove had an impact on the attitudes and concerns of the teachers but the impact turned out to be rather temporary. Later discussions and interviews with the teachers at Beechgrove — as with those at Ashton — served to confirm that matters of disruptive behaviour in the classroom were the major preoccupation of the teachers and that violence was seen as a possibility that, although real, was rather remote. On the basis of fieldwork, then, it was difficult to construe the situation at either Ashton or Beechgrove as one involving a 'crisis' of control. What was revealed instead was a situation where: (i) violence in the form of attacks on teachers did exist but was far from a common feature of school life, and (ii) disruptive behaviour was the major preoccupation of teachers, not the fear of violence.

On these points there would appear to be support for the findings of the survey-type research. However, there was another feature of control in the schools which, far from lending support to findings based on teacher self-reports, actually reinforced one of the major criticisms of such findings. It became evident that, in terms of the way control operated on a routine day-to-day basis, there was heavy emphasis placed on coping with control problems without help from colleagues and without recourse to any 'standard procedures' set up to deal with the burden of disciplinary problems. In effect, there was pressure on teachers not to publicize the control problems they encountered and this pressure consequently reinforced doubts about the accuracy of teacher self-reports as a method for estimating the extent of control problems in schools. It lent weight to the suspicion that such methods inherently underestimate the problem.

This emphasis on dealing with control problems individually and 'in private' was crucial to the nature of control exercised at Ashton and Beechgrove and it had significance in its own right, quite apart from its methodological implications. For this reason it warrants particular attention as a feature of the control practised in the schools — control at the mundane, unspectacular level of daily routine — and nowhere was this aspect of control more in evidence than in the way the house systems at the schools had become involved in dealing with disruptive pupils.

The house system and disruptive behaviour

At Ashton and Beechgrove there were certain 'standard procedures' to deal with matters of disruptive behaviour and, in both cases, these centred around the house system. Both schools had four houses — each with two 'heads of house' and a team of supporting teachers assigned to the house, and within these house systems it was clear that most of the power and the bulk of the duties rested on the shoulders of those teachers who were 'heads of house'. In fact, both in terms of their position in the hierarchy of authority and in terms of their specialist duties, the heads of house assumed a crucial role.

The houses were intended to provide pupils with a smaller unit with which they could identify and within which they could feel secure — in effect, compensating for the alienating effect of the large number of pupils in the school and providing a basis for the pastoral care and guidance of the pupils. Formally, at least, the houses were not concerned with matters of disruptive behaviour so much as the pastoral well-being of the pupils. In fact, the official guidelines for teachers at both schools made it perfectly clear that individual teachers were held responsible for control during their own lessons and the official guidelines discouraged the practice of sending a pupil out of a lesson to report to the house room, or asking a head of house to come to the classroom as a method of coping with uncooperative pupils. Such 'direct referrals' to the house system, it was argued, could undermine the teacher's authority. As the point was emphasized at Beechgrove:

> Discipline within the classroom is the responsibility of the individual teacher but heads of department and heads of houses are always ready and willing to support members of staff. However, it should be realised that in the end no useful and lasting purpose is served if too many problems arising within the classroom are referred to higher authority. This practice only serves to weaken the authority of the individual teacher in the eyes of the children. (Official Guidelines: Beechgrove)

It was acknowledged by the official guidelines and the heads of house alike that, on occasion, a situation might arise in which it was appropriate to call upon the assistance of the heads of house through 'direct referral', but such situations were limited to *emotional* problems which might flare up in the classroom situation and perhaps to those occasions where the teacher would otherwise lose his/her temper with the pupil in question. As a head of house at Beechgrove put the point:

> We don't encourage staff to send kids out of the classroom unless they really feel they can't cope. They're advised *not* to send kids out. Obviously, if the kid is just so impossible that they just can't cope, then they do.

The official stance was clear: direct referral was to be used rarely and in extreme circumstances, and never as a substitute for classroom control. Classroom control was the province of the teacher in the classroom not the house system and teachers were clearly reminded in the official guidelines in both schools that control was not to be abdicated by relying on direct referrals to the heads of house.

Such unequivocal statements should have left the teachers in little doubt about the formal distinction between the pastoral responsibilities of house staff and their own role as managers of the classroom. Yet, in practice, the house system had become heavily involved in problems of classroom control. Although proscribed by the official guidelines and deplored by the heads of house, it was acknowledged by house staff and classroom teachers alike that the heads of house were developing a 'discipline specialist' function.[8] As a result of the type of referral they received, the heads of house argued that their role was less involved with the pastoral care and guidance of (all) the pupils in the house, or even those with particular emotional problems and was, instead, being pushed towards a 'discipline specialist' or 'trouble shooter' role in which they were regularly called upon to deal with what they called 'crisis' events, such as dealing with a truculent pupil who had been sent from the classroom or having to go to another teacher's classroom to sort out a problem.

This deep involvement of the house staff with matters of classroom control might be seen as an inevitable result of the fact that the kind of behaviour which is symptomatic of a personal or emotional problem is also the kind of behaviour that the classroom teacher tends to regard as a discipline problem. As Docking (1980) points out, pupils who seem unable to cope with 'stressful situations' and those who find it difficult to 'develop meaningful relationships with school staff' are not only a problem in terms of their own welfare and development but are also likely to pose a problem in terms of orderly classroom behaviour and teacher control of the situation. But this did not seem to fully explain the way in which the house system had become involved as a back-up to classroom control because, as the heads of house argued with unanimity, the bulk of the direct referrals came from one distinct group of teachers. It was specifically the new teachers, the young, probationary, inexperienced and new arrivals who were considered to be the ones who would use the system in this 'inappropriate' manner.

One explanation for this, frequently proffered by experienced members of staff, was that new teachers sometimes were not willing enough to impose their authority and control on the classroom situation and were, in consequence, all too willing to fall back onto the services of the heads of house to back up their control of the classroom instead of coping with the problems themselves. As one teacher put it:

> Now, it may not be a criticism of teachers — it might be a criticism of the system that trains them — but many teachers coming into schools now, I feel, aren't willing to fight hard enough to get control. (The house system) is providing a feather bedding for people who aren't willing to try to win within the classroom situation. So, I get kids sent down here for various ... for very small things ... There are people in this school who will, at the slightest little thing, send a kid down here. Now you see I'm not marvellous, I have my discipline problems that I have to cope with in all the ways that I know, but sometimes people send a kid down here for chewing or not doing his work or things like that. Now I maintain that if that happens in your class, *you* ought to be able to solve these problems. (head of house (D), Ashton)

Such understanding of 'excessive and inappropriate' direct referrals coloured the way in which the heads of house dealt with the referrals. The heads of house, in practice, regarded many of the referrals as problems of teacher control rather than problems of the particular pupil and there was no automatic assumption that pupils who were referred required some counselling in order to find the cause of their disruptive behaviour because the cause of that behaviour was often attributed to the classroom control of the teacher. As another head of house at Ashton put it:

> It's my experience that house teachers spend a lot of their time dealing with high-spiritedness which the ... er ... the particular class teacher had been unable to cope with and for which there's no real need for counselling. And ... um ... it's due to a *lack of experience* on the side of the particular class teacher in charge. (head of house (H), Ashton)

The problem, in other words, was seen as the teacher not the pupil. As a head of house at Beechgrove pointed out: 'They'll often come into teacher 'A' or teacher 'B' (heads of house) very often *with problems created by colleagues and not of their own making*'.

Numerous instances were observed in the house room where direct referrals were greeted with a casual and light-hearted air which was ostensibly inappropriate. The heads of house appeared little concerned to conduct counselling or dispense punishment. An example, characteristic of such occasions, was afforded at Ashton when a 'regular' referral arrived at the room. head of house (H) laughing, asked: 'And what have we been doing today?' The boy shrugged his shoulders and another member of the house staff (D) in the room joined in the laughter. No detailed account of his referral was sought and the boy was told to sit and read for the rest of the period. The reaction was explained by the head of house: 'He's a regular. He's O.K. . . . just a bit cranky. But some of the staff can't cope with him and he plays them up and gets sent down here. It's not all his fault'.

The discretion with which heads of house acted not only reflected their understanding of the causes of the problem but also provided a possible source of conflict between the referring teacher and the particular head of house. Referring teachers sometimes felt that the pupil being referred should receive some form of punishment whilst, on the basis of their experience and pastoral expertise, the head of house considered that to punish the child would be inappropriate. The heads of house felt that, once it had been referred to them, the problem would be dealt with by them and in the manner which they saw fit.

Autonomy, experience and 'direct' referrals.

Given the discretion open to the heads of house in the way they dealt with the pupils referred to them, direct referrals had but one positive and self-evident effect on the pupils' behaviour in the classroom — to eliminate the problematic behaviours from the classroom setting. And in terms of classroom control this had particular advantages in the immediacy of its impact on disruptive behaviour. Teachers did not have to wait for a chance to pass on messages about a problem pupil and continue to suffer whilst counselling work by the heads of house filtered down into improved classroom behaviour. They could expect instantaneous beneficial results.

At first glance, therefore, direct referral to the heads of house would seem to be an enticing strategy for classroom control and it would seem reasonable to expect to see it as part of the standard repertoire of methods used by teachers for this vital part of their work. But, in practice, it was evident that the established teachers showed a marked reticence to send troublesome pupils to the house room and, as the heads of house said, it was the young and inexperienced staff who were the major users of direct referrals.

This reticence of the experienced teachers, it seemed, owed much to their unwillingness to hand over *their* problems to someone else. They were very cautious about sending pupils down to the house room or calling a head of house to deal with a pupil in their classroom because to do so might imply that they could not cope with the problem alone — and this was a dangerous implication. Calling on someone else to help in the routine control of a class suggested, to colleagues and pupils alike, that the teacher was unable to deal with matters 'autonomously' and was thus failing in a vital aspect of the job.

The heads of house themselves, were quite sensitive to this point. Because they, like the other 'experienced' teachers, felt that subject teachers should normally be able to control their own classes, they tended to regard regular calls for assistance through direct referrals as an indictment of the competence of the referring teacher. And, because of this, any intervention by the heads of house on their own admission needed very delicate handling. As one of the heads of house at Ashton put the point:

> Teachers generally would feel ... I myself as a teacher would feel ... rather than as a house teacher .. that it is important that a class teacher is able to keep control of his own class, because no matter how carefully a house teacher puts himself in a position of walking into someone else's class or being sent someone else's problem, ... however carefully he may attempt to approach the subject of why the particular teacher had to send the pupil to the house teacher, he needs to avoid the impression of ... of failure by the class teacher to discipline the child himself ... It's very difficult to escape from the fact that this is rather the impression the pupils get. They're certainly aware that some teachers send pupils to house teachers and others do not. For example, they are themselves taught by people who are house teachers, and they are aware that house teachers don't send pupils to other house teachers. They are also aware that ... many of the senior members of staff would not operate discipline in this way ... I think the pupils are aware that it's ... that teachers send them to house teachers because they themselves can't cope. It's often been the case that pupils have in fact refused to leave the room, and the teacher's had to send for a house teacher to come and take them out. There's never any trouble. As soon as house teacher arrives the pupil's perfectly willing to go ... in my experience. I think that the pupils feel that it's a shortcoming of the teacher in charge. (head of house (H) Ashton)

On this kind of occasion the relationship between the head of house and the classroom teacher became very delicate. Whether or not the heads of house felt they were impinging on the authority of the classroom teacher, they were at pains to give the impression that this was not in fact the case. The house staff felt that in these situations it was important not to exacerbate the impression which pupils may already have been fostering that the teacher had been unable to cope and had therefore to call for assistance from the head of house, and, as part of professional etiquette, the heads of house attempted to disguise the purpose and implications of their presence in order to prevent the possibility of the teacher 'losing face' in front of the pupils.

The risk of 'losing face' was heightened of course, when the head of house was less than delicate in his/her treatment of the problem. An episode at Ashton served to illustrate the point. A supply teacher had been observed for three lessons and subsequently interviewed. The methods of teaching she adopted were in her own words 'authoritarian' because, as a supply teacher, she felt this to be the best method of gaining immediate impact and control in new situations. Not long after the interview she rushed into the staffroom, in the middle of the teaching period, bursting into tears and exclaiming, 'I've never been so humiliated in all my life!' — a phrase she repeated time and again in the course of accounting for what had happened. The source of this humiliation and embarrassment was explained thus: that a particular class (acknowledged by her colleagues to be 'difficult') had been noisy and inattentive and responded to none of her pleas for order or threats of detention. In desperation, and against her normal practice, she had sought the aid of a head of house. The head of building, who was deputizing for a head of house at the time, had been unable to come immediately and the teacher had returned to the classroom. She imposed a detention and managed to start the lesson. To her satisfaction, that is, she had gained control of the class and no longer needed the support she sought. Five minutes later the head of building was alleged to have stormed into the classroom and taken a seat with the pupils. In doing so, she was effectively undermining the authority and status of the teacher by implying, in front of the pupils, that the fault lay with the teacher, not with the pupils. Being unsettled by all this, the supply teacher hesitated and faltered, in response to which the head of building grabbed the lesson notes and chalk and literally proceeded to take over the lesson. It was not only the supply teacher who was embarrassed. She emphasized later in accounting for what happened that the pupils too were very embarrassed. Pupils were so acutely conscious of the situation that those nearby apparently whispered things to the effect 'I wouldn't stand for it, Miss. I'd walk out if I was you'. She did in fact leave the room, containing the anguish of such utter humilitation until reaching the sanctuary of the staffroom where she burst into tears.

This event illustrated the possibility, which could not have escaped the notice of other members of staff, that to call upon another teacher for help was to run the risk of publicly 'losing face'. The head of building in this instance had caused humiliation for the supply teacher, and near outrage from other members of staff who became aware of the event, by showing disregard to two sensitive areas of teaching. She had implicitly challenged the competence of the teacher and she had violated the privacy of the teaching context. But the important point to note is that both aspects were opened for violation only because of the initial request for help in controlling a class. In either case, the referring teacher ran the risk of giving the impression to colleagues and pupils alike that he/she was unable or unwilling to maintain control without outside help. It could imply, in other words, a dual failing in the teacher: failure to control the class and to operate autonomously.[9]

This would explain the reluctance of experienced staff to draw on the services of the house system. Experienced teachers were wary of using it because their 'experience' allowed them to recognise the implicit failure entailed. They appreciated that it could become a 'publicly available' indicator of (lack of) classroom control. The meaning of 'experience' in this context, then, involved more than just a time-span of official appointment as a teacher. Although often associated with the number of years' service attributed to a particular teacher, in essence 'experience' concerned a way of *interpreting* the situation; experience constituted a mode of understanding and form of activity rather than a log of years in the job. And it follows that 'inexperience' involved a failure to appreciate the full *implications* of referring troublesome pupils to the house system and specifically, the way this could impugn the teacher's competence. From the teacher's point of view, what experience told them was that it was wise not to publicize the existence of control problems in their own classroom or to risk it becoming public knowledge by using 'standard procedures' available in the school.

Summary and Conclusion

Critics of standards of pupil behaviour in comprehensive schools have not generally based their allegations on substantial fact and, from what we have argued here, there are two good reasons for this. First, there have been surprisingly few attempts at rigorous investigation and second, possibly connected with this, there are certain inherent difficulties with measuring the extent of control problems. These methodological difficulties arise because (i) control problems cover a variety of situations, ranging from violence/assault to minor classroom disturbances; (ii) the existence of control problems depends on specific official definitions, particular interpretations by teachers and a willingness on the part of teachers to report such problems; and (iii) perhaps most significantly, there are strong formal and informal pressures on teachers not to publicize the difficulties they might experience.

The end result is that any attempt to identify trends or to compare different schools becomes fraught with methodological problems. Bearing this in mind, there are, nonetheless, some comments we might venture to make on the question of control in comprehensives — comments derived both from a review of the limited survey-type data that is available and from case study material focusing on teacher perceptions of control. These would suggest quite strongly that (i) violence in schools is less common than press reports might suggest and that assaults on teachers by pupils are relatively rare; (ii) from the teachers' point of view, the problem of control does not involve a fear of assault so much as anxiety about the routine problem of coping with disruptive behaviour in the classroom; (iii) experienced teachers place considerable emphasis on being able to cope with such problems without help from colleagues or outside agencies; and finally, that (iv) the idea of a crisis of control in the comprehensive school is not supported in fact. Disruptive behaviour is a serious problem facing teachers but it appears to be one that has not got out of hand.

Notes

1 Advocates of the comprehensive, not surprisingly, dismiss such allegations by pointing to the impossibility of genuine, fair comparisons or by engaging in detailed investigations to reveal the 'real' trends in academic attainments. More detailed accounts of the political and educational controversy surrounding the move towards comprehensive secondary education can be found in Banks (1955), Fenwick (1976), and Rubinstein and Simon (1973) amongst others.

2 Anxiety about deteriorating discipline and control, we should note, has focused on state schools and specifically the comprehensives. Now that 90 per cent of secondary school pupils in the maintained sector attend comprehensives (1983) the allegations have broadened to include 'state secondary schools' in general. The comparisons, as a result, are now

between 'state' and private schools rather than comprehensives and grammar schools. In either case it is the 'comprehensive' school which gets depicted as the source of the problem — its emphasis on 'non-selection' and its quality of staff allegedly causing extra problems compared with the alternative.

3 The estimate based on this research is a frequency rate of 0.10 per thousand.

4 Lowenstein (1975) makes this distinction between violence, which includes 'fairly vicious attacks on other pupils or members of the school staff', and disruptive behaviour which includes 'any behaviour short of physical violence which interferes with the teaching process and/or upsets the normal running of the school'.

5 It is also interesting to note the types of behaviour experienced by the respondents as having a 'serious effect on reasonable order' in their school. Only 23.6 per cent cited physical violence on the teacher, 21.9 per cent abusive talk to the teacher, 19.7 per cent physical violence to other pupils.

6 Examples of this approach are: Association of Education Committees (1975), Comber and Whitfield (1979), Dierenfield (1982), Lowenstein (1972, 1975), Mills (1976), Pack (1977). Notable alternatives to a dependence on questionnaire responses can be found in Hargreaves *et al* (1975), Galloway *et al* (1982), Lawrence *et al* (1977). Anecdotal accounts of the issue exist in, for example, Francis (1975) and Haigh (1976).

7 'Ashton' and 'Beechgrove' are, of course pseudonyms: 79.5 per cent of comprehensives have fewer than 1200 pupils (DES figures issued May 1983).

8 Guthrie's (1979) research serves to confirm the findings at Ashton and Beechgrove. At another London comprehensive school he notes the pressure on house staff to operate as control trouble shooters rather than agents of pupil welfare.

9 The importance of 'autonomy' for teachers is emphasized, *inter alia*, by Bidwell (1965), Denscombe (1980a, 1982), Grace (1972), Jackson (1968), Lortie (1969), and McPherson (1972).

References

ASSOCIATION OF EDUCATION COMMITTEES (1975) *Survey of Violence, Indiscipline and Vandalism in Schools*, London, Department of Education and Science.

BANKS, O. (1955) *Parity and Prestige in Secondary Education* London, Routledge and Kegan Paul.

BIDWELL, C.E. (1965) 'The school as a formal organisation', in MARCH, J.G. (Ed) *Handbook of Organizations* Chicago, Rand McNally.

CENTRE FOR CONTEMPORARY CULTURAL STUDIES (1981) *Unpopular Education: schooling and social democracy in England since 1944*, London, Hutchinson.

COMBER, L.C. and WHITFIELD, R.C. (1979) *Action on Indiscipline: a practical guide for teachers*, Hemel Hempstead, NAS/UWT.

COX, C.B. and BOYSON, R. (Eds) (1975) *Black Paper 1975: The Fight for Education*, London, Dent.

Cox, C.B. and Boyson, R. (Eds) (1977) *Black Paper 1977* London, Temple Smith.

Cox. C.B. and Dyson, A.E. (Eds) (1969–70) *Black Papers I-III* London, Critical Quarterly Society.

Denscombe, M. (1980a) '"Keeping 'em quiet": the significance of noise for the practical activity of teaching' in Woods, P. (Ed) *Teacher Strategies*, London, Croom Helm.

Denscombe, M. (1980b) 'The work context of teaching: an analytic framework for the study of teaching' *British Journal of Sociology of Education*, 1, 3, pp. 279–292.

Denscombe, M. (1982) 'The "Hidden Pedagogy" and its implications for teacher training', *British Journal of Sociology of Education*, 3, 3, pp. 249–265.

Dierenfield, R. (1982) 'All you need to know about disruption', *Times Educational Supplement*, 29 January.

Docking, J.W. (1980) *Control and Discipline in Schools*, London, Harper and Row.

Fenwick, I.G.K. (1976) *The Comprehensive School 1944–70: the politics of secondary school organisation*, London, Methuen.

Francis, P. (1975) *Beyond Control? a study of discipline in the comprehensive school*, London, George Allen and Unwin.

Galloway, D. *et al* (1982) *Schools and Disruptive Pupils*, London, Longman.

Grace, G. (1972) *Role Conflict and the Teacher*, London, Routledge and Kegan Paul.

Grace, G. (1978) *Teachers, Ideology and Control*, London, Routledge and Kegan Paul.

Guthrie, I.D. (1979) *The Sociology of Pastoral Care in an Urban School*, unpublished MA dissertation, University of London, Kings College.

Haigh, G. (Ed) (1979) *On Our Side: order, authority and interaction in school*. London, Maurice Temple Smith.

Hargreaves, D.G. *et al* (1975) *Deviance in Classrooms*, London, Routledge and Kegan Paul.

Her Majesty's Inspectorate of Schools (1979) *Aspects of Secondary Education in England*, London, HMSO.

Humphries, S. (1981) *Hooligans or Rebels? an oral history of working class childhood and youth 1889–1939*, Oxford, Blackwell.

Jackson, P.W. (1968) *Life in Classrooms*, New York, Holt, Rinehart and Winston.

Jones-Davies, C. and Cave, R.G. (Eds) (1976) *The Disruptive Pupil in the Secondary School*, London, Ward Lock.

Laslett, R. (1977a) 'Disruptive and violent pupils: the facts and the fallacies', *Educational Review*, 29, 3, pp. 152–162.

Laslett, R. (1977b) *Educating Maladjusted Children*, London, Crosby, Lockwood, Staples.

Lawrence, J. *et al* (1977) *Disruptive Behaviour in a Secondary School*, London, Goldsmiths' College.

Lortie, D.C. (1969) 'The balance of control and autonomy in elementary school teaching', in Etzioni, A. (Ed) *The Semi-Professions and their Organi-*

zation, New York, Free Press.

LOWENSTEIN, L. (1972) *Violence in School: and its treatment*, Hemel Hempstead, NAS.

LOWENSTEIN, L. (1975) *Disruptive Behaviour in Schools*, Hemel Hempstead, NAS.

McPHERSON, G. (1972) *Small Town Teacher*, Cambridge, Mass., Harvard University Press.

MILLS, W.C.P. (1976) *The Seriously Disruptive Behaviour of Pupils in Secondary Schools in One Local Education Authority*, unpublished MEd thesis, University of Birmingham.

PACK REPORT (1977) *Truancy and Indiscipline in Schools in Scotland*, Scottish Education Dept HMSO.

RUBINSTEIN, D. and SIMON, B. (1973) *The Evolution of the Comprehensive School 1926–72*, and London, Routledge and Kegan Paul.

STEBBINS, R.A. (1970) 'The meaning of disorderly behaviour', *Sociology of Education*, 44, pp. 217–236.

SWIFT, D.W. (1971) *Ideology and Change in the Public Schools: latent functions of progressive education*, Columbus, Ohio, Merrill Pub. Inc.

WILSON J.W. (1981) *Discipline and Moral Education: a survey of public opinion and understanding*, Windsor, NFER-Nelson.

Mixed Ability and the Comprehensive School

Brian Davies and John Evans

Change without Innovation

A good plan for extracting sense from most educational commonplaces (it often works too for the covering statements of other social institutions) is to turn them around until the sense drops out. They are, after all, nearly always based on only lightly empirically annotated beliefs, serving mainly to preserve interests higher up rather than lower down the hierarchy. This often means that a little new knowledge can go a long way toward unhinging them, but only if you can get the materially rooted, socially constructed, and well defended deaf to put on their conceptual hearing aids. Dialogue about education within education, however, is nearly always difficult except as a verbal love-affair between occupational clones with common outlooks.

It is not easy with those outside either, given that our capacity to defend this area rationally crumbles before the well aimed barb. Frequently the best we can do is not to answer and carry on much as before. This is what makes the particular inversion which we have in mind of such interest: our contention is that education is full of change without innovation. What comes to pass is lightly or hardly ever planned except in a minimal or reactive sense. We join bandwagons because they happen to be going our way. We could hardly flag down a vehicle for genuine change even if we wanted to, not knowing its likely colour, shape or size. Our journeys are prompted less by either destinations marked progress or timetables which tell us if anything is running our way today, than by the groundswells of child and occupational demographies. These alter at rates which we, in and out of education, are astonishingly incompetent at noticing, let alone predicting or controlling. They require constant response. Indeed, there is a sense in which, if we met them bright eyed and on our institutional toes — given our incapacity to command our central activity, pedagogy, except in poorly understood and conventional terms — we would displace even more unjustifiable energy into innovation without change. Grasping this alone will enable us to understand most of what is at stake when we feel puzzled over the amazing way in which people in and about educational activities can assert the most concrete sounding things without the slightest foundation, except their own carefully concealed feet of clay.

One further useful fact to bear in mind before we delve into a morass of mixed ability specifics is that education as discourse and practice is nearly always about somebody else's children. We do not have in England and Wales at the moment (and odd as we are, we are not unusual in all comparative terms) a single, recently achieved system of common schooling, but rather *three* systems in varying states of development: a dominant private system to which our central decision makers orient as consumers; a beleaguered and castigated public mass-system which stands only forty years from an altogether different age of standards;[1] and the massive fringes of both (but especially the latter) which our broad middle classes, new and old, colonize, subvert and hold-still in the correctly perceived interests of their children. Hackneyed though the point is, let us remember that almost all our policy makers, including those at LEA level, who exercise real control — the officers, educational theoreticians and even practitioners who work *outside* the private sector, seek to avoid the common school save in its uncommon forms.

Our first consideration *à propos* mixed ability and the comprehensive school must be, then, to ask 'what comprehensive school?' As will be shown with great clarity elsewhere in this volume,[2] the national picture is still incredibly varied as to the character and completeness of secondary reorganization. What percentage shall we put on the child cohort going to a local system from which there is minimal leakage[3] by class and ability (not to mention denomination and gender) *and* within which there is an accomplished policy of providing the common (comprehensive) school with a balanced — that is roughly equal and representative of the available distribution in the administrative area — ability intake (not to mention class, denomination, gender and ethnicity)? This may seem like a criterion designed only to avoid debate, but we make it plain that it is the only baton at the bottom of our value-filled, educational concept bag with which we feel the right tune can be conducted in a defensibly less inegalitarian society. In *its* terms, we have very few comprehensives indeed and 'balanced ability intake' is a receding rather than realizable dream in terms of recent and forseeable central government policy.[4] LEAs which have pursued it in the past have faltered under mainly class and denominational pressure. And now that we are nationally launched upon a reversionary sea of class envy and offence, the dried up politics of monetarist oppression — lubricated somewhat paradoxically by oil of our own waste — makes super-normal the voice of the standards-bearing right. The most amazing thing of all is that an industrial sphere whose dereliction has most to do with our present economic pass, can be made to appear *victim*, and not least to education's egalitarian, leftie dreams. If control of the national means to perspicacity is so speciously held, what hope can there be that the complicated voices of our poor understanding *in* education stand any chance of creating anything but tactical (even embarrassed) silence?

Mixed Ability: Meanings and Origins

Schools designated 'comprehensive', then, vary somewhat widely and far more than was the case in respect of the grammar or secondary modern schools under bipartism, particularly in pupil ability-intake terms.[5] Particularly in our inner cities, many of them have never been other than giant secondary moderns while others, particularly in our better shod, reorganized countries have effectively never parted with selective reflexes and superior intakes. The notion that 'mixed ability' should have the same 'meaning' in schools of such widely differing characters is nonsense. The working class grammar school of the fifties streamed in order to squeeze the largest net stay-on and exam gain from its clientele,[6] but its counterpart in the seventies, much more middle class dominated because it offered fewer places, and mixed abilities (such as they were) until it began to set. We do not really know at all clearly what the secondary modern did,[7] save that it tended to a top child purity principle. There is a genuine sense, of course, in which under bipartism the major grouping was done extramurally for schools. 'Streaming' becomes of interest academically as the search for the mainsprings of educability exhausts the interest in family background and moves into school. The earliest significant studies are concerned with the grammar.[8] Memoir, sub-academic proselytizing, national samples and the case study[9] moved the story over a decade or so to the point where the conventional child attainment books had been written. Empirical science was sure to show that streaming was bad for the working class child by asking that question only. No-one asked what teaching-grouping was *for*.

Reorganization forced the issue upon the natural streamers who ran our schools; that is to say, when the joining of schools changed their character, *someone* had to decide how to do grouping. They decided the issue in conventional terms. Comprehensive schools were organized by streaming and still predominantly are, in big streams called bands. Even insofar as those on the political left could be regarded historically as the protagonists of the comprehensive,[10] they certainly had no vision of internal organization on mixed ability lines until it had crept upon us. Even the true educational *avant garde* of the sixties — those without trammel of school experience, let alone licence to run schools[11] — preached individualization rather than heterogeneous grouping. Grouping maps of our system have always left a good deal to be desired even in terms of mechanical accuracy. There is not the slightest doubt that in crude 'national' terms, the whole curriculum, mixed ability secondary experience has never touched more than a third of our pupils at 11+ entry, to drop off dramatically in incidence in second and third years, especially in high status curriculum areas, as we argue below. Only a vestigial remnant of our secondary schools aim for heterogenous grouping by design in the two years to 16+, though more achieve it, in effect, by the action of our bloated option systems, especially below the curricular salt. But what is it, indeed, to know these figures without concomitant knowledge of school size and ability intake? Streaming in the elite grammar and sink secondary moderns was never in any sense 'the same thing'. How on earth could we imagine that 'mixed ability' was 'the same' in leafy suburb as in inner-city?

To offer the main part of that answer without wasting space on it, one needs to adduce the general character of educational debate. Poles rule, value positions rush in to fill empirical lacunae. To the distortion of the best which we can know, in defence of interest (which characterizes party political posturings and the only slightly more widely defined class and professional panderings of organs such as the Black Papers — whose long-time-serving chief authors have an alarming capacity for founding increasingly official sounding research and public relations forms[12] — and *Forum*, the authentic voice of the button-down left of educational centre), should be added the Theory and Practice industry, purveyors of soft-core values[13] to a sixties-swelling initial training industry which serves that brief moment of romanticism in the occupational cycle. It is still perfectly normal to go through initial and even in-service training and have ability and pastoral grouping, where dealt with, referred only to the twin rhetorics of individual and societal needs. Among the better norm-jobs aimed at teachers, we find Halsall (1973) typifying the mainstream sense in which organizing the comprehensive a decade ago conflated pastoral and teaching group issues, all along with the holy of valuational holies, staff attitudes:

> To organize houses on the basis of unstreamed teaching groups produces houses which are equal in intake as regards measured ability, but, if pastoral care is to be really good, it commits the school to unstreamed teaching groups, whatever the belief, knowledge or lack of knowledge, on this matter of teaching such groups, of the head and staff. Since it had been shown by the NFER report on streaming that the attitudes of head and staff to whatever policy is followed crucially affect its success, the conclusion one must come to is that the house system in a large comprehensive school is likely to be successful in improving pastoral care, without damaging academic results, only when the head and staff believe in unstreaming and have reoriented their teaching methods to suit it. Every other alternative appears likely to damage either academic results or pastoral care. (pp. 98–9)

Davies (1975), much persuaded of the evils of self-fulfilling selection, highlights the same note of muddled moral entrepreneurship:

> The act of faith which led many teachers to turn to mixed ability grouping in the first place has received more and more support, on the evidence of both experience and a growing body of research. From this point in the book I shall assume that the case in favour of abandoning streaming is made and concentrate on the practical implications of this at the school level. Theorising is pointless, however strong the case, if we are unable to translate our theories into effective practice at the classroom level. It is insufficient merely to change the structure if we cannot adapt our teaching and organisation in order to gain the maximum possibilities from the change. (p. 36)

Taken together, the contents of these quotes — let us emphasize, chosen for their better than average penetration in popular educational discourse — contain clues to most of the issues of relevance to us.

'Mixed ability' grouping is a product of the accelerating pace of comprehensive reorganization after 10/65. Benn and Simon's (1972) questionnaire reporting 1968 data from 673 schools (out of nearly a thousand covered by the NFER — see their Appendix 1 for details) shows only 29 (4 per cent) of schools having 'mixed ability for all subjects and pupils' in their first year, rising to 6.5 per cent on a much smaller sample by 1971 (p. 219, Table 10). Though the return was poor for our purposes, it serves as our only national baseline, and included all schools designated comprehensive. It revealed a much higher incidence of mixed ability coexisting with remedial separation and setting for subjects 'normally considered more "difficult": for instance, mathematics, a foreign language, science and sometimes such subjects as English, history, geography' (p. 218), in first year classes, but made plain that both in 1968 and 1971 streams, bands and sets, without recourse to mixed ability grouping, characterized the majority of schools in the sample (roughly 60 per cent at each date). The most significant swing between them was to banding but what is interesting about the Benn and Simon text is its systematic insinuation of the naturalness of the mixed ability end of non-streaming to the comprehensive: 'schools have tended to move over to mixed ability grouping as a result of their own experience and of educational objectives of the head and staff' (p. 226).

This is the stuff that puts educational innovation on the road — contentless necessity. Certainly school planners would have been hard pressed to emerge with design plans from the grouping research literature. From Billett's (1932) review of the literature through to Corbishley (1977) it is easy to allow absolution to researchers, not knowing enough about what they did. Lack of control of variables, differing objectives and measures, sample sizes and time-scales, all add credence to the latter's view that it is important to consider research in its time and place. It is somewhat inevitable that research will cluster round the new and interesting, argue for the coming rather than the going. This is certainly the case over fifty years in Britain and America. The view gained from only slightly lying-back must be that in respect of determining variations in academic attainment in pupils, grouping is not the prime factor. This is no advance on what we knew in the thirties and in one way indexes only the studied cerebral hygiene which we practice in respect of what little valid research we have in education.

Why did mixed ability grouping grow in respect of comprehensive schools in the late sixties and early seventies? What is certainly the case is that the answer cannot be provided in terms of simplistic notions of schools rationally scanning their own experience and framing appropriate objectives in the light of it. Indeed such a model is quite pernicious for our understanding of processes of schooling, particularly when carried through to the absurdity of notions such as the paramount importance of individual teacher and child attributes. In our mapping of grouping practices in 17 of the 21 Greater London LEAs in 1974–5, which afforded us over 90 and frequently 100 per cent returns in the secondary (and where appropriate, middle) schools of cooperating authorities, what stands out from the data is its patterning in LEA and school type terms. What stands out above all is the predominance of the first-yearness of mixed ability grouping (at around 30 per cent of our map, 40 per cent if any two from maths, science or modern language are exempted), coupled with variations from near universality in some LEAs (recently reorganized, policy-oriented toward it) to its confinement to the margin in others, especially the unreorganized or pseudo-reorganized. Excluding grammar schools, the best single indicator of mixed ability grouping was narrowness of ability intake. The thoroughly exceptional school was that with a balanced ability intake practising predominantly mixed ability grouping (across the whole subject range, save for remedial provision) in years 1–3 (until 14+). Here we are talking about rather less than 2 schools in 100. These are schools we would regard as seriously struggling with what Kelly refers to as a 'major first principle' of egalitarianism in knowledge terms — the same knowledge for as many children as possible for as long as possible, recognized to be quite unattainable once bands (streams) or sets are permitted.[14]

While we discerned a variety of overlapping, contradictory and conflicting motives professed by school decision makers — in other words, a perfectly normal set of real organizational states of affairs — in respect of 'going mixed ability' (Davies 1977) the thread that shone through interviewee *ex post facto* judgment was the systemic and technicist. Most first year secondary school mixed ability grouping (where most of it is) expresses the need for organizational moratorium and autonomy in a poorly informationally resourced and procedurally articulated system. All this is to say that when we talked to over 10 per cent of Greater London secondary schools heads or their nominees, they erected fear of sink-streams, inadequacy of 11+ intelligence, the need to 'shake' staff into new habits and the like as their 'reasons' for adopting mixed ability grouping where they had done so. What this indexed was the rise of whole-year, top-down planning for change as a concomitant of reorganization, often fixed by the promise extracted or the value impaled-upon at new headship interview. What it glossed over or incorporated unduly in the school top-person's view from the bridge was the potency of bottom- (or middle — that is, head of department) up mixed ability pressure. Ball's (1981) case at Beachside is a good example of this. Despite LEA distaste and without any other form of evident local enthusiasm, rather autonomous comprehensive school departments assumed very differing postures covering their interests (as a good interactionist, Ball calls them 'perspectives born out of subject identities') about mixed ability innovation. He sees the macro-struggle of educational forces — between academic and idealist impulses — played out in Beachside among teachers and departments.[15] Reid *et al* (1981), in a study of staggering disembodiedness, a sort of ultimate celebration of the inappropriateness of the survey and data aggregated from individuals rather than categorised per institution, rake up the same sort of patterns. On their data, setting grew at the expense of mixed ability and bands, in second and third year classes in two samples of schools surveyed for their 'predominant mode of grouping' in 1975 and 1980. 'Directed' (top-down mixed ability) innovation accounted for the change in two-thirds of those schools having mixed ability, but there is very little doubt on our data, as asserted above, that this was a second-wave phenomenon, trading on the earlier innovation predominantly pushed by idealistic and enthusiastic groups located in departments, and sanctioned by heads in a climate of ideological staff room ferment in the early seventies (Davies 1977). The 'thinkability' of mixed ability grouping was forged initially in that same school subject sector as had flirted in the sixties with integration and, as an associated minor sport, team-teaching. We can describe it as the English-as-mother-tongue-humanities-social-studies area. Demography in terms of shortage of teachers (of English) and more importantly of desirable children (as the pressures of expanding timetable demands pinched)[16] made relativistic responses possible in areas whose internal modes were characterized by topics or collections (poems aren't parsing, ain't creative writing, isn't reading stories or plays let alone drama or debate), sometimes abetted by criteria of adequacy of performance cast in high (which some would call low) individualist terms. English teaching was first, mixed ability base. History with periods and geography with regions were reluctant camp followers. Here the worksheet industry was begotten, colouring in the dinosaur after finishing the poem about it, part of common school cultural heritage. Subjects held to be more linear held off, neither lacking relatively more prestigious clientele not having as ready means of curricular reproduction in appropriate textual forms. Less willing teachers moved little in maths and science until effective individualized curricular packages appeared to make change more than what they were prone to see as ideological nuttiness.

A Comparative Study

Here it would be well to step back from the disembodied reasons/ features in general, about mixed ability in general, *pace* Reid, or theoretically overstrung preconceptions about worksheets as means to deskill teachers, mediated by Apple (1982), in the direction of the case study. In *Teacher Strategies* (see note 3) we concentrated on two mixed ability schools, both 11–18, mixed and normal sized by early seventies Outer London Borough standards, (six to seven form entry), which afforded very different routes and motives for going mixed ability, in equally different school biographic and child-material circumstances. School V, as we referred to it in Corbishley and Evans (1980) and Corbishley *et al* (1981) was a balanced ability entry, predominantly white, mixed social class school formed out of the growth of a mixed secondary modern which incorporated a girls grammar school. By 1976, the school was 'maturely' mixed ability in all subjects for two years and most for the third, with a minimal problem of remedial extraction. That is to say, it had passed the products of its regime through into the sixth, having achieved its state through an initial period of departmental enthusiasm becoming infectious and then being made mandatory. It was marked by a dominant pastoral (house) system and described both in public print and in terms fully elaborated on research site by its head as devoted, with pragmatic regard for staff capacity and outlook, to pursuing egalitarian curricular ends for motives both social and christian democratic. Under denominational licence and carefully cultivated and managed general parental consensus, it seemed to exemplify a good deal of the 'heads rule' thesis. A central part of the head's thrust seemed to focus upon the necessity to connect child and knowledge goodness, unmediated by the fallibility of teacher technique or the hierarchical message of grouping's form. Most of its classrooms were inevitably worksheet dominated. Its pupils tended to see their abilities and the pedagogic process in neutral or mildly pejorative terms. Observational data would suggest an ethos less of busyness than of *ennui*. The school, data upon which has not even yet been fully written up, must be viewed as a site which was enormously capable of attempting new things — stable, self-scanning, well-resourced, motivated and controlled by any state school standards of the early seventies — but up against the self-confessed limits (in general) of 'insufficient' mixed ability pedagogy.

School H, also called Sageton (Evans 1982, a and b) has been subjected to much fuller public analysis.[18] It can fairly stand for the experience of many inner-city 'comprehensives' of the seventies. In bare descriptive terms, it changed greatly over a twenty year period from its foundation in 1956 as a mixed four form entry (immediately taking six) high school, having space problems but enjoying in its head's terms 'good academic standards and good discipline' and good community standing. In 1967 it officially became a 13–18 comprehensive and witnessed a decline in academic, and rapid change in ethnic, composition. In 1971 it became an 'all through' 11–18, 1500 strong comprehensive, the largest in the authority, by taking in two other schools. Mixed ability innovation began in January 1974 when, in the face of successive 'depressed entries', the Academic Board narrowly adopted mixed ability and a four-period day for September 1974. In September 1975 a new head arrived, acutely aware of the need 'to change the identity of Sageton' and above all to raise the parental image of the school in order to move toward a more balanced intake. In 1977, its 198 pupil first year entry was divided into eight forms within a year system basis, which served not only as pastoral units but the mixed ability teaching groups for children in all subjects in year one, all save French (after the first term) in year two, and with maths, science and humanities also setting in year three. On NFER AH 2/3 tests the 1977 entry spread 9–28–62 per cent in comparision to the test standardization of 30–40–30 per cent, and 34 per cent of the entry had reading ages below 9 years. The school clientele was by now predominantly black and, in a period of staff and pupil conflict involving those from the three schools and the 'newcomers' coming from elsewhere to Sageton, little had been done to prepare or allow for the change. Pre-Houghton turnover, a season of three day week, unfinished buildings, prompted first a move to 'mini-schools' (upper, middle and lower) with largely autonomous heads, coexisting with departments. A further adjustment to a year system with faculties took place under the new head who also appointed a school counsellor and curriculum coordinator, as such elaboration typically decentralized and complicated the development of academic and pastoral policy and required further committee mechanisms to be developed, both for control and for consultation purposes, including a rather contradictory Policy

Forming Group.[20] The mixed ability grouping innovation, initiated largely under a rhetoric of sink-stream avoidance, control and motivation improvement, became publicly represented by the head as a sign visible and outward of Sageton caring for *all* its pupils, who might expect to benefit further in the event of the school being allowed a 'real' ability balance. Pragmatism and realism were strong. Setting was allowed when departments insisted upon it, a push was made to enhance resources (including library) and remedial extraction (and E2L provision) plentifully provided, albeit in an atmosphere of overwhelming need. In the unenviable centre of a cluster of external and internal pressures, the head's actions must be construed as aiming mainly for control. The staff room cry was 'not enough curriculum'.

In respect specifically of mixed ability, the staff experienced change at great pace, with insufficient planning and preparation. They had little expertise of any curriculum or pedagogic reform of any sort. They felt top-down pressure for concentration on control and improved assessment procedures, rather than leadership in these areas. Their experience, on the evidence of our wider sampling of London schools, was being repeated in its many parts in many other places in respect of being thrust into a form of organization by fiat, which, even if they had been asked, would not predominantly have been of their choosing. This is not to say that there was unwilling acceptance in the main. There can be little doubt that the Sageton mixed ability was mainly aiming at a moratorium space in which assembly and repair might lead to a more efficient and inevitable job of doing differentiation better (and producing a climate in which the supply of 'differences' to work with might become more normally distributed by altered external supply). There was little by way of the egalitarian, *noblesse oblige* or teacher-reconstructing about it (*inter alia*, motives located elsewhere). The sign on the front of its bandwagon said 'control' and on the back 'going up-market'. That it, like many other schools attempting similar change, was reactive victim to demographic cuts and thrusts born societally and *amplified* locally, goes, for us, without saying. Streaming and whole-class pedagogy were, although best evolved techniques of another age and school character, strangling their reorganized efforts. In British terms, only a year before Dahllof (1971), reflecting on the Swedish and particularly Stockholm experience of comprehensivization and ability experiment, could say that the costs of heterogeneity in less work and lower standards might be worth the 'better social climate, more positive attitudes, a greater and socially broadened recruitment to higher education', mitigated by an abandonment of 'the

old class-centred pattern of teaching in favour of increased individualization within the comprehensive class' (pp. 92–3). Stevens
(1970), in highly characteristic British voice, while recognizing that
'comprehensive teaching units ... because formal and orthodox
teaching is impossible' may lead to 'adventurous and exhilarating new
ways of working', fears with much feeling that 'children of the new
generation — those who have good ability but lack the social predis-
position and the verbal equipment to take readily to abstraction and
generalization and formal method' — might not profit:

> The very evident feeling of the first-generation grammar-
> school children of the succour of a community of learning, and
> the strong tendency of children in streamed comprehensive
> schools to choose friends not merely in their own but in closely
> adjacent streams, indicates that one needs like-minded compan-
> ions in order to endure 'the unsupportable fatigue of thought'.
> (pp. 183–4)

Our contention is that it is the Stevens rather than the Simons,
Bantocks or Boysons of the world who stand closest to the most
important recent historical strand in secondary-teacher consciousness.
In a system oriented to the twin gods of mastery and failure, *mass*
education in its common twitch had rapidly to improvize change which
foreswore disorder. But it — and our data on the tiny Sageton corner
attests this — lacks the sheer wherewithal (neither vocabulary nor
practice) to effect mass *education*, if by that we mean prolonged, willing
(even if largely calculative) engagement with public knowledge forms
beyond the merely self assignedly relevant (O! slippery term) for all
children. Stevens the English educator talks about 'original and personal writing, the making and use of recordings and films, fieldwork, the
employment of new materials and new uses of the old, heuristic
methods in science' as examples of new and exciting comprehensive
ways. The Swede Dahllof, in different tongue and voice, reports that in

> comprehensive [mixed ability] classes the bright pupils reach
> the same level of objective in the same effective time as their
> counterparts in the positively selected [homogeneous ability]
> classes. Having done this they must wait in some way or other
> for their slower peers in the steering criterion group [those the
> teacher uses to decide how fast to go, usually around 75th
> percentile]. This waiting time may be filled with other types of
> work ... through so-called enrichment exercises ... more

difficult problems of the same general type as in the common core ... [which] ... very soon become overlearning ... The pupils of this area of the ability distribution may be busy, and certainly do not cause any disciplinary problems, but they are not learning anything more of substantial value. (1971, p. 82)

We quote these apparent educational culture-poles at length not only because they focus on that same central fear — doing justice to the able, particularly of the fragile sort — while coming to roughly opposite (insofar as they are comparable) conclusions, but also because they sum up a great deal of discursive Sageton data. They also capture the pierced form of British comprehensivization at large, an organizational form lost in search of true pedagogy, goaded by demographic cut after surfeit, despised or neglected by too many of its masters. Our data persuade us on a subject basis that pupils cannot properly be talked about as alienatedly rejecting knowledge which they have not been effectively offered. To put it starkly, they all too often do not confront the different knowledge contents which most of us, not yet having fully succumbed the *trahaison des clercs*, regard as the goodness which justifies schooling's mission as opposed to its functions which in all societies serve to reproduce differences invidiously ranked in social — including economic and political — form. Indeed, we recognize that legitimized equality and inequality within and without education are empirically linked. Demographic change *qua* jobs — changing types and availabilities — fundamentally conditions the motivations of educands as to the effort they put forth, as school assumes and changes external 'meaning'. Dumping 10 per cent or more of the workforce into unemployment designed (or not resisted) to cure inflation and put the lower orders back into their pre-Keynsian place, reacts rather powerfully on the way children about to be quite disproportionately unemployed think about proper classroom performance and educational participation, as well as enabling the state to insinuate an increasingly unreformed educational voice, where 'how we've done it best' with the Few becomes the superhetted model for 'how we'd better do it again' with the Less.

The common school's logic, if we grant that social institutions are not merely boring facades for the class in hegemonic residence, is that of the Many. Doing the Many nicely no doubt requires a fundamental demographic reform concerning the ordinariness or incidence of those deemed to be successful at the final examinations, or their functional equivalent. Though this brings us close to the name which decent

Thatcher- and several otherites in education dare-not-speak, teachers know half the answer which is called 'abandon existing forms of assessment and size of flows out of school to more educational (but necessarily different from what we now have) experience.'[21] The rest is still silence but we must begin to think of it, on our data, in terms of improving the modes of transmission (MOT), which first of all presupposes an understanding and ability to elaborate their meaning. Detailed investigation of subject classrooms at Sageton scratches the surface of the teaching process in suggestive ways. Where mixed ability *grouping* is the innovation, there cannot be dramatic classroom change save in some of the surface features of the technology of teaching (heaven knows these have led to speculation enough about the meaning of the worksheet, from Apple, 1981, and Buswell, 1982, who appear to substitute macrospheric profundity for microscopic depth), rather than in terms of any basic departure from assumptions embodied in whole-class method and homogeneous grouping. The written word of the worksheet as opposed to teacher's mouth as the main mode of transmission promotes literacy over listening but does not challenge instructional limits. Orientation to middling-low ability and time pressure of pacing perpetuate material conditions of pedagogy and learning which throw up less able counter-steering groups (those you are not using to 'pace' but who, from lower down, force themselves upon attention) who 'challenge'. Social class in Sageton, as in Lumley, will not glibly explain away the issue. Lack of variety in and poor understanding of the nature and means to enhance differing classroom strategies or modes of transmission will account more properly for such phenomena. When worksheets rule, for example, pupils are less dependent upon teacher, but differentially, according to the levels of skills with which they are predisposed to work independently. Pupils still depend on teacher for getting 'unstuck', which further presupposes their command of skills which recognize stuckness-appropriate-to-hailing-teacher and command of means of getting non-pejorated attention. The teacher must distinguish folly from procedural contingency, from more or less deep-seated conceptual difficulty or blockage. The rate at which these problems potentially emerge, even with fairly horrid worksheets, makes whole-class teaching look like the conceal-ment-caper of all time. The decent one merely threatens to make normal — rational and explicit — the difficulties which children, right across the ability range, encounter minutely with 'getting at' classroom knowledge when 'collective piloting' is delegitimized. Where it is no longer normal for 'being taught' as a whole class without necessary reference to 'gaining understanding' to be sufficient, then the whole framework of ordinary convention about shutting up and 'getting on with it' unless bidden otherwise, threatens to collapse as unsuited to the mode.

Teachers at Sageton, as elsewhere, are deeply socialized into the ordinariness of whole-class teaching, with its reliance on common pacing, skills of listening, recording and responding to directed questions — the primacy of mastering the linear text in silent choral learning. They are *not* socialized into understanding the minutiae of what the mode presupposes, that is to say, what it takes to be in a position, as a pupil, to reveal competence as required by the recitation MOT or any sense of obligation to provide for lacks revealed. Indeed, only at the very front end of schooling — the nursery and early infant level — is teaching and learning truly conceptualized in terms of MOT and even there the 'naturalness' of pupil inability tends to win the effective battle for teacher beliefs against the apparent house ideology of child beneficence. Junior and secondary children are already judged in terms of capacity or irreperable lack, and indeed they are lacking in the face of MOT as poorly conceptualized and stereotypically performed as ours.

Let us labour the point quite explicitly. We are now rather good at developing curriculum content after two decades of funded public endeavour[22] (and the watchful eye of our ever aspiring Nelkons and Ridouts) and can run it across ages, stages and ability. We are freshly aware of the power of evaluation, with MSC pushing the rhetoric of 'skills' capable-of-measurement as all-we-need, graded tests talked about as sure-fire motivators and profiles as way of catching every achieved breath (long or short — as well as some suspiciously-ascribed ones too).[23] But they are, in a sense, major frames on either side of the ongoing classroom mystery about what it is that we do when we invite work from children in terms of specific classroom strategies. In Sageton, differing departments all worked under general pressure to assess fully: they adopted various curricular contents to provide the basis of mixed ability teaching (SMP work cards, a Nuffield-type science adapt, more home-grown humanities topic schema, a generally specified teacher-eclectic English syllabus that started to move in the direction of more individualized and individuated commercially and departmentally based materials). But although these contents frequently involved *forms* (MOT) quite different from recitation, this was a change little understood (that was not to say that the procedural *necessity* of moves to individualization for example, by the use of

worksheets was not recognized). It was consequently experienced as a
new sea of troubles to be resolved variously in terms of fuller
revelations of child capacity or through relatively technical aspects of
the materials (not always trivial, for example, the reading-age entailed),
or in terms of the way in which strategies enhanced or lessened
ubiquitous control problems. The undefeated end of conventional
wisdom defined best solutions in terms of a combination of 'variety'
and keeping them at it. Indeed, in the absence of being able to make
MOTs 'work', 'time on task' probably remains the only safe criterion
for those bent on attainment maximization. However, keeping noses to
the grindstone can only produce sour sharpness if the content is
inappropriately delivered.

> They don't teach you in the first place ... what's the point of
> teaching you if you don't know how to put it in a sentence ...
> that's dull. They ask you the question ... but they don't teach
> you the French ... (Pupil 10, Class 1P) (Evans, 1982, pp. 245)

Mixed Ability and Control

Our argument, then, is that mixed ability appeared as an organizational
form in our common schools for reasons which had rarely to do with
the provision of appropriate curriculum or pedagogy but everything to
do with system and control needs. It evoked pedagogical groupings for
suitable individualized media whose nature was no better understood
than the whole-class recitation mode which they replaced. They carry
new problems of unfamiliarity and lack of elaborated sub-strategies for
dealing with emerging problems and pathologies (as well as recognizing their 'success'!). Much of the reversion from mixed ability — and
there has certainly been an increase in the tendency to top-and-tail
where it is practised — represents an acceptance of pedagogical failure.
Where it has been persevered with, it has at best led to widening of
definitions of appropriate teaching strategies (ordinary worksheets as
staple diet lead to educational malnutrition as great as the whole-class
method alone), improved participation in subject opportunity structures and a clarified vision of the undue narrowness of existing
curricular forms and paces of life. These all presuppose widened
definitions of appropriate pupil ability and constitute, in the main,
progress by default. It was hardly in many original mixed ability
coping intentions to complicate ideas of pupil ability, but rather to
exploit old forms in new ways. Continuing pupil disaffection, more

intimately experienced by teachers, has sometimes forced the rise of more sophisticated insight into what pupils can do rather than simply perfecting correctionalist stances of yesteryear. It is these tendencies, to be viewed, as ever in our fascinatingly and maddening decentralized system, only in a few schools (Hail Coombe Martin, enter Stantonbury, next please...?) where perseverance and critique have held together to provide an inkling of the broadened participation, without mere relativization of content and achievement to the point of generational trickery, which is possible. But there is no real necessity why the common school must be made to work, in the traditional sense of providing ladders of opportunity into an effervescent and changing occupational pool. If work is dead for increasing numbers who cannot defend their patch (or drained shallow end!) then education will be increasingly pressured to serve as ultra-competitive site for its entry by those who still bathe daily. It will take an effort of political and class altruism and imagination of hitherto unknown proportions in education to alter direction. It augurs badly unless we can grasp that the present *disconnection* between school and work, for the majority of our children, provides the opportunity for radical moves away from early specialization and traditional mastery, high early achievement criteria which now ensure mass failure. But us without them won't go.

Notes

1 It is hardly ever realized, it seems to us, even in the specialized world of the history of education text, that we stand barely two generations from the mass elementary school, where only a minority went to secondaries — all selective, whether grammar, central or whatever — and where the dominant principle of grouping for teaching was not ability within age grades but attainment *transcending* age: you passed on from a standard when you had made the grade. Hadow's arguments in favour of streaming must be read in this context of tides or floods, within what we would now regard as the primary stage, bearing bright children on, relatively regardless of chronology toward the scholarship class. Only with the institutionalization of separate institutions for Spensian secondary school scholars was the Hadow recommendation of the Detroit triple-track system translated into the metaphor of three types of child to match what the 1943 White Paper saw as three types of school — the grammar, modern and technical. It was within these that the modern drama of streaming began. For plain accounts see Hyndman (1978) and Barton (1980).
2 See particularly the Introduction.
3 Data for 1974–5 based on the Greater London boroughs suggests that the total secondary leakage to all forms of out-county and private provision

can rise to over 30 per cent of the age cohort. We will expand this data as part of our final report to the SSRC in respect of *A Preliminary Study of Unstreaming in London Secondary Schools* and the sequel *Teacher Strategies and Pupil Identities in Mixed-Ability Curricula: a case study approach* HR4998/1, late in 1983. We gratefully acknowledge the support of the SSRC in respect of our capacity to write this article.

4 The 1980 Act with its strengthening of 'parental choice' and the introduction of special places are blatant cases of organized class-based reversion, which the failure to enforce reorganization on 'recalcitrant' LEAs like Bexley, Kingston and the rest, and the national fudge — below which any LEA might behave almost exactly as it wished over settling secondary intakes by fiat — stand as a more continuous lifeline back to 'freedom of choice' for the self-assigned educogenic minority. This minority can insist upon academic repeaters for their offspring, and is able to press wisely, and if necessary site nicely, to get it (see Ahier and Flude, 1983).

5 In our Greater London data we try, so far as is possible in the face of varying (or absent) 11+ ability measures, to evaluate school intakes on an ABC (30, 40, 30 per cent) distribution. There were schools in 1974–5 with, for example, as few as 5 per cent of their intake from the 'top' group and as many as 60 per cent from the bottom group.

6 For demonstration of this point, see Brandis and Young (1971).

7 Characteristically, the major institutional studies we originally had to make do with in England and Wales — Stevens (1960) on the grammar, and Taylor (1963) on the secondary modern — had very little to say on grouping, although Stevens (1970) does.

8 See, for example, Halsey and Gardner (1953) and onward.

9 For example Partridge (1965) for memoir; Pedley (1963) for advocacy shading into respectability, more properly attaching to the Daniels (1961), Douglas (1964) and Barker-Lunn (1970) surveys and the case-studies of Lacey (1970), Hargreaves (1967) and the most unfortunately underpublicized Lambart (1970).

10 The battle is continuously fuelled by within-left revisionist guilt. For the fairest but still remorse-tinged decent brief account see Rubenstein (1984). The extended literature on the rise of the comprehensive in administrative terms is now pretty extensive.

11 James (1968) is still *sans pareil* in this respect, in our view.

12 Cox's abound and not only continue to abuse academic manners with using established positions in other specialisms as the cloak for their tendentious and maximally media-oriented writings on the necessity of regression in education (see Marks, Cox and Pomian-Srzednicki, 1983, as the latest example), but we now see overt manifestations of their nearness to patronage in forms ranging from personal honours to the witting choice of official and licenced sounding agencies such as the Centre for Policy Studies.

13 For example, Wragg (1976), or Kelly (1978) where in the latter, albeit in the midst of eminently more sane statements, we are invited to accept the argument 'that the introduction of comprehensive education requires not only common schools but also common classes. For the principle of both is

that every pupil should be given access to education in the full sense of the word and offered as many educational advantages as he or she is capable of profiting from. The move to mixed ability classes then must be seen as a major contribution toward the move away from the stratification of knowledge with its resultant social divisions and towards a greater measure of equality of educational opportunity for all. This must be regarded, therefore, as another major first principle of teaching mixed-ability classes' (pp. 43–4).

14 An unusually clear headmagisterial expression of this, though he never brought it off in a full form during his office at Thomas Bennett, is to be found in Daunt (1976), where he argues that mixed ability grouping is a logical concomitant of the equal-value principle to which he is, and he would like to see all comprehensive educators, committed.

15 See Ball (1984) for his most recent discussion, but see also the guiding ideas in his Introduction to *Beachside* (1981).

16 No-one has yet made a decent fist of exploring the underlife of secondary school internal child-markets, not least in respect of options. If there are 'high' and 'low' status subjects then the departments which supply them no doubt get part of their standing from the way in which they effectively demand the high status, i.e. predominantly able pupil or not.

17 We have reflected upon our difficulties in this respect in Davies *et al* (1983).

18 We anticipate publishing the case study late in 1984. The following analysis is based upon Evans (1982a)

19 As Lumley (Hargreaves, 1967) was overwhelmingly, so Sageton was by now predominantly working class.

20 This generated widespread staff resentment. On the one hand they felt that they were being asked for very large amounts of involvement in planning and consultation, only now to be faced with the hidden hand made iron fist.

21 There is absolutely no doubt that when you scratch the secondary school teacher, looking for heart inscriptions as to what it is really about, the dominance of public exams looms so large as to blot out all other constraining rays. The alternative vision about 'how else?' is not as strongly distributed; fears about abandoning traditional assessment forms (for example for profiles) and ranges (particularly the meaning of including the 'least able') are pervasive. Moreover, the traditional depth of the feeling that most pupils are not 'worth' extended education is great although only the instantly seducible or those with their eyes on the resources to grab are detained for a moment by the unscrupulous *New Initiative* for Autumn 1983 and on.

22 This is now of course also misrecognized and spoiled-meat on the part of our present political masters who might have been expected to grasp that an organization like Schools Council was just beginning to get it right after an inevitable bad trip with RD and D models which keep commercial innovators happy but do not work when consent cannot be reduced to the calculus of the corporate piggy-bank.

23 See the bated scepticism of the NUT publications, for example, on these matters. Perhaps the one bit of unambiguously good news from the

Brian Davies and John Evans

assessment quarter is the way in which APU, conceived as a mixture of cock-up and control, has resisted urges merely to calibrate the castigation of the masses.

References

AHIER, J. and FLUDE, M. (Eds) (1983) *Contemporary Education Policy*, London, Croom Helm.

APPLE, M. (1982) *Education and Power,* London, Routledge and Kegan Paul.

BALL, S.J. (1981) *Beachside Comprehensive: A Case Study of Comprehensive Schooling*, Cambridge, Cambridge University Press.

BALL, S.J. (1984) *Inside the School: Internal Organization of Comprehensive Schools,* Unit 8/9, Block 2, 'Conflict and Change in Education', E205, Milton Keynes, Open University Press.

BARKER-LUNN, J.C. (1970) *Streaming in the Primary School*, Slough NFER.

BARTON, D.K. (1980) 'Mixed Ability Grouping — a consideration of the factors contributing to the move away from streaming and the emergence of mixed ability grouping', MEd (Science Education) dissertation, University of London, Chelsea College.

BRANDIS, W. and YOUNG, D. (1971) 'Two types of streaming and their probable application in comprehensive schools' in COSIN, B.R. *et al* (Eds) *School and Society: A Sociological Reader*, London, Routledge and Kegan Paul and Open University Press.

BENN, C. and SIMON, B. (1972) *Half Way There, Report on the British Comprehensive School Reform*, 2nd edition, Hardmondsworth, Penguin.

BILLETT, R.D. (1932) *The Administration and Supervision of Homogeneous Grouping*, Columbus, Ohio, State University Press.

CORBISHLEY, P. (1977) 'Research findings on teaching groups in secondary schools' in DAVIES B. and R.G. CAVE (Eds) (1977).

CORBISHLEY, P. and EVANS, J. (1980) 'Teachers and pastoral care: an empirical comment' in BEST, R. *et al* (Eds) (1980) *Perspectives on Pastoral Care*, London, Heinemann Educational Books.

CORBISHLEY, P., EVANS, J., KENRICK C. and DAVIES, B. (1981) 'Teacher strategies and pupil identities in mixed-ability curricula: a note on concepts and some examples from Maths' in BARTON, L. and S. WALKER, (Eds) (1981) *Schools, Teachers and Teaching*, Lewes, Falmer Press.

DAHLLHOF, U. (1971) *Ability Grouping, Content Validity and Curriculum Process*, New York, Teachers College Press.

DANIELS, J.C. (1961) 'The effects of streaming in primary school, II: a comparison of streamed and unstreamed schools' *British Journal of Educational Psychology*, 31, pp. 119–126.

DAUNT, P.E. (1975) *Comprehensive Values*, London, Heinemann Educational Books.

DAVIES, B. (1977) 'Meanings and motives in going mixed ability', in DAVIES, B. and R.G. CAVE, (Eds) (1977) *Mixed Ability Teaching in the Secondary School*, London, Word Lock.

DAVIES, B. (1976) 'Piggies in the middle — or "Who Sir? No, not me Sir" ' in

JONES-DAVIES. C. and R.G. CAVE, (Eds) (1976) *The Disruptive Pupil in the Secondary School*, London, Ward Lock.

DAVIES, B. and CAVE, R.G. (Eds) (1977) *Mixed Ability Teaching in the Secondary School*, London, Ward Lock.

DAVIES, B., CORBISHLEY, P., EVANS, J. and KENRICK, C. (1983) 'Integrating methodologies: if the intellectual relations don't get you, then the social will', paper presented to *Qualitative Methodology and the Study of Education, SSRC, Whitelands College Workshop, July*.

DAVIES, R.P. (1975) *Mixed Ability Grouping: possibilities and experiences in the secondary school*, London, Temple Smith.

DOUGLAS, J.W.B. (1964) *The Home and the School*, London, MacGibbon and Kee.

EVANS, J. (1982a) 'Teacher Strategies and Pupil Identities in Mixed Ability Curriculum: A case study', PhD Dissertation, University of London Chelsea College.

EVANS, J. (1982b) 'Teaching, control and pupil identity in mixed-ability curricula: a case study of science teaching', paper presented to *Ethnography and History*, St. Hilda's Conference.

HALSALL, E. (1973) *The Comprehensive School: Guidelines for the Reorganisation of Secondary Education*, Oxford, Pergamon.

HALSEY, A.H. and GARDNER, L. (1953) 'Selection for secondary education and achievement in four grammar schools', *British Journal of Sociology*, 4, pp. 60–75.

HARGREAVES, D.H. (1967) *Social Relations in a Secondary School*, London, Routledge and Kegan Paul.

HYNDMAN, M. (1978) *Schools and Schooling in England and Wales*, London, Harper and Row.

JAMES, C. (1968) *Young Lives at Stake*, London, Collins.

KELLY, V. (1978) *Mixed Ability Grouping: Theory and Practice*, London, Harper and Row.

LACEY, C. (1970) *Hightown Grammar*, Manchester, Manchester University Press.

LAMBART, A. (1970) 'The Sociology of an Unstreamed Urban Grammar School for Girls', PhD Dissertation, University of Manchester.

LAMBART, A. (1976) 'The Sisterhood' in HAMMERSLEY, M. and P. WOODS, (Eds) *The Process of Schooling: A Sociological Reader*, London, Routledge and Kegan Paul and Open University Press.

MARKS, J., COX, C., and POMIAN-SRZEDNICKI, M. (1983) *Standards in English Schools — an analysis of the examination results of secondary schools in England for 1981*, London, National Council for Educational Standards.

NUT (1983) *Pupils Profiles: a discussion document*, London, National Union of Teachers.

PARTRIDGE, J. (1965) *Life in a Secondary Modern School*, Harmondsworth, Penguin.

PEDLEY, R. (1963) *The Comprehensive School*, Harmondsworth, Penguin.

REID, M., CLUNIES-ROSS, L., GOACHER, B. and VILE, C. (1981) *Mixed Ability Teaching: Problems and Possibilities*, Windsor, NFER-Nelson.

RUBENSTEIN, D. (1984) 'Equal Educational Opportunity: the tripartite system and the comprehensive school 1944–64' Unit 6, Block 2, 'Conflict and Change in Education', E205, Milton Keynes, Open University Press.

STEVENS, F. (1960) *The Living Tradition*, London, Hutchinson.

STEVENS, F. (1970) *The New Inheritors*, London, Hutchinson.

TAYLOR, W. (1963) *The Secondary Modern School*, London, Faber.

WESTBURY, I. (1973) 'Conventional classrooms, "open" classrooms and the technology of teaching', *Journal of Curriculum Studies*, 5, 2, pp. 99–12.

WRAGG, E.C. (Ed) (1976) *Teaching Mixed Ability Groups*, Newton Abbot, David and Charles.

Defining a Subject for the Comprehensive School: a Case Study

Ivor Goodson

'The Elimination of Separatism'

One of the questions in the emergence of comprehensive schooling that has been relatively neglected is how school subjects weathered the transition from the tripartite to the comprehensive system. The subjects taught in the grammar schools were normally distinctively different in content and pedagogic orientation from those taught in the secondary moderns. Hence, for the comprehensive ideal to be implemented, substantial curriculum renegotiation might have been envisaged and attempts made to initiate major curriculum reforms. The belief that broad-based curriculum reform, with a range of associated political and pedagogical implications, was indeed underway was commonly held in the early era of comprehensivization following the 1965 circular. Professor Kerr asserted in 1968 that 'at the practical and organizational levels, the new curricula promise to revolutionize English education' (Kerr, 1971, p. 180). Likewise in 1973, following ROSLA (Raising of the School Leaving Age), Rubinstein and Simon envisaged a range of curriculum reforms which effectively married the characteristics of the best secondary modern and grammar school curricula to provide a new synthesis suitable for the comprehensive school.

> The tendency is towards the development of interdisciplinary curricula, together with the use of the resources approach to learning, involving the substitution of much group and individual work for the more traditional forms of class teaching. For these new forms of organizing and stimulating learning mixed ability grouping often provides the most appropriate methods; and partly for this reason the tendency is towards the

reduction of streaming and class teaching. (Rubinstein and Simon, 1973, p. 123)

The 1965 circular had sought to 'eliminate separatism in secondary education' (DES, 1965, p. 1). But a close reading of the circular implies that the prime concern, perhaps understandably at the time, was with eliminating the separatism of different school types and buildings. What was unclear and unspoken was whether the logic of providing a comprehensive education for all in the common school would be pursued into also providing a common curriculum. The grammar schools and secondary modern sectors distinguished 'two nations' of school children and this was to be eliminated, since separatism — at least separatism of buildings — was thought unfair. But the differentiation into 'two nations' took place both by the designation of separate schools *and* by the designation of separate curricula. On the elimination of separate curricula the 1965 circular was silent.

Indeed there were clear indications that far from expecting a new synthesis of curricula along the lines defined by Rubinstein and Simon, the main concern in 1965 was to defend and extend grammar school education. The House of Commons motion which led to circular 10/65 was fairly specific:

> This house, conscious of the need to raise educational standards at all levels, and regretting that the realization of this objective is impeded by the separation of children into different types of secondary schools, notes with approval the efforts of local authorities to reorganize secondary education on comprehensive lines which will preserve all that is valuable in grammar school education for those children who now receive it and make it available to more children'. (DES, 1965, p. 1)

This hardly hints at a new synthesis of common and comprehensive curricula — was there nothing valuable in secondary modern education to be preserved and merged? 'Grammar school education for *more* children', but not *all* children; what about the children still left outside? The concern it seemed was rather with spreading grammar school education a little more widely.

Even at the time some commentators were warning that the curriculum patterns emerging in the new comprehensive schools might merely facilitate a new curriculum for inequality. The preservation of grammar school education for some (although 'more') pupils implied that the new curricula would be essentially aimed at the 'other' pupils.

This interpretation was fostered by the close association of many of the curriculum reforms with the new pupil clienteles arising from ROSLA and with the 'new sixth form' groups unsuited to the traditional courses.

Marten Shipman argued that the curriculum reforms were in danger of perpetuating the two nations approach inside the educational system, what he called a 'curriculum for inequality'. He spoke of the 'unintended consequences of curriculum development':

> Coming less from actual content than from the introduction of new courses into a school system that is still clearly divided into two sections, one geared to a system of external examinations, the other less constrained. The former is closely tied to the universities and is within established academic traditions. The latter has a short history and is still in its formative stages. It is the consequences of innovation into these two separate sections rather than the curricula themselves which may be producing a new means of sustaining old divisions. (Shipman, 1971, pp. 101–2).

He summarized the distinction into two nations of curricula in that 'one emphasizes a schooling within a framework of external examinations, the other attempts to align school work to the environment of the children' (p. 104).

The long legacy of a dual curriculum stretched back to the origins of the state system in the nineteenth century. There had always been not only separate schools but separate curricula. Eliminating separate schools would not then of itself eliminate separate curricula. Indeed the Norwood Report which inaugurated the tripartite system had been quite clear on the link between separate school types and separate curricula. It had argued that throughout Europe, 'the evolution of education' had, 'thrown up certain groups, each of which can and must be treated in a way appropriate to itself'. In England three clear groups could be discerned. First, 'the pupil who is interested in learning for its own sake ... he is interested in the relatedness of related things, in development, in structure, in a coherent body of knowledge'. These pupils form the continuing clientele of the traditional subject-based curriculum, for, as Norwood states, 'such pupils, educated by the curriculum commonly associated with the grammar school, have entered the learned professions or have taken up higher administrative or business posts' (Norwood Report, 1943, p. 2). The needs of the intermediate category — 'the pupil whose interests and abilities lie markedly in the field of applied science or applied art' were to be fulfilled by the technical school. Finally, Norwood states with a very partial view of educational history, 'There has of late years been recognition, expressed in the framing of curricula and otherwise, of still another grouping of occupations'. This third group was to provide the clientele for the new secondary modern schools:

> The pupil in this group deals more easily with concrete things than with ideas. He may have much ability, but it will be in the realm of facts. He is interested in things as they are; he finds little attraction in the past or in the slow disentanglement of causes or movements. His mind must turn its knowledge or its curiosity to immediate test; and his test is essentially practical. (p. 3)

This curriculum 'would not be to prepare for a particular job or profession and its treatment would make a direct appeal to interests, which it would awaken by practical touch with affairs' (p. 6).

If a government report had so recently identified different curricula for different pupil types, such pervasive features could hardly be wished away by gathering all the categories under one roof through comprehensive reorganization. Clearly then the question remained as to how the different curricula and associated pupil clienteles would be merged or prioritized in the comprehensive school. On Norwood's analysis, academic O and A level subjects were best suited only to the minority entering elite positions. Following Shipman, Marsden (1971) had warned what would happen if the 'academic category' were given priority:

> If we give the new comprehensive the task of competing with selective schools for academic qualifications, the result will be remarkably little change in the selective nature of education. Selection will take place within the school and the working class child's education will suffer. (p. 26)

To understand how the curriculum was negotiated and devised for comprehensive schools after 1965 the following case study looks at one curriculum area, rural studies. Teachers of rural studies were closely allied to 'attempts to align school work to the environment of the children' and in 1965 were beginning to face the challenge of the new comprehensive schools. A case study should provide valuable insights into the process whereby the categories of curricula and pupil clientele identified by Norwood were merged or prioritized in the comprehensive system. Rural studies had a long history of involvement in Norwood's category three, and were primarily found in secondary modern schools. The whole history of the subject had proceeded through 'a direct appeal to interests, which it would awaken by practical touch with affairs'. Rural studies then hardly seemed fertile ground on which to sow the fears expressed by Marsden about a take-over by 'academic qualifications'. A curriculum case study in this area should provide evidence of how one subject was 'translated' from one sector of the tripartite system to the comprehensive. By viewing this process of translation in evolutionary profile we can assess the curriculum values and pupil categories which were to achieve primacy in the comprehensive system.

Rural Studies: A Case Study

The origins of rural studies

Although the early origins of rural studies are both conceptually and chronologically widely spread it is possible to distinguish two paramount themes. Firstly there were those advocates who stressed the *utilitarian* aspects of education allied to husbandry and agriculture. For instance, in 1951 Samuel Hartlib proposed in his 'Essay for Advancement of Husbandry Learning' that the Science of Husbandry should be taught to apprentices (Adamson, 1951, pp. 130–31). Later, alongside Britain's 'agricultural revolution' in the eighteenth and early nineteenth centuries, a number of private schools began to teach agriculture.

The second group advocated the use of the rural environment as part of an educational method: they were concerned with the *pedagogic* potential of such work. Rousseau summarized the arguments in his book *Emile*, written in 1767. He believed that nature should teach the child, rather than the classroom teacher with his formal methods.

In England ideas about rural education had their main influence in the elementary schools and in their curricula; the utilitarian rather than pedagogic tradition was followed. The tradition emerged in the schools of industry set up in the last decade of the eighteenth century and related to the Poor Law Act passed in 1834. The curriculum of these schools included gardening and simple agricultural operations, amongst other activities, such as tailoring and cobbling for the boys, and lace-making for the girls. They were seen as vocational schools for the poorer classes (Carson, 1967, p. 4).

The Board of Education did later show some interest in rural studies but in 1904, when the secondary school curriculum 'Regulations' were issued, rural studies was omitted. Rural education was still taken seriously within the elementary sector with emphasis on those pupils not expected to proceed to secondary education. In keeping with this view secondary examinations (from 1917 known as 'School Certificates') did not include rural studies.

The publication of a memorandum on 'The Principles and Methods of Rural Education' by the Board of Education in 1911 stressed that the movement to implement rural education was designed to make teaching in elementary rural schools:

> ... more practical, and to give it a more distinctly rural bias; to
> base it upon what is familiar to country children, and to direct it
> so that they may become handy and observant in their country
> surroundings. (Board of Education, 1911, p. 7)

The Board of Education's statistics evidence a substantial growth in school gardens:

1904–5	551 schools
1907–8	1171 schools
1911–12	2458 schools

In the last year, twenty 'departments' of gardening or rural education are recorded (Board of Education 1939).

The pre-war growth of rural studies in school was summarized as 'an attempt to use education to further the interests of rural industry in ways similar to those in which it was being used in the city' (Selleck, 1968, p. 150). The most obvious methods of supporting rural industry was to retain the labour force that emerged at the age of 13 from the elementary schools. Many of these children joined the 'drift from the land' which seriously threatened the viability of the rural economy. Fabian Ware argued that developing an interest in his natural environment through education 'would not only make a better worker of the agriculturalist, but would strengthen him morally against, at any rate, the lower attractions of town life' (Ware, 1900, p. 62).

This theme was reiterated in the inter-war years. In the influential circular on 'Rural Education' of May 1925, which inaugurated a new series of national and local circulars on the subject, the Board of Education stressed that 'liking and aptitude for practical rural work are dependent on early experience, and an education which tends to debar children from gaining such experience has a definitely anti-rural bias and is liable to divert them from rural occupations' (Board of Education, 1925).

Rural studies in the tripartite system

At first the changes in the educational system following the 1944 Act did not lead to any great changes in rural studies teaching. There were, however, some innovations and attempts to organize the whole curriculum around investigations of the environment. In 1950, A.B. Allen saw rural studies at the centre of the curriculum in country schools:

> Taking agriculture and horticulture as our foundation subjects, we see the interrelationship within the curriculum. Agriculture leads into elementary science, general biology, nature study, world history and world geography. It also leads into mathematics with its costing problems, mensuration and balance sheets. Horticulture leads into elementary science (and so is linked with agriculture), and local history. (Allen, 1950, p. 16)

In some of the early secondary modern schools this vision of rural studies as the 'curriculum hub' connecting school to environment and life had a marked influence.

An example of such a school was Wrotham Secondary School in Kent. In 1949, A.J. Fuller, a keen gardener, was given the headship. He appointed Ronald Colton to teach sciences, and Sean Carson to teach rural science. The new school consisted of three huts in a field. Carson taught 4F — ie 4th year farming. There were also 4P (practical) and 4A (academic). However, since there were no examinations the farming class often attracted some of the brightest pupils. The agricultural apprenticeship scheme had just started: 'The best boys, the most able, who today would be in the sixth form, went into farming gladly. Good farms, good employers!' Carson built the activities of the class around the rural environment. 'I think the inspiration probably came from Fuller' . . .

> Also I can remember I did a lot of walking about the orchards in Kent and talking to farm workers and I can remember lots of occasions when the attitude of these people struck me very much. I had a strong feeling that education wasn't just book learning . . . it involved commonsense applied to a problem — I talked to many farmers there . . . I still correspond to one now,

who would talk about the kind of intelligence a farm worker would need to apply to his job.

Carson had 4F for all subjects except science, which Colton taught, and woodwork:

> I taught them maths, English, history, etc. All tied in completely with the rural environment ... for example maths I based as much as possible on the farm activities. In fact I used a series of books which were popular then called *Rural Arithmetic*. (Sean Carson, interviews)

As the tripartite system of education gradually emerged in the form of new school buildings and modified curricula, it became clear that rural studies and gardening were developing solely in the secondary modern schools. In 1952 a questionnaire survey of gardening and rural studies teachers in Kent produced, with three exceptions, the response from grammar and technical schools of 'subjects not taught', whilst in 63 of the 65 secondary modern schools the subject was given an important position in the curriculum (*Kent Journal*, April, 1953, pp. 4–6).

In 1957 the Hertfordshire Association of Teachers of Gardening and Rural Subjects, worried by the loss of status and influence of the subject, carried out a similar survey to the Kent one. This time, significantly, questionnaires were sent only to secondary modern schools. The financial treatment of rural studies showed clearly that by this time the priorities of secondary modern headmasters had moved away from rural studies towards other subjects. 'It is surprising to learn ... that some schools allow the rural science department no money at all while others are so small that the financial pinch entails great worry to the teacher.' Of the 39 schools that returned questionnaires, 15 had no classroom allotted for rural studies. 'Generally the standard of provision for rural subjects appears to be below that of other practical subjects. Few schools are equipped satisfactorily with the items required for a good horticultural or agricultural course at secondary school level.' Of the 53 teachers involved, 26 were unqualified in gardening or rural studies (Hertfordshire Association, 1957, *mimeo*).

Promoting the subject: early initiatives

The 1957 survey illustrates the general point that from the late 1950s onwards the position of rural studies in the secondary moderns rapidly deteriorated. Primarily this was because of the take-up of specialist examinations within secondary moderns. More parents began to realize that certification led to better jobs, teachers found examinations a useful source of motivation and heads began to use examinations as a means of raising their schools' reputation and status. For some heads, support for GCE may have stemmed from an initial rebellious non-acceptance of the whole tripartite philosophy. But soon 'success in this examination started a national avalanche' (Gibberd, 1962, p. 103). In 1961–63 when Partridge studied a secondary modern school, the competitive nature of the 'examination race' was clearly apparent: 'With the public demand for academic attainments, reflecting the fact that education has become the main avenue of social mobility in our society, GCE successes would immeasurably enhance the repute of the such a school, and hence the standing and status of the headmaster' (Partridge, 1968, p. 68).

The take-up of GCE and a wide range of other examinations in secondary moderns led to an exhaustive inquiry by the Ministry of Education which culminated in the Beloe Report. As a result of the Report's recommendations in 1965 the CSE was inaugurated. The growing emphasis of specialist subject examinations and their effects on rural studies in the secondary modern are a harbinger of the patterns which emerged later in the comprehensive schools. But the debates which finally pushed the subject towards specialist examination took place in the mid-sixties when the comprehensive system was being rapidly developed.

By this time rural studies teachers were beginning to respond to the dual challenges posed by the spread of specialist examinations and the prospects of comprehensivization. The first response was the formation of a National Rural Studies Association to promote rural studies as a specialist subject worth of 'parity of esteem'. The inaugural meeting was in 1960 when six County Associations that had been formed previously met together to form the Association. By 1961 eleven new County Rural Studies Associations had been formed and affiliated.

The second response was to scrutinize the whole question of examinations, particularly the new CSE. By 1962 leaders within the subject had begun to realize that the National Association would never get 'parity of esteem' for the subject without accepting external examinations and thereby transforming the very basis of the subject. The spread of the CSE drew attention to the dilemma that faced advocates of rural studies. A good deal of the energies of the Association centred on gaining more facilities, time and better qualified staff

Ivor Goodson

for the subject. But in the increasingly exam-conscious secondary
moderns little success could be hoped for in a non-examinable subject.
To break out of the cycle of deprivation faced by the subject the only
way forward seemed to be in defining an examinable area. By 1962
Carson had realized the cul-de-sac which the National Association's
efforts had entered:

> We never forgot our aims were to see this subject get taught to
> *all* children ... that facilities should be better, etc. Then it
> became increasingly obvious to me and one or two others, that
> it wasn't going to get anywhere! That however many good
> ideals we might have, in fact it was not going to be realized.
> (Carson, interview)

As a result the Association initiated a major experiment by which to
test a new rural studies exam. The experiment was reported in the
Hertfordshire Journal:

> Following a meeting of representatives of Rural Study Associa-
> tions, the panel of HM Inspectors for rural studies and Dr.
> Wrigley of the Curriculum Study Group of the Ministry of
> Education, a joint experiment has been held in schools in North
> Hertfordshire, Nottinghamshire, Staffordshire, Lincolnshire
> and East Sussex to test the validity of sections of our examina-
> tion scheme. This is being evaluated by the Ministry of
> Education's Study Group. (*Hertfordshire Journal*, October, 1963)

Sean Carson was involved in the experiment: 'It was an attempt to find
out whether exams were a good thing. We were trying to find out
whether we should remain outside or whether we should have anything to do with them' (Carson interview). The moves to devise an
examination in the subject posed a number of problems for rural
studies. For behind the rhetoric of the advocates and subject associations, alongside the significant but exceptional innovatory schools and
teachers, most rural studies teachers continued to base their work on
gardening. The subject's essentially practical assignments were not
easily evaluated by written examinations.

Preparing for the comprehensive school

The formation of a national association for the specialist subject of rural
studies and the scrutiny of external examinations was to be the

186

watershed in the development of rural studies. Sean Carson, who had set up the meeting which founded the National Association, had now emerged as a leading spokesman for the subject and also had become an adviser for rural education in Hertfordshire. He was aware that 'rural education' as an integrating focus for the whole education of secondary modern pupils was about to be abandoned: 'By this time I'd really given up hope of getting rural studies seen in the way I'd taught it in Kent. Then I saw it as a specialist subject which had weak links':

> My alternative vision ... was that a lot of kids don't learn through paper and pencil and that we do far too much of this. A lot of kids could achieve success and use all the mental skills that we talk about in the classroom such as analyzing and comparing through physical activities.... With the farm it was a completely renewing set of problems and the fact that it was a farm was incidental. You were thinking in educational terms of process with these kids. (Sean Carson, interview)

In embracing the specialist subject, the National Association played a symbolic role:

> The object of that (forming the association) was really to raise the status of rural studies and get the facilities for the subject which other subjects got. For example, we used to constantly compare what was given to cookery, metalwork and woodwork, and we had got practically nothing whereas they had properly equipped classrooms.... This is what we set out to do and we achieved it to a certain extent, but the situation was never there to achieve any more than that it was specialism in a school and should be adequately supported. (Sean Carson, interview)

Carson's final sentence here summarizes the situation which rural studies had come to occupy by 1957. As the *Kent Journal* noted, 'with the building of large secondary schools within the last few years, full-time specialists are needed'. (*Kent Journal*, September, 1958, p. 1). Rural studies was just one of a range of specialisms in the secondary modern schools. Moreover it was of low status and historically poorly organized.

But if the fact of becoming a specialist subject was now inevitable the kind of subject was still a matter of urgent debate among rural studies teachers, advisers and the Inspectorate. In this debate we see the potential utilitarian and practical (and to some extent the optimistically pedagogic 'rural education') traditions within the subject facing the implication of joining in the process of academic certification. The whole genesis, evolution, intentions and practice of rural studies made the subject uniquely ill-suited to playing this academic role whether in the secondary moderns or in the comprehensive school.

The early reports were outspokenly frank about this. The first report on the possibility of a CSE in rural studies stated that: 'rural studies teachers are by nature opposed to the competitive and restrictive aspects of examinations in school.' But more specifically a practical subject like rural studies was utterly unsuited to a mode of written examination borrowed from academic grammar school subjects. To set examinations of this sort amounted to a renunciation of the intentions of most of the teachers of the subject and of the pupil clientele for whom it had historically catered. The reports drawn up by rural studies teachers put the problem of the renunciation of subject tradition as diplomatically as possible: 'Few examinations included much practical work and rarely was there any assessment of the candidate's practical ability and achievement over a period of time'. These examinations produced 'unfavourable backwash effects in the teaching of rural studies': 'In order to produce candidates who would be successful in the written examination teachers felt that they had to concentrate on written work to the neglect of practical activities which are the essential features of Rural Studies' (Rural Studies Draft Report, 1966).

Following the 1965 circular the pace of comprehensive reorganization began to quicken. With respect to examinations the debate was speedily transformed from an uncertain response to the suitability of written examinations at CSE level to a realization that in fact only an even more basic reorientation to O and even A level would ensure survival.

Confined within the secondary modern school sector rural studies was especially vulnerable to comprehensive reorganization. In 1966 the NRSA Journal carried its first report on the 'The place of rural studies in the comprehensive system', produced by a working party set up at the Spring, 1966 Conference of Wiltshire Teachers of Rural Studies. Within the report there is some evidence that the Wiltshire teachers were extremely concerned about the fate of their subject in the comprehensive school. The change to comprehensives was taking place against a background of decline in the subject which had begun in some areas in the late 1950s. By the early 1960s Sean Carson saw the decline setting in in Hertfordshire: 'it was already happening inside some schools. Where a teacher was leaving, they didn't fill the place, because they gave it to someone in the examination set-up' (Carson, interview). In 1966 the Wiltshire teachers were advising:

> The urgent necessity is for us to persuade teachers and education authorities that the omission of the facilities for teaching Rural Studies in new schools and in buildings which are being adapted to a comprehensive form of education would be a mistake. (*NRSA Journal* 1966, p. 4)

The problem was partly explained by the fact that:

> 'as many of the new heads of comprehensive schools were being appointed from grammar school backgrounds these heads had little or no experience of the value of rural studies in the education of the secondary child. Because of this lack of knowledge, rural studies as an examination subject was being equated with rural biology, agricultural science or even pure biology. In addition there was little demand for rural studies as a post O level subject'. (NRSA Policy Committee Report to Council.

The teachers themselves saw clear evidence of broadbased decline and by November 1967 one was writing of a 'general air of defeatism among rural studies teachers'. (George Wing to Sean Carson, 12 November, 1967). A Hertfordshire teacher recalled this period:

> A few years back, rural studies was being phased out . . . it was getting itself a poor name . . . it was . . . you know, losing face . . . it was being regarded as not the subject we want in this up-and-going day and age. And we had awful difficulty in getting examining boards and universities to accept it at O level and A level . . . mainly because of its content . . . I could see that I was going to have to phase out rural studies because the demand for it in the school was going down . . . it was being squeezed out in the timetable and the demand for it at options level in the fourth year was going down. (Gordon Battey, interview)

Not only was rural studies less in demand but those areas of the curriculum where the subject may have expanded were being taken over by other subject specialists. In the comprehensives rural studies was often not included or was being confined to the 'less able'. In a position of rapidly falling demand and closing options, rural studies was faced with extinction, certainly in those counties where comprehensive education was rapidly pursued. Carson in Hertfordshire was convinced that rural studies was 'a dead duck' ... 'it would rapidly have disappeared', and Topham, who was later to devise an A level, thought that at this time rural studies 'was finished'.

Whither rural studies: practical subject or academic discipline?

The inauguration of CSEs and the rapid changeover to comprehensive schooling meant that rural studies was engulfed by a rapidly changing situation which threatened the very survival of the subject. On one point those seeking subject promotion now began to agree: what was needed was not just a new 'emphasis' or even a specialist subject, but a 'discipline'. The rhetorical requirement of a discipline symbolized the dual purpose of redefinition — a new synthesis of knowledge but also one which afforded higher status and could be offered to a new clientele covering a higher ability spectrum than the previous clientele for whom CSE was the highest aspiration.

Sean Carson, whose research had begun for an MEd at Manchester, initially concerned with the CSE, began, in the autumn of 1966, to perceive the need for 'a discipline' of rural studies for the following reasons:

> The lack of a clear definition of an area of study as a discipline has often been a difficulty for local authorities in deciding what facilities to provide and more recently in having rural studies courses at colleges of education accepted for the degree of B.Ed. by some universities. It has been one of the reasons for the fact that no A level course in rural studies exists at present.

Further, in commenting on the Report the Study Group on Education and Field Biology he noted: 'because rural studies was not recognized as a discipline at any academic level, even at O level, the Group were prevented from giving it serious consideration' (Carson, 1967, p. 135).

Carson's judgments were passed on to the Schools Council Working Party on Rural Studies set up in 1965 who reiterated them in the report to the Council of June, 1968. The working party perceived 'the need for a scholarly discipline'. The discipline would spread 'across the present system of specialization' and might 'take the form of an integrated course of study based upon environmental experience in which rural studies has a part to play'. (Schools Council 1968, p. 19).

This recommendation hinted at a change of title from rural studies to environmental studies which was to emerge later.

The most common pattern for defining new 'disciplines' of knowledge in the essentially hierarchical education system in England has been through the work of university scholars. Unfortunately at this time there was very little academic activity in this field for the rural studies advocates to build upon. Since a new disciplinary definition of rural or environmental studies was not forthcoming from scholars in the higher education sector, the process of definition had to be undertaken at the secondary level as an A level subject. One of the pioneers of the A level syllabus later claimed that the process of curriculum development undertaken 'is schools-based and is the result of initiatives taken together by practising teachers with the support of their local authority. Such self-generated work offers a viable way of developing an area of the curriculum' (Carson, 1971, pp. 7–8). Thus in the schools-based model the academic discipline is developed because classroom teachers perceive the need for a new area of knowledge and then set about involving academics in its construction.

The growing perception of such a need among rural studies teachers can be discerned from the beginning of 1967. In February, 1967, Mervyn Pritchard as Secretary of the Research and Development Sub-Committee of the National Rural Studies Association reported that: 'We wanted to discover how rural studies experience can help students with gaining entry to Colleges of Education, and what value post O level qualifications in rural studies would have for this purpose'. In the discussion which followed this report John Pullen, HMI, said 'Several questions required answering', among them:

— Do we consider an A level course should be included in rural studies?
— What do we do about the reaction, 'We do not want people with A level in rural studies?'
— What parts of rural studies should be treated as aspects of other disciplines?

At the same meeting the Policy Committee reported that a sub-committee had been formed 'to find existing curricula for able children leading to at least O level in the rural studies field' and 'to produce evidence that there is a need for rural studies up to O level, i.e. to show that the subject is of benefit to able pupils' (NRSA Files, Meeting on 11 February, 1967).

In March a 'statement of evidence' was presented by the National

Association to the Schools Council Working Party on rural studies. The definition of rural studies advocated was almost identical to that established in Carson's Manchester research:

> The study of the landscape, its topography, geology and pedology, the ecological relationship of the plants and animals naturally present, together with the study of man's control of this natural environment through agriculture, horticulture and forestry. (Carson, 1967, p. 369)

In advocating this definition of rural studies and adding as an objective 'The development of an awareness and appreciation of the natural surroundings', the National Association contended: 'There is a growing demand for examinations at 'O' and 'A' level based upon the Studies described ... we are certain that if such examinations are introduced they will be used increasingly'. Finally they asserted that the content which they had defined 'provides a unified and clear area of study and a valuable academic discipline' (*NRSA Journal*, 1968, p. 38).

At this time a small group of HM Inspectors interested in rural studies, among them John Pullen, also saw a need for a discipline of rural studies in schools. They argued in an article published in the house journal, *Trends:*

> Work now being attempted at many schools could justifiably claim to reach this level. It is true that some schools with strongly developed rural studies courses find, as one might expect, that older pupils turn very naturally and successfully to A level courses in chemistry, biology and geography and often gain university entrance on the standards they have achieved. Nevertheless the time appears to be ripe for the introduction of 'A' level courses in agriculture, agricultural science, and in the wider field of rural studies. (DES, 1967, pp. 30–31)

The changeover to comprehensives encouraged a number of teachers, who had previously worked with CSE, to define rural studies at O and A level. The 1968 *NRSA Journal* noted that schools in Yorkshire, Nottinghamshire and Hertfordshire were campaigning for such exams (*NRSA Journal*, 1968, p. 44). Reporting on 'Rural Studies in the Comprehensive School', Topham argued that 'rural studies should be so organized within the comprehensive school that no child, boy or girl, of whatever ability, is denied the opportunity to participate' (p. 45). The rural studies teachers in a comprehensive school should aim to offer:

i   a course leading to an O level GCE
ii a course leading to CSE
iii an integral course
iv to participate in a general studies course
v   a course leading to the A level GCE and, when established, to a certificate of further secondary education.

Consequently, 'in a large comprehensive school one can envisage generous allocation of staff to the department' (p. 46).

The Schools Council Working Party on Rural Studies had reported that one of the paramount problems facing teachers of the subject was dealt with in the section on 'status': 'there is no doubt that a substantial proportion of rural studies teachers do find themselves in a difficult position because of the demanding nature of the task, the lack of ancillary help, and the attitude which regards the subject as a sublimating exercise for the less able' (Schools Council, 1969, p. 15). Elsewhere the report noted: 'The old concept of the subject predominantly as gardening, often gardening for the backward boys only, did not die easily' (p. 5). The remedy for this situation was clearly perceived: 'Examinations in rural studies have helped to improve the image of the subject and to give it a certain status in the eyes of the pupils and their parents. Acceptable A levels could raise the status still further (p. 12).

By the late 1960s rural studies faced a dilemma: the choice was clear but bitter in its implications. Within the comprehensive schools the subject was in sharp decline, its very survival turning on whether it could be presented and accepted as a valid academic qualification. But its practitioners were in large majority trained and aligned to a concept of rural education which was above all practical in orientation. To embrace academic examinations meant a stark renunciation of the history of the subject and the main intentions of the teachers, a renunciation of its traditional pupil clientele. In effect its teachers were being asked to renounce their priority commitment to this style of learning and this group, Norwoods category 3, in favour of a style of examination suited to a different mode of learning and pupil clientele, Norwoods stage 1. To not so renunciate would be to face extinction.

The period is fascinating because of the wealth of evidence that at the time many of the teachers knew precisely what was at stake: they knew the renunciation that was being demanded. The following short extract written in 1967 for the Hertfordshire Rural Studies Journal by Mr. P.L. Quant of Baas Hill Secondary Modern School summarizes the stark reality of the choice and speaks for significant sections of rural studies teachers who saw the implications of the suggested changes:

> I do not think my fears are entirely groundless. The state needs to tap the resources of schools with increasing urgency, and consequently the new schools will be expected to fill their halls at speech day with the successes they have turned out. But what praise for the unintelligent now? Are we to make a mockery of our mode three liberty in order to gloss over the realities of this urgent problem?

> True education is not for every man the scrap of paper he leaves school with. Dare we as teachers admit this? Dare we risk our existence by forcibly expressing our views on this? While we pause after the first phase of our acceptance, are we to rely on exams for all, to prove ourselves worthy of the kindly eye of the state? Dare we allow to leave some of our charges who have been once more neglected and once more squeezed into a forgotten heap of frustrating unimportance?

> My knowledge of rural studies teachers leads me to say how lively and stimulating they are in their enthusiasm for the subject. Then let us not shirk from the sum total of our responsibility towards *all* our children. (P.L. Quant, 1967, pp. 11–13).

In fact the points made by Quant were privately conceded by the main advocates of academic examinations who were so influential in causing the National Rural Studies Association to move rapidly to embrace the academic discipline route to better resources and status. Topham, whose course became the model for the A level in environmental studies, said at the time 'I firmly believe that success in examinations is not really indicative of the value of any subject and this is especially true of rural studies' (Topham, interview). Likewise Carson felt 'by embracing academic examinations we forever abandoned the aim of education for *all*' (Carson, interview).

Embracing the academic examinations: the price of comprehensivization

From the acknowledgement among rural studies advocates, advisers, the Inspectorate and Schools Council that a 'scholarly discipline' was needed, events moved rapidly. A range of O levels in rural and environmental studies was devised and accepted by a number of examination boards. Other initiatives aimed to develop A levels in Rural Studies, most notably in Hertfordshire and Wiltshire. The history of the promotion of the Hertfordshire A level has been told in detail in *School Subjects and Curriculum Change* (Goodson, 1983). It began in Shepalbury School in Hertfordshire in 1967 where the rural studies teacher, Paul Topham, with the strong support of the head, Dr. Jack Kitching, set about devising an A level. Both felt rural studies had outlived its usefulness. The headmaster had not previously encountered the subject and saw little use for such a practical subject aimed only at the less able. By now in this new comprehensive, 'everyone was very much concerned with achievement and what bit of paper was going to unlock the golden gate to college, university and employment' (Topham, interview). Topham devised a prospective A level course which was circulated in February 1967 to universities, colleges and professional bodies. Initially the response was rather unfavourable but the proposal gained new momentum when Paul Topham became an advisory teacher under Sean Carson. By this time Carson was convinced that rural studies could achieve new status by aligning itself with the new 'environmental lobby'. The National Rural Studies Association had that year, very much at Carson's initiative, embraced the new title environmental studies (in 1971 it became the National Association of Environmental Education). The new title, like the aspiration to become a scholarly discipline, summarized the desire to leave for ever the low status enclave of traditional rural studies in favour of a new well-financed niche as an A level subject.

Topham and Carson developed a strategy for an environmental studies A level using Topham's original rural studies A level proposal. Topham was clear on the rationale for this:

> I think that we had got to prove that environmental studies was something that the most able of students could achieve and to do something with it ... if you started off there all the expertise and finance that you put into it will benefit the rest — your teaching ratio goes up, etc, and everyone else benefits — the side effects that people don't mention sometimes.

To establish environmental studies in this way a new strategy was evolved:

> So we decided we should be A level ... that we should think up the right syllabus and then that we should bring together the teachers of Hertfordshire, critically examine it, develop it ...

> take advice from people, ... so we did this, there was the first
> meeting of the Working Party. (Topham, interview)

Sean Carson adds a number of reasons for the founding of the Working
Party of Hertfordshire teachers:

> In talking to Paul, we decided that the only way to make
> progress was to get in on the examination racket ... we must
> draw up an examination.... We decided that the exam was
> essential because otherwise you couldn't be equal with any
> other subject. Another thing was that comprehensive education
> was coming in. Once that came in, no teacher who didn't teach
> in the fifth or sixth form was going to count for twopence. So
> you had to have an A level for teachers to aim at. (Carson,
> interview)

The Hertfordshire Working Party duly completed the construction
of an A level syllabus after detailed consultation with a range of
academics, advisers, inspectors and examination board officials. The
proposed A level now encountered 'fierce opposition from the geo-
graphers in particular. Their opposition was mounted both within the
examination boards to whom the A level was submitted and then in
Schools Council subject sub-committees. Above all, the opposition
turned on whether environmental studies was really a 'discipline',
especially as it did not have subject scholars based in universities: with
no prospects of a scholarly discipline of environmental studies coming
from the universities, the Hertfordshire advocates had been forced into
attempting to define 'a discipline' from school level. This allowed
opponents of the new subject, whilst broadly conceding its value to the
young and less able, consistently to deny that it could be viewed as in
any sense a 'scholarly discipline'.

The result of the subject opposition was to deny the environmental
studies A level any chance of broad-based take-up. In the event two
'experimental' A levels were agreed but they were not to be taken with
geography. The subject group's 'filibuster' delayed acceptance until
1973 when much of the momentum of the environmental lobby had
passed.

The rural studies advocates having finally indicated their willingness to renunciate their practical origins in favour of O levels and
especially A levels in environmental studies were thereby blocked at the
last hurdle. The new subject was left somewhat in limbo with the range
of new O levels, which had been accepted, but without the unequivocal

A level status that would have finally ensured the finance, resources and high status careers that were so urgently sought.

Comprehensive Schools, Divisive Exams

The evolution of rural studies presents us with a range of insights into the curriculum values and pupil categories which achieved primacy in the comprehensive school. The subject moved from utilitarian and practical origins through a similar pattern in the early secondary modern period (alongside a small minority of innovative schools which built on the practical tradition to develop an integrated model of rural education) towards an embrace of academic examinations in the comprehensive school. The sudden renunciation of the practical and utilitarian heritage of rural studies and its traditional pupil clientele was because 'if you didn't, you wouldn't get any money, and status, and intelligent kids!' (Carson, interview).

Within the comprehensive schools a clear hierarchy of school subjects developed. The hierarchy was based on the primacy of grammar school subjects which were naturally given such priority by the grammar school staff who largely took over the headships and head of department posts. But the hierarchy was crucially underpinned by patterns of resource allocation. This took place on the basis of assumptions that 'academic' subjects were suitable for 'able' students whilst other subjects were not. These academic subjects, Byrne (1974) has shown, were thought to require longer periods to be taught, more highly paid staff and more money for equipment and books. She notes that the primacy of academic grammar school subjects was not challenged after comprehensivization. Hence the 'academic' grammar school subjects and 'able' pupil clienteles continued to enjoy financial priority in the comprehensive school. Separatism of buildings was eliminated, separatism of curricula maintained. Indeed not only did academic subjects retain their dominance; they extended it. From now on, 'academic' rules were extended to the mainstream curriculum of all comprehensive schools.

That comprehensive schools do place overwhelming emphasis on academic examinations, in spite of the growth of ROSLA type courses and pastoral systems, has been recently confirmed in Ball's (1981) study of 'Beachside Comprehensive'. He notes that 'once reorganized as a comprehensive, academic excellence was quickly established as the central tenet of the value system of the school' (p. 16); 'academic achievement tended to be the single criterion of success in the school'; and 'teacher resources within the comprehensive school are allocated differently according to the pupils' ability ... the most experienced teachers spend most of their time with the able pupils' (p. 18).

   The curricular implications of this academic dominance can be readily viewed in the case of rural studies. Rural studies advocates were persuaded by the structuring of material interests and career prospects to renunciate their practical, utilitarian origins and traditional clientele. The promoters of rural studies showed no inclination or interest in defining a new common curriculum for *all* abilities of pupil. There was no effort to develop an 'alternative road' leading in an integrated manner from the practical to the academic. From the beginnings of comprehensive reorganization rural studies was in flight from its practical origins and clientele towards a new 'academic scholarly discipline' that would ensure finance, resources, the subject's survival and the teachers' careers. For the teachers the renunciation of their traditional pupil clientele was the price for survival and status improvement in the comprehensive school.

   But for many pupils the predominance in comprehensive curricula of academic examination subjects and their disproportionate share of resources was to have severe implications. Sir Keith Joseph's current concern for the 'bottom 40 per cent' reflects a situation which arises less from intrinsic pupil problems than from the systematic production of an under-class by the curriculum structures and associated patterns of resource allocation embraced by comprehensive schools.

   As in the tripartite system so in the comprehensive system, academic subjects for able pupils are accorded the highest status and resources. The triple alliance between academic subjects, academic examinations and able pupils ensures that comprehensive schools provide similar patterns of success and failure to previous school systems. For the teachers who have to cater for all kinds of pupils this concentration on a particular kind of pupil and a particular kind of educational success poses the same dilemma voiced by the rural studies teacher in 1967 in face of the 'looming inevitability of the comprehensive school': 'True education is not for every man the scrap of paper he leaves with. Dare we as teachers admit this? Dare we risk our existence by forcibly expressing our views on this?' This case study of rural studies provides a definitive answer to his questions.

References

ALLEN, A.B. (1950) *Rural Education*, London, Allman and Sons.

ADAMSON, J.W. (1951) *Pioneers of Modern Education 1600–1700*, Cambridge, Cambridge University Press.

BALL, S.J. (1981) *Beachside Comprehensive: A Case Study of Secondary Schooling*, Cambridge, Cambridge University Press.

BOARD OF EDUCATION (1911) Memorandum on the Principles and Methods of Rural Education, London, HMSO.

BOARD OF EDUCATION (1925) Rural Education Circular 1365, London, HMSO.

BOARD OF EDUCATION (1939) Report for 1904–1939, London, HMSO.

BYRNE, E.M. (1974) *Planning and Educational Inequality*, Slough, NFER.

CARSON, S. (1967) *The Use and Content and Effective Objectives in Rural Studies Courses*, MEd thesis, University of Manchester.

CARSON, S. (1971) (Ed) *Environmental Studies, the Construction of an 'A' Level Syllabus*, Slough, NFER.

DES (1965) 'Organisation of Secondary Education', Circular 10/65, London, HMSO.

DES (1967) 'Rural studies in schools', *Trends in Education*, London, DES, October.

GIBBERD, K. (1962) *No Place Like School*, London, Michael Joseph.

GOODSON, I.F. (1983), *School Subjects and Curriculum Change: Case Studies on the Social History of Curriculum*, London, Croom Helm.

HERTFORDSHIRE ASSOCIATION OF TEACHERS OF GARDENING AND RURAL SUBJECTS (1957) 'Report on Rural Subjects and Gardening in Secondary Schools in Hertfordshire', *mimeo*.

KERR, J. (1971) 'The Problem of Curriculum Reform', in R. HOOPER (Ed) *The Curriculum Context, Design and Development*, Edinburgh, Oliver and Boyd.

MARSDEN, D. (1971) *Politicians, Equality and Comprehensives*, T.411, London, Fabian Society.

THE NORWOOD REPORT (1943) *Curriculum and Examinations in Secondary School*, London, HMSO.

PARTRIDGE, J. (1968), *Life in a Secondary Modern School*, Harmondsworth, Pelican.

QUANT, P.L. (1967) 'Rural Studies and Newsom Courses', *Hertfordshire Rural Studies Journal*.

RUBINSTEIN, D. and SIMON, B. (1975), *The Evolution of the Comprehensive School 1926–1972*, London, Routledge and Kegan Paul.

RURAL STUDIES DRAFT REPORT, 'The Certificate of Secondary Education Experimental Examination', *mimeo*.

SELLECK, R.J.W. (1968) *The New Education: the English Background 1870–1914*, Melbourne, Pitman.

SCHOOLS COUNCIL (1969) 'Rural Studies in Secondary Schools', *Working Paper* 24, London, Evans/Methuen Education.

SHIPMAN, M. (1971) 'Curriculum for Inequality', in HOOPER, R. (Ed), op. cit.

WARE, F. (1900) *Educational Reform*, London, Methuen.

Headship: Freedom or Constraint?

Robert G. Burgess

> The British headteacher has the greatest freedom in the world to put into practical operation his personal educational philosophy. (Archdiocese of Westminster, 1975, p. 7)

> The greatest advantage to being a head is that you can do what you bloody like. (Headmaster, Bishop McGregor Comprehensive School)

Leadership, power, authority and freedom are all terms that are considered to be synonymous with the headteacher. Indeed, comments from such diverse groups as Her Majesty's Inspectors (HMI), academics, LEA officials and headteachers themselves indicate that they consider the head to be the pivot and focus of the English school system (cf. Baron, 1955).

When the Inspectorate reported on *Ten Good Schools* in the secondary sector they were agreed that while the secondary schools they visited did exhibit many differences 'what they did all have in common is effective leadership' (HMI, 1977, p. 35). Indeed, they continued to explain that 'without exception, the most important single factor in the success of these schools is the quality of leadership' (HMI, 1977, p. 35). Among the comprehensive schools that they visited they were able to report that they had seen headteachers who could apply their educational philosophy to the particular circumstances in which they found themselves. Headteachers were able to deal firmly with parents, to give leadership to staff and pupils, to take executive action when required and to establish structures of cooperation between staff and pupils. In short, they considered that headteachers had imagination and vision tempered with realism, for they saw 'good' heads as: public relations officers, diplomats, negotiators and personnel managers who 'appreciate the need for specific educational aims, both social and intellectual and have the capacity to communicate these to staff, pupils and parents, to win their assent and to put their policies into practice' (HMI, 1977, p. 35).

The importance of the headteacher was also emphasized by the government Green Paper, *Education in Schools: A Consultative Document* (DES, 1977) which, in reviewing the evidence from the Inspectorate, stressed the point that 'The character and quality of the headteacher are by far the main influences in determining what a school sets out to do and the extent to which it achieves those aims' (DES, 1977, p. 32). However, within this document there was clear recognition by central government that the roles and relationships of headteachers and associated staff had undergone some change; it was argued that serious consideration should be given to

> the continuing need for the training of senior teachers, especial-
> ly heads of department and headteachers for the complex tasks
> of school organization and management, including the design
> and planning of the curriculum, to help them make the most
> effective use of all available resources, not least the talents of the
> school staff itself, in providing for the diverse needs of their
> pupils. (DES, 1977, p. 30)

Indeed, in the same year the tenth report from the expenditure committee (Select Committee, 1977) quoted the Secretary of State for Education and Science as saying that heads nowadays 'have laid upon them a degree of management responsibility which is quite unfamiliar with what heads were required to do. It is not enough to be a large scale teacher, one often has to be an administrator as well' (Select Committee, 1977, p. xlvi). Embodied within these statements is the idea that the headteacher is an organizer and manager who is called upon to implement decisions relating to teachers and pupils.

Such statements suggest that headteachers in the English school system have the power and the freedom to promote programmes on school organization and the curriculum. Indeed, Morrison and McIntyre (1969) have argued that heads are given freedom by LEAs to exercise power within institutions. However, we might ask what kind of freedom do headteachers actually have? A recent account of headship in secondary schools by a headteacher points to the fact that heads in secondary schools have freedom to do no teaching, to sit in a prestigious office and to take coffee whenever they wish (Honeyford, 1982, p. 32). To such a list might be added the power to regulate hair length, and the wearing of jewellery and school uniform, for headteachers have, in practice, relatively little control over such matters as the curriculum and external examinations.[1]

Yet we might ask what do we know about headship and about headteachers? In 1981 the Department of Education and Science collected data on comprehensive school headteachers (see Table 1).

Table 1   Comprehensive school headteachers in England and Wales in March 1981

	Graduates	Others including non-graduates	Total
Male	2578	496	3074
Female	355	155	510
Men and Women	2933	651	3584

Source: Extract from Table B129: 'Full time teachers in maintained nursery, primary and secondary schools: grade and graduate status, analysed by sex and type of school', DES, 1981a, p. 25.

In 1981 there were 200,118 teachers in comprehensive schools, of which 112,098 were male and 88,020 were female. Clearly, these data, like the data in the NUT/EOC (1980) survey (using data from *Statistics in Education* for 1976), also demonstrate that women are under-represented among headteachers. For although in 1981 women consti-tuted 44 per cent of the teaching force in comprehensive schools, they only held 14 per cent of the headships that were available.[2] Such evidence supports Warwick's view (1974) that sex is a greater determi-nant of career success than subject specialism. He utilizes evidence from a DES survey published in 1968 on the curriculum and deployment of teachers in secondary schools which showed that former students of languages and literature had one and a half times the chance of former students of science and mathematics and four times the chance of former students of music and drama to become heads.[3]

Apart from statistical data on headteachers in comprehensive schools, what else do we know about them? Such a question will meet with little response from educational researchers for they have collected relatively little empirical data on comprehensive school heads. In the early 1970s Bernbaum (1974) did collect data on the social origins and educational background of headmasters in the East Midlands who were members of the Headmasters Association. But most educational studies of comprehensive schools only provide brief glimpses of the head-teacher in relation to other areas of school work. For example, Richardson (1973; 1975) discusses the headteacher's tasks in relation to other duties of the senior management team at Nailsea School, while King (1973) introduces some data on heads in relation to his survey of secondary schools with the result that we do at least get a portrait of the headteacher in school assembly, if nowhere else. Even ethnographic studies with their emphasis upon portrayal have not done much more, for Ball (1981) only introduces the headmaster into his account of Beachside Comprehensive to provide something of the context of the school and to give some background information on the role of innovation (Ball, 1981, pp. 169–171). However, in the course of studying a new Roman Catholic comprehensive school that I called Bishop McGregor (Burgess, 1983) I focused on the headmaster, providing some account of his social and educational background and some detail on the way in which he established a new purpose-built co-educational comprehensive school. Here, the focus was not so much on the office and the office holder as upon the activities of that individual in the day-to-day life of the school (Burgess, 1983, pp. 26–51). My purpose was to portray the headmaster's conception of the school.[4]

With such a slight empirical base it is not surprising that basic texts on the sociology of education devote relatively little attention to headteachers. Indeed in a recent book on this subdiscipline, Meighan (1981) only uses the example of the headteacher's office to discuss the use of space in educational institutions (Meighan, 1981, pp. 44–45), while Shaw's survey of the field contains three chapters on teachers which make no mention of headteachers (Shaw, 1981). However, if educational researchers have lacked evidence it has not stopped specula-tion for they have provided accounts on the role of the head (Bern-baum, 1976; Hughes, 1976), on changes that confront headteachers in comprehensive schools (Taylor, 1973) and discussions of heads as lead-ers, managers, and sources of authority (King, 1968; Easthope, 1975; Taylor, 1976). In these accounts typologies abound. Basically sociolo-gists are agreed that there are three major dimensions to the role of the head: the instrumental — focusing on administrative tasks, the expres-sive — focusing on relationships between teachers, pupils and parents, and the symbolic — focusing on the head as a symbol of authority both within and outside the school.[5] However, beyond this typology there is disagreement about how comprehensive school heads interpret their roles. For King (1968) has argued that heads will retain the instrumental dimension but delegate the symbolic, while Burnham (1968) suggests the head will delegate the expressive. Meanwhile, Taylor (1968) considers that the head will retain the expressive but delegate the instrumental. Despite these differences they all agreed that comprehen-sive schooling would result in changes in the role of the head.

The traditional way in which educational researchers have perceived the role of headteacher has been well summarized by Banks who remarks:

> Traditionally, the headmaster or headmistress of an English school is expected to function as a leader rather than as a part of an administrative bureaucracy. All the teaching methods and procedures, all matters relating to curricula, the relationships with parents and the control of teachers and their duties are recognized as matters for the head to decide and education committees will rarely try to interfere. (Banks, 1976, pp. 134–135)

However, such a model had evolved in the English school system in schools which had at maximum no more than 400 children (cf. Baron, 1955). Accordingly, a shift towards large comprehensive schools with over one thousand pupils demanded some movement away from an autocratic concept of headship (Secondary Heads Association, 1983, p. 1). The implications of such changes in the size and complexity of comprehensive schools for headteachers have been summarized by Taylor when he remarks:

> It is no longer so easy for the head to be in close personal contact with the staff and pupils, to be able to claim that he knows everyone in the school. He must necessarily delegate a good deal to senior colleagues. The skills involved in coordinating the work of several departments and house units, in interpreting the school to the community which it serves, in initiating innovation and encouraging others to innovate, all become of greater importance; the head must add managerial skills to his existing commitment to educational objectives and the needs of children. (Taylor, 1973, pp. 11–12)

Such remarks give rise to a number of questions that need to be stressed about headteachers in comprehensive schools: What are their duties? What expectations do LEAs have of heads? What are their powers? What constraints are there upon their roles? What kind of problems confront the headteacher? How does a headteacher work in a comprehensive school? In what way is the role of headteacher interpreted? We will attempt to address some of these questions by focusing on basic social processes associated with headteachers using two sources of data; first, sets of 'further particulars' for the position of headteacher that have been obtained from various LEAs;[6] secondly, case study material on the headteacher of the school that I called Bishop McGregor. The result is that we will focus upon those data that illustrate the way headship is defined by local authorities and the way in which it is defined within one school. The analysis therefore takes the form of a case study that highlights the processes and problems that confront some comprehensive school heads. Clearly, it is not generalizable to all comprehensive school heads who may serve in schools in different circumstances: rural or urban, purpose-built or split site, co-educational or single sex and so on. It is, therefore, an exploratory study that begins by examining the way in which headship is defined by LEAs.

Headteachers and Local Education Authorities

Headteachers are appointed by the LEA and in the case of voluntary aided schools by the school governors. In all cases the appointment of teaching staff, the way the school shall be conducted and the duties of the head are prescribed in articles of government which are issued in respect of every school in England and Wales. While they may contain slight variations depending on local circumstances, they are broadly uniform, having been based upon models that were issued following the 1944 Education Act. Within these articles of government there is some definition of the responsibility of the headteacher for the organization and curriculum of the school in relation to the governors and the local education committee. Such articles state:

> The Authority shall determine the general educational character of the school and its place in the local educational system. Subject thereto and subject to any direction of the Authority on any matters which in the Authority's opinion may affect educational policy, the Governors shall in consultation with the Head Teacher have the oversight of the conduct and the curriculum of the school. (Articles of Government, Norbury Manor High School, Croydon Education Committee)

Such a statement establishes the position of the headteacher in relation to the local authority and the governors to whom the head has to work and in whose framework the school has to operate. However, this represents an ideal situation, for in practice it is often acknowledged that curriculum matters are devolved onto the headteacher and the staff (DES, 1981b, p. 3).[7] Indeed, further specification on the duties of the head is given in the following terms:

Subject to the provision of these Articles the Head Teacher shall control and conduct the curriculum, the internal organization, management and discipline of a school, the choice of books, the method of teaching and the arrangement of classes: and shall exercise supervision over the teaching and non-teaching staff. He shall have the power to suspend pupils from attendance for any cause which he considers adequate, but on suspending any pupil, he shall forthwith report the case to the Chairman of the Governors and to the Director of Education. (Articles of Government, Norbury Manor High School, Croydon Education Committee)

On this basis, it would appear that 'running' a school is a joint enterprise between the governors and the head who are accountable to the LEA for the curriculum and the general conduct of the school, but beyond this there is no detail about what a headteacher should be doing. Indeed, even the head's contract of service with the LEA has little to say about the duties of headship, apart from remarks on conditions of service and terms of employment. On this basis, we might then turn to advertisements, sets of further particulars and application forms to see what clues they provide on the duties of a headteacher and the expectations which LEAs have of potential heads of comprehensive schools. A recent survey by Morgan, Hall and Mackay (1983) indicated that advertisements did not specify the criteria for application too precisely (cf. Secondary Heads Association, 1983, p.7). Furthermore, their survey of application forms for secondary headships in sixty LEAs revealed only 30 per cent who used a specific form, while the remainder provided general teaching application forms where few of the questions were relevant. Meanwhile, they found that sets of further particulars rarely provided a full job description but instead described schools in terms of type, size, historical background and their main organizational and curricular features.

Among the sets of further particulars that I obtained, it was common to provide some statement about the reason for the vacancy and whether the job had occurred through the retirement or resignation of the current holder or whether other circumstances such as reorganization or the establishment of a new school accounted for the availability of the post. Accordingly, the situation was often described in the following terms:

Applications are invited from experienced teachers for the post of head of the John Fernley High School, Scalford Road,

Melton Mowbray, Leicestershire LE13 1LH. The vacancy is from August 1983 and is due to the retirement of the present head. (Leicestershire Education Committee)

Such statements were in general followed by descriptions of: the school, staffing, organization, accommodation, the management structure of the school, the curriculum, pastoral care, links with the community and the LEA together with any special circumstances related to the post. In addition, some indication was given of the kind of headteacher that was required. However, this was often limited to a few sentences (cf. Morgan and Hall, 1982; Secondary Heads Association, 1983).

Among the documents that have been examined there were general statements on headship, comments on leadership, on management and the specific requirements of a comprehensive school. The general requirements for a headteacher are well summarized in Solihull's advertisement for comprehensive school heads which takes the following form:

Applications are invited from suitably qualified and experienced teachers for this appointment (Head Teacher) tenable from 1st September 1983. (Solihull Education Committee)

However, more detailed specification resulted in requests for leadership, management and qualities that were associated with particular aspects of comprehensive school organization.

On leadership, LEAs not only made requests for leaders in general terms but also in relation to curriculum matters by stating:

The Governors and the LEA are anxious to appoint to the Headship a person who will lead the school into the next phase of its development as a comprehensive school, whilst maintaining the high standards that have already been established. (East Sussex County Council)

and

It is hoped to appoint a Head Teacher who will continue to provide a vigorous and imaginative leadership in the development of the curriculum and who will maintain the high standards of academic attainment which have been achieved over the past years. (Kent Education Committee)

Meanwhile a set of particulars for a school in Waltham Forest was more expansive on the qualities of a future head by indicating:

A Headteacher of vision, drive and enthusiasm is sought, who is prepared to work hard to meet the needs of all pupils. The personality and potential of the candidate will be rated as highly as strict academic qualifications or detailed experience. (Waltham Forest Education Department)

Clearly, candidates for these headships were subject to personal as well as academic demands (cf. Morgan, Hall and Mackay, 1983). In addition to qualities of leadership, management and managerial skills were also required, as suitable experience was equated with 'appropriate experience at senior management level'.

The phrase 'suitably qualified teachers with substantial and recent experience' was discussed in terms of leadership and management as, in addition to 'a sound teaching record', it included:

qualities of leadership, managerial flair and a grasp of and sensitivity to the many issues posed for schools by such developments as overall contraction in pupil numbers and accelerating social and technological changes in the years ahead. (Wolverhampton Education Committee)

Another authority summarized its requirements in similar terms by indicating:

The Authority wish to appoint a well qualified graduate teacher experienced in senior levels of school management, used to working with pupils of differing abilities and aptitudes and conversant with the various teaching styles demanded in a comprehensive school. It is essential that the successful candidate continues the technological innovations so prominent in the school's present curriculum. (London Borough of Bromley Education Committee)

Despite all these calls for 'leadership' and 'management' there are few indicators as to what counts under these headings except on application forms where applicants were asked to comment on particular aspects of management structure concerning deputy heads, heads of departments and heads of year or heads of houses. Further details were also requested on policy-making and decision-making in curriculum areas and pastoral care.

In advertizing the post of headteacher in one comprehensive school, Kent Education Committee stated:

Since its amalgamation, Woodlands School has become a school which provides a stimulating working environment for both

> pupils and teachers. It is now very well established within the
> community, and it is hoped to appoint a Headteacher who will
> continue to provide a vigorous and imaginative leadership in
> the development of the curriculum and who will maintain the
> high standards of academic attainment which have been
> achieved over the past years. (Kent Education Committee)

Here, the curriculum was interpreted in terms of 'high standards of
academic attainment' which implied that the 'vigorous and imaginative
leadership' had already been defined. Indeed, such a description suggests an academic orientation in the comprehensive school which
would result in the under-representation of some curriculum areas
(Calouste Gulbenkian Foundation, 1982; Hargreaves, 1982).

Nevertheless, it is popularly imagined that heads are given freedom to develop schools. However, on inspection of sets of particulars
it is evident that candidates are provided with LEA policy, together
with details on the current patterns of school organization and details of
the curriculum structure. Accordingly, LEA policy was provided on
such diverse areas as community education, multi-cultural education
and school structures which a head would be expected to operate.
Indeed, where a new school was under construction in Devon,
candidates were told:

> The buildings are designed in such a way that a Lower School
> Unit has been incorporated to enable a particular approach to
> education in Years 1 and 2 and the Authority hope to appoint a
> Head whose philosophy will tie in with this and who will foster
> its development through its curriculum and the organisation of
> the School.

Indeed a job description for the head of a secondary school in Devon
provided details on four areas of responsibility: the curriculum, the
organization and management of the school in all its aspects, and
accountability and external relations (see appendix). At first glance it
might appear that the head has maximum flexibility to identify,
determine and evaluate the curriculum; to develop, define, motivate
and supervise staff and pupils and co-ordinate, determine, present and
establish external relationships. However, the section on accountability
puts the head's role in perspective when it states that this includes:
'working in accordance with the policies of the Education Authority.
Attending and reporting to Governors' meetings. Liaising with the
chairman. Embracing governors' views in school policy'. Such a

statement does not depart from the clues that have appeared in the materials produced by other LEAs as it highlights the limitations that are placed on the 'freedom' of the headteacher in the comprehensive school.

Furthermore, it places emphasis on managerial skills that are also demanded for many other headships. Indeed, Morgan and Hall (1982) and the Secondary Heads Association (1983) also point to the rise of managerialism and managerial vocabularies to describe the task of headship in the contemporary comprehensive school. Accordingly, we might ask: how does a headteacher lead and manage? To what extent is a headteacher free to organize a school? In short, how does a headteacher define headship? To address these questions, we now turn to an analysis of headship in a comprehensive school using case study material.

Headship in a Comprehensive School

The material that is presented in this section of the paper is taken from an ethnographic study of a purpose-built, co-educational Roman Catholic comprehensive school that I called Bishop McGregor (Burgess, 1983).[8] We begin by providing a brief description of the school and introducing the headteacher, Geoffrey Goddard, before presenting his conception of headship and the way in which he defined his role within the school.

Bishop McGregor School

Bishop McGregor School is a co-educational 11–18 Roman Catholic comprehensive school with just over 1200 pupils and 69 full time staff. The school is located in the city of Merston and has been established on the Merston authority's structure for comprehensive schools with a house system for pastoral care and departments for subject work. The head is a practising Catholic in his mid-forties who has previously been head of a science department in a comprehensive school and headmaster of a secondary modern school for boys before coming to McGregor.

As head of a new school it may appear that he had maximum freedom to establish structures and develop staff. However, local authority policy was such that after appointing a deputy head he had to appoint house heads who were to be the next level of senior staff, after which appointments could be made to departments. While the authority gave a points allocation that allowed four house heads to be appointed on the highest scale for assistant teachers, no such allowance was forthcoming for the departments. Indeed, Goddard remarked: 'I was very disappointed that the Authority could not give me the number of points (scale posts) to recruit heads of departments at the start, just as I recruited heads of houses'.[9]

As a consequence, when the school opened, only one head of department could be appointed; all other departments being the responsibility of house heads. For Goddard this was critical as in his view this influenced major decisions in the first three years and subsequent developments in the next ten years. Indeed, this view was shared by many heads of departments who considered that the fact that departments had initially been organized by house heads and that house staff were senior to department staff influenced the tenor of relationships between these two groups of teachers (Burgess, 1983, pp. 52–83). In turn, this structure also influenced Goddard's style of headship.

A style of headship

When Goddard was appointed to Bishop McGregor School he had already been a head for five years. Before that he had derived ideas about headship from his father who had been a headteacher and from heads for whom he had worked in grammar, secondary modern and comprehensive schools. However, this was not the only source of his ideas about headship as he explained:

> I think I'm a bit of a pragmatist. I tend not to work to a whole theory. The coat is not made of one piece. It's a bit of a patchwork quilt. No one school of thought, no one man has a theory. I have, therefore, drawn from books I have read, conferences I have attended, from institutions I have seen and from people I have talked to. I have mixed them. I am a sort of educational supercook.

In these terms, Geoff Goddard could not be neatly defined as a leader or a manager. Indeed, he argued that he had deliberately chosen not to be a dictator but decided to 'give the impression of being a democrat'. Accordingly, he saw it as his task to get others to participate, to listen, to probe and to think through their ideas. However, we need to consider how he attempted to achieve this task. Just as the literature on headship contains military analogies so Goddard was taken with such comparisons; he often referred to his job as one of running a 'happy ship' where pupils knew where the railings were so that they would not fall overboard. Meanwhile, his own position was likened to a field officer where leadership was essential. Indeed, he summarized the style of his headship as that of 'a field officer, not a staff officer. I lead from the front and it works for me'.

When it came to operationalizing leadership, Goddard considered that this could only be done by means of personal demonstration to the staff and pupils. For him teaching was the key way in which he could demonstrate those things which he considered important, qualities which he wanted to develop in his staff as well as a way of getting to know more about the school and its members. For him this was the key to headship as he explained:

> When a head puts himself on the timetable it must be more than just getting out of the office, of doing what he did well as a young man. He must be tasting and testing what is going on in his school. It is a great help if the head can be round the school so that people expect him. It is a way staff can see him. In a developing school with a young staff they are going to have to listen to a load of old guff from the head so it's a great help if they get a class from him that they know he can teach. If he teaches, what he teaches shows what he thinks is important. If he teaches religious education, he says in this school religious education matters. If he teaches sixth form general studies he does not just say sixth form is important but general education is important. If I teach Newsom (the less willing and the less able) I show it is important and then if I ask someone else to do it, it's not because you're the last man on the timetable but because I think you have a contribution to make. If you ask someone to sweep a street you've got to be prepared to do it yourself.

As a consequence, Goddard saw himself as the main participant who through the act of teaching could lead, manage, co-ordinate and plan. Furthermore, he maintained that this put him in a position where he could seek advice from individual teachers and consult with them. However, the head's participation in the school was not limited to personal contact, for he also communicated regularly with teachers and pupils through sets of written documents which included a weekly news bulletin and two sets of occasional information sheets known as standard operational procedures (STOPS) and advice, information and routines (AIRS). The result was that the head established school policy and defined the roles, rules, and routines which were part of the day-to-day life of members of the school. Indeed, he acknowledged that 'The school, whether I like it or not, or whether I want it or not, is at least in fair measure shaped by me.' However, he continued by indicating that there were many areas that he could not control and therefore it was his task to be 'an arranger, a fixer and a compromiser' who was involved in leadership through the management of crises in the school.

The headmaster of Bishop McGregor School, therefore, considered that there were a number of dimensions to his job which resulted in him leading, managing and defining school activities. When these ideas were operationalized it resulted in situations in which the head dealt with crises, produced memoranda, took school assembly, taught classes and chaired meetings, for it was by personal example that he led, managed and defined school activities.

Headship and the definition of the situation

In a new school with new staff (many of whom had not worked in a comprehensive school before) Goddard decided to provide a framework around which daily routines could be established for staff and pupils. Accordingly, this process was conducted through discussion papers on areas such as sanctions, remedial education, option schemes and educational visits; informal meetings and regular committees. While all staff were involved in consultation it was heads of houses and heads of departments to whom he turned for advice as he held regular meetings with these groups on a fortnightly basis throughout each term. However, they were consulted by the head; they were not bodies that took collective decisions, for the head chaired all the meetings, often acted as the minute secretary and produced the log of decisions that were taken and subsequently made available to teachers.[10] Collective meetings of all staff were rare except in emergencies and at the start of each academic year. Accordingly, it was usual for staff to receive details of the way in which the headmaster expected the school to operate through information contained in circulars that were issued each week. In turn, this information was often reinforced through a talk that was given by the headmaster in school assembly

which he used to address teachers and pupils. For as Goddard remarked: 'School assembly is a straight exposition of my ideas, about
the school, about behaviour such as spitting, about charity and about
religion'. In short, talks given by the headmaster in school assembly
were a principal means by which he communicated ideas that he wished
to promote. While I was in the school I attended school assembly and
recorded examples of talks in which the head promoted positive aspects
of pupil behaviour (the pastoral dimension of the school) and subject
work (the academic dimension).

In one assembly that I attended I made the following record of the
headmaster's talk:

> Mr. Goddard began by saying that as it was just four and a bit
> weeks from the end of the term he wanted to talk about several
> things which could be summed up as 'school spirit'. First, he
> said, 'All pupils from this school, by their bearing and carriage
> give an impression of the school. You are representatives of the
> school as you make your way home'. On this basis he explained
> that it was important to give the neighbours an accurate
> impression of what the school was like. Secondly, he said that
> in the athletics competition that took place the previous Satur-
> day he was pleased to see that pupils who represented the school
> went on to the track proud to wear their school colours. He
> added 'I hope that we are all proud to wear the school colours
> and to keep to the school uniform'. He said that he was
> prepared to make uniform part of the competition for the house
> trophy and that each house would, therefore, be awarded a
> mark out of ten for their appearance between now and the end
> of term. 'It will', he said, 'give you the opportunity to show
> your school spirit through your house.' Thirdly, he said that
> school spirit could be demonstrated through help and support
> that pupils might give to the annual fete by doing something or
> bringing something. He added that half of the profits from the
> fete would go towards a school bus which would result in free
> trips next year. Finally, he summarized what he had said by
> indicating that there were three things they should remember:
> behaviour on the way home, behaviour and school uniform,
> and the fete and field day. With this he said 'good morning' and
> closed his part of the assembly.[11]

This assembly is illustrative of the way in which the headmaster
reinforced the work of houses and house staff by discussing the

behavioural norms for which they were directly responsible. While it may appear that these remarks were directed at pupils, they were also directed at department staff who were not always prepared to support house staff (Burgess, 1983, pp. 52–83) on issues such as school uniform. In this respect, teachers as well as pupils were being reminded about a dimension of schooling which the head wished to promote, especially at a period close to the end of the term and the academic year when such issues were often lost from view.

As well as giving support to house staff through talks in school assembly the head also supported the academic side of the school which he also promoted in assembly. In an assembly with fourth and fifth year pupils I made the following record in my fieldnotes:

> The headmaster began by saying that he had gathered together all the fourth and fifth years because they were the senior part of the school and they could give leadership to the rest of the school. He said that he thought the fourth year could learn from the fifth year. 'If the fifth had listened last year this time (summer term) they wouldn't at this stage be concerned about their examinations. It is a time when one group can learn from another'. He suggested that if both groups wanted to talk about their future in examination classes they should talk with department staff, their tutors, their heads of houses and with himself. Finally, he indicated that if anyone would like to engage in a special project at the end of term 'I will be happy to spend two days making the arrangements'.

This assembly talk, like all others was conducted in the presence of teachers as well as pupils. On this occasion the head highlighted academic values which were expressed in terms of external examinations.[12] In addition, he reminded pupils of teachers with whom they should be able to consult; this in turn provided him with another opportunity to highlight the structure of the staff and the areas for which they were responsible. Finally, he indicated the value that he placed upon the pupils' academic activities by indicating his willingness to be involved in consultations with pupils in establishing their programmes of work.

These two assemblies reflect the way in which the headmaster communicated his ideas about the way in which the school should work by discussing areas of the pastoral and academic curriculum with teachers and pupils. Each of these examples relate to aspects of the school structure and to situations which were defined by the head in the course of handling day to day events. However, Goddard considered that the real test of headship concerned the management of crises, to which we now turn.

Headship as crisis management

When the school opened Goddard had taken into account that he would need to prepare for major emergencies. Indeed he considered that attempting to anticipate crises should be a central feature of school management for he stated: 'My job is not to manage today's crisis, but to manage the crisis of four months time. The settlement of today's crisis is by principles established four months before. If it isn't something has gone wrong with forward planning'. Accordingly, one of the early documents that he prepared was a set of notes on wise and effective action that could be taken by teachers when injuries, accidents and emergencies were involved. In particular he had prepared a set of general principles when fires, crashes, explosions and other situations occurred, as he argued, 'however remote the possibility ... we (the staff) need some ideas of what to do'.[13] The main principles were:

i   Each teacher will be responsible for checking their group and getting the children in his or her care to either their house block or a place of safety.

ii   If teachers are injured the nearest teacher/responsible adult conducts unharmed children to a place of safety.

iii At the same time the head and deputy head are to be informed. The head will get to the scene of the accident, the deputy head will go to the administration block to take charge of organizing outside help and receiving reports from the rest of the site. Mr Jackson [teacher in charge of safety] will join the deputy head.

iv   As soon as possible after delivering children to a safe place and handing them over to a responsible adult, heads of houses will conduct a register check and at the earliest opportunity will notify the deputy head of any missing children. They will remain with the children of their house until further instructions are given.

v   Other teachers will, when practical, join their head of house. Assistant heads of house will inform the deputy head of any staff missing. The reporting to the deputy head in iv) and v) is *essential*.

vi Mr Penfold and Mr Dare will as soon as they have handed over their children report to the head at the scene of the accident.
vii All roads and paths must be kept clear for emergency service vehicles.

Action by secretaries: a) care of those sent to rest room; b) phoning for ambulances etc; c) contacting parents whenever a child is going to hospital; d) collecting, issuing information under the guidance of headmaster/deputy head; e) ensuring that accident reports are completed and appropriately distributed.

To assist in c) it is very helpful if telephone numbers for contacting parents are available not only at house level but also in the main office, and heads of house are asked to ensure that as many phone numbers as possible are given to the secretary.[14]

While this provided an outline of the ideal procedure which the head expected the staff to follow, it also indicated how his plans were moulded by the basic structure of the school staff. In particular, it was house heads rather than departmental staff who were to provide the basic support for the head who was to be the main participant in any emergency. Indeed, if critical situations were to arise the head had already nominated himself, as the person who would take charge, for in his view this would involve taking critical decisions which was what he considered being a headmaster was about.

While I was in the school I witnessed three situations that were considered by the teachers to be crises. They consisted of a series of bomb scares, a mass walk out by 600 pupils who were complaining about the fact that they had not been given a holiday to celebrate the wedding of Princess Anne and a series of events at the end of the summer term (Burgess, 1983, pp. 84–119). In each of these situations it was the head who took control. Indeed, even in his absence during one of the bomb scares, his plan of action was adopted and adapted by the deputy head in association with other teachers (mainly drawn from the houses). In these terms, the leadership shown by the head in each of these situations while needing to be responsive to the particular circumstances basically related to the structure of the school that had been established by the LEA. It would appear, therefore, that the head was constrained by the structure within which he was located.

Conclusion

This paper has been concerned with the dynamics of headship in the comprehensive school. It began by considering accounts from sociologists and educationalists that place stress upon leadership, management and freedom, all of which are popularly associated with headteachers. However, an analysis of sets of further particulars together with a case study of headship in one comprehensive school casts doubts on these notions and points to a series of issues that require further investigation.

On the basis of the data presented here it is difficult to draw firm conclusions. Indeed, this is an exploratory account, for if we are to understand more about the culture of headteachers a systematic programme of research needs to be established. First, some analysis is required of the way in which LEAs and school governors define the duties of the head.[15] Secondly, more detailed analyses are required that take the head rather than the school as the focus of the study. Here, questions need to be addressed about what counts as 'management', 'leadership' and 'decision-making'. Furthermore, heads need to be viewed in relation to education officials, governors, unions, parents, employers, teaching and non-teaching staff. For it is only when such work is attempted that we will begin to have some understanding of the position of headteacher in the contemporary comprehensive school. Meanwhile, the evidence that has been assembled suggests that headteachers do not have 'freedom to do what they bloody like' but have to operate within the constraints that are established by their LEAs. Indeed, the critical cases of Michael Duane who was removed from Risinghill School (Berg, 1968) and R.F. Mackenzie who was sacked from Summerhill School by the Aberdeen Education Committee in 1974 (Mackenzie, 1977) are further indications of the limited powers of the head. Furthermore, in the light of financial restrictions, falling rolls, teacher redeployment and the amalgamation of comprehensive schools, LEAs may increase their control over the action and activities of headteachers. For decisions taken by local authorities may have implications for school organization and for the curriculum. Certainly, further control has been advocated by the DES for many years. Indeed, in the tenth report from the expenditure committee (Select Committee, 1977) it was suggested that the DES should persuade LEAs to provide management training for heads and establish criteria for their selection. Furthermore, it was recommended that 'the DES should seek by all the means possible tò promote the concept of limited tenure for head-teachers on the understanding that there would be previously agreed criteria for evaluation' (Select Committee, 1977, p. xlvi). Since 1977 these views have been reinforced and restated in numerous documents on the curriculum and on the education service (cf. *Teaching Quality*, DES, 1983). However, those who seek maximum freedom within the English educational system might take the advice of the headmaster of Bishop McGregor by working in a church school, as he argued that 'You have to give offence to church and state simultaneously before they chop you'.

Acknowledgements

I would like to thank Hilary Burgess, Margaret Threadgold and the headmaster of Bishop McGregor School who provided helpful comments on an earlier version of this chapter. In particular, I am very grateful to Stephen Ball for his editorial support and detailed comments which I found most helpful. However, any weaknesses in this chapter are my own. The study of Bishop McGregor School was made possible by a postgraduate studentship from the SSRC.

Notes

1 For a discussion of attempts to control the curriculum in schools see HMI (1980), DES (1981b) and for a commentary see, for example Lawton (1980), White *et al* (1981).
2 Such a situation means that in general women have less status and have lower salaries than their male counterparts in comprehensive schools (cf. Acker, 1983). Furthermore, it also holds implications for the role models that are presented to girls in schools (cf. Deem, 1980; Delamont, 1980, 1983).
3 In a report on the arts (dance, drama, music, visual arts, literature) it was recommended that teachers of these subjects should aim for headships in order that these areas should become better represented in the school curriculum (Calouste Gulbenkian Foundation, 1982). A similar point has also been made by Hargreaves (1982) who has noted the way in which such subjects are under-represented in comprehensive schools.
4 For a similar account from the USA based on an elementary school principal see Wolcott (1973).
5 A slightly modified and extended typology has been advanced by Morgan and Hall (1982) on the basis of evidence from an empirical study of headteachers (the POST project on selection procedures used for secondary

school headteachers). Their views are based on an analysis of managerial roles in which they argue that there are four tasks involved in headship: technical tasks concerned with education, conceptual tasks based on operations management, human relations tasks based on leadership, and external management tasks based on community relations and accountability. However, this typology has considerable overlap with the sociologists' categories.

6 This analysis is based upon thirty-five sets of further particulars for headships that were advertised in *The Times Educational Supplement* in February 1983. These data are used as the basis of an exploratory analysis. If this kind of investigation were to be pursued the methodology would need to be developed using a wider range of data sources. However, this small scale investigation reveals similar findings to the survey by Morgan, Hall and Mackay (1983).

7 For a similar view in relation to primary education see the Auld report on William Tyndale School (Auld, 1976).

8 For the study see Burgess (1983) and for a methodological commentary see Burgess (1982, 1984a, 1984b).

9 Except where indicated all the extracts that are quoted are from tape recorded interviews with the headmaster.

10 As in many comprehensive schools, Goddard relied on these heads of houses and heads of departments who were his 'middle management'. For further discussion of such groups see Maw (1977), Ball (in this volume) and Sikes (in this volume).

11 Extract from fieldnotes — summer term, 1974.

12 This highlights the importance of academic values that were dominant in sets of further particulars and which Hargreaves (1982) has identified as forming the ethos of many comprehensive schools. Indeed, at Bishop McGregor School, the head defined the Newsom course as being for those pupils regarded as less willing and less able in terms of their limited abilities in academic work and public examinations (Burgess, 1983, 1984c).

13 Extract from document on 'Emergencies' written by the headmaster.

14 *Ibid.*

15 A start has been made with this kind of research by Morgan, Hall and Mackay (1983).

Appendix: Job Description for the Head of a Secondary School in the County of Devon.

The head of the school has responsibility to the LEA and to the Governors for deciding and guiding the internal organization, curriculum and discipline of the school and for managing and supervizing the teaching and non-teaching staff, subject to the provisions of the Articles of Government and such policies as the LEA may from time to time determine.

These responsibilities are defined in the four areas of:—
    1 the curriculum
    2 the organisation and management of the school in all its aspects
    3 accountability
    4 external relations
as follows:—

1 The curriculum

i Aims and objectives
    Identifying, in consultation with LEA, governors, teaching staff and other interested parties, aims and objectives on which the work of the school as a whole and its specialized departments will be based.
ii Academic curriculum
    Determining a curriculum relevant to the learning abilities, aptitudes and needs of all pupils. Allocating curricular responsibilities to departments, staff members and pupils.
iii Pastoral curriculum
    Determining a policy of organization for pastoral care including the social context in which norms of behaviour and discipline for pupils and staff will be established.
iv Evaluation
    Evaluating standards of teaching and learning and progress in all aspects of school policy generally by establishing measurement criteria and instruments. Using the results to initiate appropriate developments.
v Pupil records
    Ensuring that the policies of the authority are effectively carried out.

2 Organisation and management of the school in all its aspects

i Planning, organization, co-ordination, and control
    Determining the procedures for all internal school policy-making and management control, including the delegated responsibilities of the Senior Management Team. Securing the effective dissemination of school policy, news of activities and events, and effective channels of two-way communication.
ii Staff deployment
    Defining staff tasks and writing job descriptions. Selecting and appointing staff within the terms of the Articles of Government.

iii Staff development
Developing policy and procedures for the professional development, work enrichment and support of staff.

iv Leadership
Motivating staff and pupils by personal influence, incentives and concern for individual needs, health, safety and working conditions generally. Solving problems and resolving conflict by applying chairmanship, negotiation, arbitration and reconciliation skills.

v Capital resources
Supervising and security and maintenance of the physical plant. Controlling the financial affairs of the school including the allocation of capitation allowances and responsibility for school funds.

vi Returns and records
Maintaining adequate and appropriate records including the keeping of registers, statistical returns and school annals.

3 Accountability

Working in accordance with the policies of the Education Authority. Attending and reporting to Governors Meetings. Liaising with the chairman. Embracing governors' views in school policy.

4 External relations

i Other institutions
Coordinating the school's provision with that of feeder schools, other secondary schools, FE and HE institutions.

ii Parents
Determining a policy to achieve the support and involvement of parents in the work of the school.

iii Media and local community
Presenting news of the school to the local community and gauging community expectations for the school.

iv Employers
Establishing communication with employers and ensuring that there is understanding within the school of employers' expectations and employment opportunities.

v External agencies
Linking the school with supporting external agencies.

Robert G. Burgess

References

ACKER, S. (1983) 'Women and teaching: a semi-detached view of a semi-profession', in WALKER, S. and L. BARTON, (Eds) *Gender Class and Education*, Lewes, Falmer Press.

ARCHDIOCESE OF WESTMINSTER (1975) *Your First Headship*, London, Archdiocese of Westminster.

AULD, R. (1976) *Report on the Inquiry into William Tyndale School*, London, Inner London Education Authority.

BALL, S.J. (1981) *Beachside Comprehensive: A Case Study of Secondary Schooling*, Cambridge, Cambridge University Press.

BANKS, O. (1976) *The Sociology of Education* (3rd edn), London, Batsford.

BARON, G. (1955) 'The English notion of the school', unpublished paper, University of London, Institute of Education, *Mimeo*.

BERG, L. (1968) *Risinghill: Death of a Comprehensive School*, Harmondsworth, Penguin.

BERNBAUM, G. (1974) 'Headmasters and schools: some preliminary findings', in EGGLESTON, J. (Ed) *Contemporary Research in the Sociology of Education*, London, Methuen.

BERNBAUM, G. (1976) 'The role of the head', in PETERS, R.S. (Ed) *The Role of the Head*, London, Routledge and Kegan Paul.

BURGESS, R.G. (1982) 'The practice of sociological research: some issues in school ethnography', in BURGESS, R.G. (Ed) *Exploring Society*, London, British Sociological Association.

BURGESS, R.G. (1983) *Experiencing Comprehensive Education: A Study of Bishop McGregor School*, London, Methuen.

BURGESS, R.G. (1984a) *In the Field: An Introduction to Field Research*, London, Allen and Unwin.

BURGESS, R.G. (1984b) 'The whole truth? some ethical problems of research in a comprehensive school', in BURGESS, R.G. (Ed) *Field Methods in the Study of Education*, Lewes, Falmer Press.

BURGESS, R.G. (1984c) 'It's not a proper subject: it's just Newsom', in GOODSON, I.F. and S.J. BALL, (Eds) *Defining the Curriculum*, Lewes, Falmer Press.

BURNHAM, P.S. (1968) 'The deputy head', in ALLEN, B. (Ed) *Headship in the 1970s*, Oxford, Basil Blackwell.

CALOUSTE GULBENKIAN FOUNDATION (1982) *The Arts in Schools: Principles, Practice and Provision*, London, Calouste Gulbenkian Foundation.

DEEM, R. (Ed) (1980) *Schooling for Women's Work*, London, Routledge and Kegan Paul.

DELAMONT, S. (1980) *Sex Roles and the School*, London, Methuen.

DELAMONT, S. (1983) 'The conservative school?' in WALKER, S. and L. BARTON, (Eds) *Gender, Class and Education*, Lewes, Falmer Press.

DEPARTMENT OF EDUCATION AND SCIENCE (1977) *Education in Schools: A Consultative Document*, London, HMSO.

DEPARTMENT OF EDUCATION AND SCIENCE (1981a) *Teachers in Service in Maintained, Assisted and Grant Aided Schools and Establishments of Further Education in England and Wales, 1981*, London, HMSO.

DEPARTMENT OF EDUCATION AND SCIENCE (1981b) *The School Curriculum*, London, HMSO.

DEPARTMENT OF EDUCATION AND SCIENCE (1983) *Teaching Quality*, London, HMSO

EASTHOPE, G. (1975) *Community, Hierarchy and Open Education*, London, Routledge and Kegan Paul.

HARGREAVES, D.H. (1982) *The Challenge for the Comprehensive School*, London, Routledge and Kegan Paul.

HER MAJESTY'S INSPECTORS (1977) *Ten Good Schools*, London, HMSO.

HER MAJESTY'S INSPECTORS (1980) *A View of the Curriculum*, London, HMSO

HONEYFORD, R. (1982) *Starting Teaching*, London, Croom Helm.

HUGHES, M.G. (1976) 'The professional-as-administrator: the case of the secondary school head', in PETERS, R.S. (Ed) *The Role of the Head*, London, Routledge and Kegan Paul.

KING, R. (1968) 'The headteacher and his authority' in ALLEN, B. (Ed) *Headship in the 1970s*, Oxford, Basil Blackwell.

KING, R. (1973) *School Organization and Pupil Involvement*, London, Routledge and Kegan Paul.

LAWTON, D. (1980) *The Politics of the School Curriculum*, London, Routledge and Kegan Paul.

MACKENZIE, R.F. (1977) *The Unbowed Head*, Edinburgh, Edinburgh University Students Publication Board.

MAW, J. (1977) 'Defining roles in senior and middle management in secondary schools', in JENNINGS, A. (Ed), *Management and Headship in the Secondary School*, London, Ward Lock.

MEIGHAN, R. (1981) *A Sociology of Educating*, New York, Holt, Rinehart and Winston.

MORGAN, C. and HALL, V. (1982) 'What is the job of the secondary school head?', *Education*, 159, 25, pp. i-iv, 18 June.

MORGAN, C., HALL, V. and MACKAY, H. (1983) 'Selecting heads: the POST Project', *Education*, 162, 2, pp. i-iv, 8 July.

MORRISON, A. and McINTYRE, D. (1969) *Teachers and Teaching*, Harmondsworth, Penguin.

NATIONAL UNION OF TEACHERS/EQUAL OPPORTUNITIES COMMISSION (1980) *Promotion and the Woman Teacher*, London, National Union of Teachers.

RICHARDSON, E. (1973) *The Teacher, the School and the Task of Management*, London, Heinemann.

RICHARDSON, E. (1975) *Authority and Organization in the Secondary School*, London, Macmillan.

SECONDARY HEADS ASSOCIATION (1983) 'The selection of secondary heads: suggestions for good practice' *Occasional Paper, 2.*

SELECT COMMITTEE (1977) *The Attainments of the School Leaver*, Tenth Report from the Expenditure Committee, London, HMSO.

SHAW, B. (1981) *Educational Practice and Sociology*, Oxford, Martin Robertson.

TAYLOR, W. (1968) 'Training the head', in ALLEN, B. (Ed) *Headship in the 1970s*, Oxford, Basil Blackwell.

TAYLOR, W. (1973) *Heading for Change: The Management of Innovation in the Large Secondary School*, London, Routledge and Kegan Paul.

Robert G. Burgess

TAYLOR, W. (1976) 'The head as manager: some criticisms', in PETERS, R.S. (Ed) *The Role of the Head*, London, Routledge and Kegan Paul.

WARWICK, D. (1974) 'Ideologies, integration and conflicts of meaning', in FLUDE, M and J. AHIER, (Eds) *Educability, Schools and Ideology*, London, Croom Helm.

WHITE, J. *et al* (1981) 'No minister: A critique of the DES paper "The School Curriculum" ' *Bedford Way Papers*, 4, University of London, Institute of Education.

WOLCOTT, H. (1973) *The Man in the Principal's Office*, New York, Holt, Rinehart and Winston.

Becoming a Comprehensive? Facing Up to Falling Rolls[1]

Stephen J. Ball

Introduction

One of the points that is constantly reiterated in discussion of the impact of financial cuts on educational provision is that the effects or the severity of the effects vary considerably from one LEA to another and from one school to another. Some LEAs are facing a massive decline in their school age population which is requiring them to undertake a radical reconstruction of their educational provision. (For example, the London Borough of Croydon faces a 43 per cent decline in the secondary age population between 1981 and 1986.) Others with rather different demographic and socio-economic structures are coping with only minimal readjustments. Similarly, there are tremendous differences between schools; in some cases a rise in school population does much to soften the blow of cutbacks in local authority expenditure. But it is important not to fall into the trap of assuming that the problems caused by falling rolls are somehow separate from the financial issues, that they are some kind of unwelcome but inevitable blight upon the education service. The deleterious effects of falling rolls arise, to a great extent, from the financial decisions which accompany them. In particular the decision, forced on most LEAs by cuts in government grants, to enforce a strict relationship between numbers on roll and staffing. While there are clearly diseconomies of scale there is no inevitability, other than financial inevitability, that falling rolls must lead to teacher redeployment, the non-replacement of vacant posts, early retirements and redundancies.

We are only just beginning to become aware of the full range of consequences attendant upon the application of strict staffing formulae in schools. Recent reports (for example, the HMI report 'On the Effects on the Education Service in England of Local Authority Expenditure Policies — Financial Year 1980–81' and the NAS/UWT 1983 survey, 'Cuts in the Education Service') have begun to sketch a situation of enormous complexity, where cutbacks in existing staffing, in capitation, in support services and in new entrants into teaching are producing inter-related and compounding effects in many schools. For example, the direct effects on teachers include: a loss of promotion prospects, a reduction in non-contact time (for preparation, marking, administration), fewer opportunities for in-service training, reduced support from advisers and educational psychologists (since cuts, normally referred to as 'savings', are also being made in these areas), greater demand for teaching in more than one subject area and fewer resources available to support classroom work. The indirect effects of these changes in working conditions are then felt in the loss of morale and commitment from the teachers, an increase in work-load and stress and concomitantly a poorer standard of teaching for pupils. These personnel effects are then exacerbated by the organizational changes which are made to cope with a situation of fewer staff and reduced material support. For example the HMI report cites a 'reduction in the number of teaching groups within a school, leading both to increase in class sizes and to groups combining pupils of much wider abilities and needs, including mixed-target groups in major subjects for public examinations' (p. 12).

The reduction in staffing in many schools combined with the attempts made to limit the necessity for redeployment and redundancy also have consequences for the curriculum provision. Subjects which lie on the periphery of the curriculum have come under particular pressure. The HMI report found 'actual loss of some subjects and opportunities, including foreign languages, some of the humanities, music, craft, design and technology, swimming' (p. 12). The NAS/UWT survey revealed a loss of services in 'areas of special need including multi-cultural education, careers education and the integration of pupils with special handicap' (p. 2). The HMIs add to this that many of their 'returns indicated a reduced or non-existent specialist cover for minority subjects such as classics, Russian, Italian or geology and reductions in remedial work' (p. 4). Added to these are a variety of what might be called marginal consequences: 'the existence of a disproportionate number of temporary staff in some departments, including major ones like English' (HMI report, p. 4). Children from low income families may suffer disproportionately; 'charging for instrumental music tuition or for swimming has taken these activities out of the reach of some children' and 'the growing dependence of some primary schools on parental contributions' were both noted by the HMIs (p. 4). Lack of materials and cash is also having an impact on the way in which particular subjects are taught and the range of activities in which pupils are involved, 'loss of individual practical work in science; limitations in materials in art, crafts, needlework, CDT, [Craft, Design and Technology], home economics; lack of field work in geography, and more generally, limitations on homework and individual enquiry for want of sufficient and appropriate books and other source materials' (p. 12).

Speaking for teachers Fred Smithies, General Secretary of the NAS/UWT summed up the implications of his union's survey in this way:

> At a time when shorter working hours, longer holidays and better working conditions are the general trend, teachers are being asked to work harder in return for reduced pay. Local authority employers justify this by saying teachers are better off than the unemployed. I cannot refute this callous logic but I say that such an attitude must breed discontent which bodes ill for the education service. (p. 2)

However, Mark Carlisle, Secretary of State for Education when the HMI report was published, took a different view of the implications of the cuts. He commented that:

> This does not mean that the fabric of education is disintegrating or is about to disintegrate. The report makes it clear that in many respects and in many places the quality of service observed continues to be satisfactory. The staffing observed was assessed as satisfactory in nearly 80 per cent of the schools visited and 70 per cent had a satisfactory book supply.

Putting this another way, 20 per cent of schools visited had unsatisfactory staffing and 30 per cent had too few books. This general picture of the impact of reduced spending on education in comprehensive schooling gives some indication of the complexity of the difficulties facing heads and teachers coping with 'the cuts'. But as I pointed out initially, there must and will be enormous differences between schools. Furthermore, this catalogue of general trends and effects tells us little about the meaning of 'the larger historical scene' for the 'inner life and the external career of a variety of individuals' (Wright-Mills 1970 p. 11). Reversing the direction of Wright-Mills' sociological imagination I want to try and relate and connect this account of educational and economic policy to the 'personal troubles' and 'personal uneasiness' of individual teachers in 'the welter of their daily experience' (p. 11). In doing so it may still be possible to achieve something of Wright-Mills' project in demonstrating some of the ways in which individuals 'become falsely conscious of their social positions' and perhaps also something of the limits to that false consciousness.

The case study material presented here is concerned with the impact of falling rolls in one school. And two stances or perspectives towards this problem are explored; the individual responses and concerns of teachers, and the institutional implications and consequences. The effects of falling rolls in the case in question constituted a major institutional trauma with which teachers and, to a certain extent, pupils had to cope. Furthermore, I wish to argue that in this case the effects of falling rolls imposed massive and profound constraints upon the process of becoming a comprehensive school. Not all of the 'problems' identified below are direct consequences of falling rolls, but they were all related, in one way or another, to those consequences. In examining the micro-politics of the school it is rarely possible to separate off one issue and treat it in isolation.

The Case of Casterbridge High School[1]

Casterbridge High School was opened as a comprehensive school in September 1979, the product of the amalgamation of three existing schools — Melchester Grammar School for Boys, Egdon Heath Secondary Modern for Boys, and Shottsford Road Mixed Secondary Modern. There is one other comprehensive in the town which was also created by the amalgamation of existing schools.

The reorganization in Melchester town was, in fact, the last stage in the process of comprehensivization in Whyshire LEA. The relative lateness of the reorganization of the Melchester division in fact heralded a final defeat for the opponents of comprehensivization in the town, who had fought a long and hard campaign for the retention of the Melchester Boys' and Girls' Grammar Schools.

Casterbridge High School opened on the site of the Boys' Grammar School and Shottsford Road Mixed Secondary Modern which, conveniently enough, were based in adjacent buildings not more than 100 yards apart. The Grammar School building (the East Block) was used to house the upper school (years 4–7) and the secondary modern (the West Block) years 1–3. The Egdon Heath site was closed.

The school serves a mixed catchment area; within walking distance are to be found both a range of large detached houses, some of the most expensive dwellings in Melchester, and a large inter-war council estate (which had previously been served by Egdon Heath). The school buildings and playing fields are surrounded by an estate of semi-detached private 1920s houses. Casterbridge High takes its name from the nearby National Hunt racecourse.

Falling rolls and redeployments

From the mid 1970s in common with many other areas in the country, Melchester experienced a significant decline in its school age population. Local authority projections for the South Whyshire division, of which Melchester is a part, estimated that 'there will be some 7000 surplus school places' by 1986. In Melchester itself the figures for 'surplus places' were given as shown in Table 1.

Table 1   Surplus places in Melchester schools

	Primary	Secondary
1981	860	580
1986	1190	940
1991	960	1180

Casterbridge thus faced a period of falling rolls at least until 1991. At the governors meeting held in March 1982, the headmaster reported that 'by the time the school had felt the full effect of falling rolls the staff would have been reduced by nearly 50 per cent since reorganization in 1979'. He added that 'The staff are bitter at having to undergo this so soon after reorganization'. The minutes recorded that 'It was felt that statements made at reorganization either failed to look at the facts, or were misleading by suppression of the facts. The governors agreed that the school ought to be considered as a special case and supported the staff's plea for some extra cushioning and generosity on the part of the Authority in dealing with early retirements'. It was the policy of the Whyshire LEA, in common with many others, to respond to falling rolls by cutting staff on the basis of estimated pupil numbers. However, it should be said that this policy was interpreted, with regard to

Casterbridge High at least, with some degree of flexibility. In March 1982 the Chief Education Officer of Whyshire wrote to the head of Casterbridge in the following terms:

> I write to confirm that your allocation of teaching staff in 1982/83 will be 69.8 FTE [Full Time Equivalent] staff. This figure is made up of a basic allocation of 61.8 FTE on the estimated pupil numbers in January 1983, with an addition of 8.0 FTE for falling rolls, based on the number of pupils shown on form 7 for January 1982. There are currently 80.2 full-time equivalent members of your staff and a reduction of 10.4 FTE therefore has to be made. In view of the size of this reduction I feel that it will be necessary to consider the redeployment of some members of your existing staff.

In the first instance the headmaster was able to respond to the LEA by indicating that two resignations were anticipated from women teachers on maternity leave, and that there would be the redeployment of a science teacher on an LEA contract, a teacher secondment, three possible early retirements and one teacher who had expressed an interest in voluntary redeployment. The CEO noted these possibilities and replied:

> Having taken account of all the above factors I have decided that formal redeployment measures will need to be taken in respect of the reductions which are sought in history/sociology, mathematics, science, art, and remedial. In accordance, there-fore, with paragraph 1.3 of the Authority's Code of Practice on the Redeployment of Teaching Staff I am writing to ask you formally to seek volunteers for redeployment in the subject areas mentioned where, in my view, it appears unlikely that the reduction can be achieved by any other means.

The letter went on to say that

> In applying section 3.3, I propose that every teacher who has a major teaching commitment in one of the five subject areas listed earlier who is employed on scale 1 or scale 2 should be interviewed by ..., the Area Secondary Adviser.

The interviews duly took place and for the remainder of the school year the redeployment issue became a major focus of conversation, specula-tion, gossip and disgruntlement among the staff on scale 1 and scale 2 posts. The interviews themselves were not well received by some of the teachers involved. One history teacher explained this to me in the following way:

> We got through the pally bit, 'nice to see you again, how are you', and then 'what teaching do you do in the school?', 'What responsibilities do you have?' Then came the crunch question. 'Can you justify yourself?' 'What value are you to the school?' he said. 'What have you done for the school?' Well I got a bit narked by that time and I turned around and pointed out of the window. 'See that minibus out there, the new one, I collected one sixth of that'. I wouldn't do it again mind you. They walk all over you. Like Alan Atlas with the summer fair last year. 'A young teacher' they said 'it would be good experience for you and all that' and not a word of thanks. And this year they've got John Bunsen doing it and he's now been nominated for redeployment. I would go, I would go to Crabtree Community. Its a lot more friendly than it is here.

Another member of the history department, who was eventually nominated for redeployment commented on her interview that 'It was a formality, they always redeploy the scale 1s. They only interviewed the others to make it seem fair'.

The flow of information to the interviewees and the handling of the subsequent procedures were also criticised by the teachers involved. An English teacher explained:

> Its always the same. They don't tell you anything. It was three weeks before Karen Thimble got a letter after her interview with the Adviser and then they sent her for an interview at the Church School and offered the other candidate the job while they were both in the room. Morale is at rock bottom.

And another colleague said of Ms. Thimble: 'She says that she could not teach properly for a month after the interview with the Adviser'. And the headmaster came in for particular criticism. Typically, a languages teacher said:

> This redeployment thing is demoralizing for people — and the head, I don't know, I would think that he would keep people more informed about what is going on. He's playing it that the Authority are the villains, but he must have some say in the appointment of his own staff, about who is to be redeployed. He's very approachable but he doesn't take time to find out

about people. He's not good at initiating. Its a pastoral function really. People are fed up about not knowing when decisions are being made and what stage has been reached about their redeployment. He's very rarely over here (the West Block). We're beginning to feel like an imperial outpost on which the sun never sets.

There are many other examples of this kind of talk which could be quoted. Grumbling about the head seems to be an almost universal characteristic of staffroom talk in schools, and at Casterbridge disgruntlements about leadership style were freely aired during the redeployment crisis. But it would be a mistake to dismiss these grumbles as either simply examples of personal discontent or as reflecting the failings of an individual head. They illustrate a more general shift in the role of the headteacher and in staff-head relationships, a shift that is being brought about by the increased level of intervention by local authority officials in areas of policy and decision-making previously left to the responsibility of the headteacher.

Briault and Smith (1980), from their study of schools hit by falling rolls, make the point that:

> In the many difficult decisions to be made, which in total result in the size and character of the staff establishment of the school, the role of the head is bound to involve some conflicts of loyalty, particularly when the roll falls and staff reductions are required. Is the head primarily responsible upwards towards his employing authority or downwards towards his school? (p.127)

Hunter (1979) adds the point that 'the head thinks in terms of general rules and uniform events; teachers think in terms of concrete situations, unique individuals and extenuating circumstances' (p. 133–24).

The views, attitudes and response of the threatened staff at Casterbridge to the actions of the LEA and their interpretation of the headmaster's role demonstrate both an apparent weakening of normative and professional commitment to the school and an increasing exposure of and recognition of the straightforward employee-employer relationships within which they worked. Much of the teachers' knowledge and understanding of the process of management was based on gossip and hearsay and they resented the lack of consultation and communication. The separation of policy making and executive decision-making from the day-to-day work of teaching revealed for some, perhaps for the first time, the contradictions in their view of themselves on the one hand as being 'professionals' while on the other labouring 'according to the dictates of those with authority over them'. To a great extent the professional mythology (see Bailey, 1982, p. 97 on school mythologies) through which the teachers had interpreted their work relationships and attendant sense of personal autonomy was being stripped away by the de-personalizing experience of the redeployment crisis. Even the role of the unions, at least for those teachers on scales 1 or 2, seemed to be merely that of providing an agreed procedure, which gave them a minimum of personal protection and security. Interestingly, one teacher at least saw the teaching unions as too 'gentlemanly' and deferential: 'The dockers are getting £22,000 apiece for 15 years service. Perhaps they've got a better union than ours. Ours is always too pleased with anything they can get. "Yes sir, thank you very much sir" '.

There was little evidence of collective strategies of defence at work in Casterbridge High, although collegial relationships among the younger staff did provide psychological and emotional mutual support and commiseration. But the decisions were being taken elsewhere. Wallace et al (1983) report a similar lack of coherent response to cuts among middle school teachers they interviewed. As Ozga and Lawn (1981) suggest, 'even teachers who totally reject any parallels between their situation and that of British steel workers ... are learning the extent of their vulnerability when they no longer fulfil a function useful to capital' (p. 139).

It is important, however, to see the headmaster's role in the redeployment process not only in terms of the dilemmas involved in his position in relation to the teachers and the local authority, but also in relation to the pupils: 'How can he best serve the interests of his pupils? Within the school, is his first concern to be the curriculum or the teachers?' (Briault and Smith, 1980, p. 128). The Casterbridge head was keenly aware of this dilemma, but equally saw his options as severely limited.

> In this situation, first of all, to make a happy staffroom, it's advisable to keep the number of redeployments down to the basic minimum, which means that if you do have a high turnover of staff because they retire or they get jobs elsewhere this in fact does help the situation ... but equally the priority above all is to safeguard the curriculum, so that with every person leaving, the first question is, from the curriculum point of view, must I replace this person? ... The authority are

> sympathetic, in that they are prepared to spend time coming to
> the school, from the advisory level and the officers, they
> appreciate the dilemma, the need to protect the curriculum. At
> the same time, in the end, it is quite clear that they say to me
> 'you've got to get down to that number of staffing'.

As he saw it, the first priority lay in maintaining and, where feasible,
developing the existing curriculum provision in the school. His planning lay at the centre of a number of contending pressures. First, the
authority's requirement that numbers of staff be reduced. Second, the
need to safeguard the school curriculum. Third, the problem of
maintaining staff morale by keeping redeployment to a minimum, and
by responding as best he could to individual career aspirations. Fourth,
to balance decisions about curriculum coverage and individual redeployments against the somewhat unpredictable pattern of staff resignations (early retirements, promotions and pregnancies all played their
part in this calculus of uncertainty). One outcome of these contending
pressures, from the point of view of individual members of staff was an
inevitable disjunction between personal problems, career and institutional planning. (Thus, Ms Thimble, who was nominated for redeployment and sent for an interview at another school and then not
offered the post, was eventually removed from the redeployment list
when another woman teacher became pregnant and decided to resign.)
In terms of Briault and Smith's (1980) analysis of the management of
falling rolls, Casterbridge fits the 'plan, redevelop and appoint' (p. 120)
type of management behaviour. What Briault and Smith fail to
recognize in their analysis of this process, from a management perspective, is the impact that such a strategy may have on the motivations,
self-esteem and commitment of the teachers, like Ms Thimble, who are
caught up in the mixture of executive decision-making and pure
chance.

Indeed, looking more widely, in line with the recent flight into
management training for school administrators (the DES has allocated
£6 million for this purpose, of which £350,000 has gone to the
University of Bristol to establish a National Educational Management
Centre), the major trend in educational research and writing on falling
rolls is concerned almost exclusively with *managing* falling rolls. The
emphasis is on dealing efficiently with the technical and managerial
problems thrown up by falling rolls rather than with the personal and
human problems created for the individuals involved (see, for example,
Butterworth, 1983; Lynch and Wright, 1983, and Shaw, 1980). While

in many respects there is nothing at all wrong with efficiency as an organizational goal, Braverman's (1974) point that management itself is not a neutral technology, is worth reiterating here. Management is one form of organization control, based on executive control of labour, but not necessarily the only available one. Nor is it necessarily the most efficient form of organizational control and decision-making for coping with rapidly changing conditions (Burns and Stalker, 1961). Participative procedures are an alternative which a few schools have attmepted (Scrimshaw, 1975). It is tempting to suggest that the recent (1983) commitment of DES funds to school management training is not unconnected with the problems of falling rolls and financial cutbacks being faced by schools. To go further, it might be suggested that these two phenomena are ideologically and politically related.

Clearly, in one way it is possible to portay the circumstances faced by Casterbridge High as an inevitable consequence of the financial decisions being taken outside the school by national and local government, but the handling of staff reductions is done within schools by responsible senior postholders. Again the headmaster is not unaware of the problems he faced or the effects of his actions on his staff:

> The effect on morale shouldn't be underestimated at all. There aren't many things apart from another reorganization that can actually disturb the morale of a staff more than a falling roll. Redeployment, not getting promotion and this frustration of not seeing any way up, even if you stay in the school. All of which combines to dampen the enthusiasm of sometimes very good and enthusiastic teachers, it's a very worrying time indeed ... It is sometimes the most conscientious teachers who are affected most by this, they feel perhaps they are being undervalued.

One group of teachers who in particular expressed strong feelings of being undervalued in the school were women teachers. The original basis of the reorganization in Melchester created Casterbridge High out of two boys schools and one mixed. When the reappointment process was completed the senior posts were overwhelmingly dominated by male staff. By the third year of the existence of the comprehensive school there were 84 staff in all (full and part time), 52 men and 32 women, but in senior posts there were just 3 women in all (one assistant head, one year tutor and one major departmental head). Thus there was only 1 woman out of 7 members on the senior management team, 2 women members out of 13 on the academic board, and 6 women members out of 21 on the pastoral board. Consciousness was raised and resentment heightened by the fact that a series of internal promotions made in the second and third years after reorganization all went to men. A group of women teachers based in the West Block got together to write a letter to the headmaster to express their concern.[2]

> We wrote a letter to the head last year and got about thirty signatures on it ... it seems that there *are* no career prospects for good women in the school and we did ask in the letter whether the powers that be felt that they did not have any good women in the school ... The response from the Head was that the right people had been given the jobs. (English teacher)

Feelings were running particularly high in the summer term of 1983 when two internal appointments made in the same week both went to male candidates. As the outcome of the second appointment became known in the West Block staffroom, one of the women's group declared aloud to the assembled staff: 'What do you expect, it's the same everywhere; in commerce and in industry. In a time of crisis it's women back to the kitchen.

For the women teachers at Casterbridge (and newly appointed young men) the declining prospects of promotion inside the school, and locally and nationally outside, created a situation of 'career truncation'. And 'they could not see any future possibility of movement up the career ladder and no way out of their career impasse' (Riseborough, 1981, p. 28). Such realizations, Riseborough suggests, can have profound implications for 'perceptions of self and role performance'. In particular, for the married women, as is the case in other occupations, there was a double handicap to be faced. Not only were there fewer posts being advertised but most of the married women saw themselves as limited to local opportunities by their husband's employment and their children's schooling. The cutting of part-time posts as a first recourse in the efforts to meet reduced staffing numbers also affected women teachers disproportionately.[3]

The Competitive School

One of the other factors that further complicated and exacerbated the problem of falling rolls at Casterbridge was the coming into force in 1981 of the provisions of the 1980 Education Act. In effect Casterbridge was in competition with other schools and colleges in Melchester and the surrounding area for a share of a decreasing pool of secondary age children. The Act required that: 'Every local education authority shall make arrangements for enabling the parent of a child in the area of the authority to express a preference as to the school at which he wishes education to be provided for his child' (section 6, paragraph 1). Subsequent regulations issued by the Secretary of State required publication of 'information as to the public examinations for which pupils at the school are entered and as to the results obtained by such pupils' and 'of particulars where there are arrangements for parents considering sending their child to the school to visit it'. Thus, by implication at least this competition between schools was not to be passive; schools were being encouraged to present themselves as best they could to their potential pupils.

The effects of this competition with neighbouring schools were felt at Casterbridge at both ends of the school. Potential first year entries were being lost, in small numbers, to the nearby Church comprehensive. This particular source of losses was raised and discussed at a meeting of governors.

> The Headmaster expressed his concern at the greater number of pupils being admitted to Church Comprehensive and was particularly disturbed with reference to the criterion 'practising Christians'. The governors spent some time discussing this problem and it was agreed that the chairman should bring to the notice of the county Education Officer the governors' concern on this matter.[4] (minutes of the governors' meeting)

At the sixth form end of the school, pupils were lost to the sixth form colleges in the next town and to a lesser extent to the further education college there. One senior member of staff, an ex-grammar school teacher, explained the situation thus:

> We've got a problem now as well. You see, in the grammar school virtually no one went to the sixth form college, partly because although they had to stay in uniform, they knew exactly who was teaching them . . . and for various reasons they just didn't leave. Despite the fact that we had them in school uniform until they were nineteen, and they could have gone up to the sixth form college and goodness knows what. We lost the occasional one who had hennaed his hair and things like that. But we're in trouble now you see, because they leave by the thirties. Partly I think to start with because the grammar school parents got a bit peeked, and thought, you know, 'If

Stephen J. Ball

they're going to demolish the grammar school, we'll take our
children away and see if we can't demolish them! There must
have been an element of spite I think. But once that starts of
course it spreads ... we're getting left with the dregs, with the
secondary modern children ... It'll get to a stage where we'll
have to join with the school down the road to have one sixth
form or the whole sixth form will go to one or another school
and the other become an 11–16 school.

This decline in the popularity of and the 'quality' of the sixth form was
seen by the ex-grammar school staff as a direct consequence of
comprehensivization and a further threat to the academic standards
achieved in the grammar school days. The grammar school staff spoke
with pride of the school's record in obtaining Oxbridge scholarships,
recorded in gold paint on the rolls of honour in the East Block hall. The
possible loss of the sixth form was also a threat to the work satisfactions
and self-conceptions of the ex-grammar school staff, among whom A
level teaching, and preparation for university entrance was considered
to be a major part of their expertise as teachers. In the grammar school
tradition the sixth form is the major bastion of academicism and is
associated with a special relationship, based on close personal contact,
between teacher and pupil (see Reid and Filby, 1982). Woods (1979)
points out that '... tradition can no longer vouchsafe a reasonably
watertight world within the institution with its own isolated conceptions of respect, honour and identity' (p. 248). The school was keenly
aware of the need to compete in a 'buyers market' and make best use of
new necessities, like the requirement to hold 'open evenings'. And
every opportunity to advertise and display the school's range of
activities and especially its competitive successes were to be seized. To
quote again from the minutes of a governors' meeting (November
1981): 'It was suggested that some favourable publicity would be in the
school's best interests and the question of contacting the Press Office at
County Hall was discussed, also the possibility of suitable publicity in
the new publication The Melchester Citizen'.

One of the ploys aimed, in part at least, at encouraging more
pupils to stay on into the sixth form was the introduction of City and
Guilds vocational preparation courses. These courses were intended to
attract pupils to stay on who might otherwise either have drifted into
unemployment or would have been attracted to vocational courses at
the nearby further education college. With some difficulty the headmaster, whose idea the City and Guilds courses had been, obtained

240

£600 from the LEA to fund the initiative. The other schools in Melchester and its neighbourhood, especially the sixth form colleges — the nearest being in the next town (in fact less than two miles from Casterbridge), undertook similar developments and initiatives in order to safeguard their own student numbers and if possible attract customers away from their rivals. It was not long before the further education college hit back. Early in 1983 a pamphlet was circulated to all the schools in the Melchester area, headed: 'WHAT NEXT AFTER SCHOOL? Start with the further education college ... the alternative sixth form.' The pamphlet went on to argue that:

> For many years commentators have been drawing attention to what they believe to be a 'British Disease'. They have complained that a lot of our degree courses are too academic — that the study of pure science, for example, with its accent on the pursuit of knowledge, has been considered by many educationalists to be 'better' than technology. These commentators have included many of those from the forefront of industry and commerce who have been concerned that many academics rank the ability to design, manufacture and sell below the ability to debate and analyse ... A large number consider that the narrow curriculum followed for examinations in some sixth forms have contributed to this ... At the further education college we have always recognised that for many students there are limitations imposed by the conventional A level courses. For those who have a reasonable understanding of what they are going to do after A levels, we offer several interesting courses which really do set out to help cure the 'British disease'. Our courses include selected packages at A level studied alongside courses which really do show the application of theoretical work in real life.

Lightfoot (1978) sees such activities and the attitudes and forms of relationship that they encourage as further examples of the deleterious effects that the financial interpretation of falling rolls are having upon schools:

> Competitiveness will be a feature of individual teachers' relations with one another as well as the constant pressure of the need to attract pupils to secure the health, possibly the survival, of institutions. As this pressure continues, a downward spiral can be anticipated ... one of lowering morale, distrust, institutional friction and that debilitation which comes from the

Stephen J. Ball

feeling that futures can scarcely be influenced and cannot be controlled. (p. 38).

It is tempting to relate this state of affairs to the free market dogmatism of Thatcherite economics. The principle which says that in periods of economic recession 'the weakest will go to the wall', can be applied as well to schools as it can to businesses.

Conclusions

Clearly, it would be difficult to argue that the problems and traumas faced by Casterbridge are, in the particular form experienced, typical of comprehensives generally. However, considered separately the problems of falling rolls, of redeployment, of competition for pupils and loss of staff morale are 'facts of life' currently being faced in many comprehensives.

For Casterbridge, this concatenation of 'effects' has had a decisive impact upon the sort of comprehensive school it has and will become. The impact of falling rolls coming so soon after the reorganization has produced a set of circumstances which weigh heavily against the possibility of institutional change and in favour of a high degree of carry over from the bipartite system in Melchester. More specifically, the redeployment procedures have a number of consequences for the staffing and ethos of Casterbridge High, which are being experienced in very similar ways in many other comprehensive schools. These can be listed under eight headings.

   i   There was an increased top loading of the staff; redeployments were limited to teachers on scales 1 and 2, although there were a number of early retirements at the other end of the scale structure. In some departments this produced a situation where a high proportion of staff held other posts of responsibility. In humanities for example, of the five staff, four held scale 4 posts or above (three year tutors and a deputy head) the other teacher, on scale 1, was redeployed.

   ii   Related to this top loading, one of the school's union representatives described the redeployments as having the effect of leaving the 'tired' staff in the school while removing the 'innovative, enthusiastic new staff' — that is to say, those with most recent experience of teacher-training and therefore those most likely to have been trained in comprehensive schools elsewhere were most likely to be redeployed.

242

iii Furthermore, the continued viability of the redeployment scheme within the LEA as a whole meant that 'staff who would not be acceptable in other schools for various reasons' (headmaster) remained at Casterbridge. The Headmaster was certainly aware that if he, or any other head, used the redeployment scheme to 'offload' tired, weak or unsuccessful staff onto other schools then the credibility of the scheme in the eyes of 'receiving' heads would quickly be destroyed.

iv The redeployment of younger staff also had the effect of leaving in place a majority of older bipartite staff with their existing conceptions of teaching and curriculum more or less unchallenged by new inputs.

v The 'stability' of the senior staff, 'the hierarchy' as it was often referred to by junior staff, also reduced the possibility of internal promotions. Scale points were held by established staff unlikely to move to new posts. And as the size of the school roll fell an actual points surplus began to accumulate.

vi The top-heaviness of the school, both in terms of its age structure (with the implications that that has for innovatory potential) and its administrative structure (senior management, the pastoral system and other posts of responsibility remained intact) began to highlight the separation between the younger staff whose work was mainly concerned with their teaching duties and older staff with responsibility allowances who had a lower timetable commitment and who 'were seemingly able to fulfil their obligations without much effort' (Hunter and Heighway 1980, p. 70). Hunter and Heighway found this to be the case in a number of middle schools they studied.

vii The initial staffing of the school, the 'stability' of the senior posts, and the promotion appointments made internally, produced a situation where women members of staff felt undervalued and unfulfilled. They felt the lack of promotion prospects in a particularly acute way which was exacerbated in most cases by limitations upon the possibilities of applying for other posts out of the area. While the pupil population at Casterbridge was adjusting itself to a more even mix of boys and girls, the senior staff posts continued to be dominated by men teachers.

viii Perhaps most striking of all at Casterbridge (and widely reported elsewhere) was the impact on staff morale and commitment to the school. The institutional factors, outlined above, and the general climate of uncertainty and insecurity produced by the redeployment process, the increased competitiveness and demands for external accountability, the declining resources and lack of promotion prospects, produced a sense of disaffection and malaise in the school's staffrooms. It is much more difficult to say what effect, if any, these symptoms may have had in the classroom. Several of the findings and conclusions reported by Rutter *et al* (1979) would suggest that the loss of morale and degree of disaffection evident in the Casterbridge staffrooms *would* have had some impact on school 'outcomes'. Rutter *et al* note, for example, that outcomes were related to decision-making structures in the schools they studied: 'it seemed necessary that teachers should feel that they had some part in the decision-making processes but also that they had sufficient confidence in the staff group as a whole that they were content for their opinions and suggestions to be expressed by someone else' (p. 193). Neither could be said to be the case here. Rutter *et al* also comment that 'Doubtless, too, pupils are likely to make less satisfactory progress when teaching staff are discontented or in conflict' (pp. 193–4).

I shall leave the last word on Casterbridge High to the headmaster:

I believe we are trying to develop a comprehensive school in possibly the most difficult circumstances that man could actually devise. And it's ironic that the first talks about reorganization in Melchester, I understand, took place about sometime like 1965, and it was put off several times I think, twice even when a date had been set, because at the time it was said that, 'We haven't got the money available to do it properly, we must defer it and do it properly'. We've now reorganized at a time of falling rolls ... which makes the development of courses extraordinarily difficult to achieve.... We can see needs, as the school develops, for different types of courses to suit different types of pupil. We sometimes can't provide them because we are losing staff and not appointing them.

Notes

1 I am most grateful to the headmaster of Casterbridge High School for his willingness to discuss openly with me the problems caused by falling rolls and for his comments on and responses to a previous draft of this paper.
2 Initially, this group consisted of four ex-Shottsford women who were frequently critical of various aspects of the school regime, but as the redeployment and promotion issues gained ground they were joined by other women teachers in private and general staffroom discussions.
3 The women teachers at Casterbridge found themselves confronted with a set of compounding factors which served to raise and reinforce an awareness of their subordinate position in the school:

— the initial basis of the amalgamation, two boys schools and one mixed, had produced a male dominated 'hierarchy';
— the lack of staff mobility had meant that few opportunities arose for women to gain promotion either inside the school or by moving elsewhere;
— many women found themselves limited to local promotion opportunities because of the unquestioned priority of their husband's work ties and children's education;
— a number of internal promotions, which had arisen, had gone to male teachers;
— as the proportion of girls in the school increased some women found themselves dealing with pastoral problems raised by girls who were unwilling to talk to male teachers, there were few women in pastoral posts;
— also as the number of girls increased, some of the female staff became concerned about the lack of women in senior positions who might thereby act as role-models.

4 The headmaster's concern here was not with losses as such, for the school continued to be over-subscribed, but rather the implication that the Catholic school was the only secondary school in the Melchester area which would meet the needs of practising Christians.

References

BAILEY, A.J. (1982) *The Pattern and Process of Change in Secondary Schools: a Case Study*, Unpublished DPhil thesis, Education Area, University of Sussex.
BRAVERMAN, H. (1974) *Labour and Monopoly Capital*, New York, Monthly Review Press.
BRIAULT, E. and SMITH, F. (1980) *Falling Rolls in Secondary Schools*, Windsor, NFER.
BURNS, T. and STALKER, G.M. (1961) *The Management of Innovation*, London, Tavistock.

BUTTERWORTH, I. (1983) *Staffing for Curriculum Needs: Teacher Shortages and Surpluses in Comprehensive Schools*, Windsor, NFER.

DEPARTMENT OF EDUCATION AND SCIENCE (1981) 'Report by HMI on the effects on the Education Service in England of Local Authority expenditure policies — financial year 1980–81', London, HMSO.

HUNTER, C. (1979) 'Control in the comprehensive system', in EGGLESTON, J. (Ed) *Teacher Decision-Making in the Classroom*, London, Routledge and Kegan Paul.

HUNTER, C. and HEIGHWAY, P. (1980) 'Morale, motivation and management in a middle school' in BUSH, T. *et al* (Eds) *Approaches to School Management*, London, Harper Row.

LIGHTFOOT, M. (1978) 'The Educational Consequences of Falling Rolls' in RICHARDS, C. (Ed) *Power and the Curriculum*, Driffield, Nafferton.

LYNCH, J. and WRIGHT, D. (Eds) (1983) *The Management of Education in Contraction*, London, Croom Helm.

NAS/UWT (1983) *Cuts in the Education Service*, Birmingham, NAS/UWT.

OZGA, J. and LAWN, M. (1981) *Teachers, Professionalism and Class*, Lewes, Falmer Press.

REID, W. and FILBY, J. (1982) *The Sixth: An Essay in Education and Democracy*, Lewes, Falmer Press.

RISEBOROUGH, G. (1981) 'Teachers' careers and comprehensive schooling: an empirical study', *Sociology*, 15, 3 (August), pp. 352–80.

RUTTER, M. *et al* (1979) *Fifteen Thousand Hours*, London, Open Books.

SCRIMSHAW, P. (1975) 'Should schools be participant democracies?' in BRIDGES, D. and SCRIMSHAW, P. (Eds) *Values and Authority in Schools*, London, Hodder and Stoughton.

SHAW, K. (1980) 'Managing the curriculum in contraction' in FINCH, B. and SCRIMSHAW, P. (Eds) *Standards, Schooling and Education*, London, Hodder and Stoughton.

WALLACE, G., MILLER, H. and GINSBURG, M. (1983) 'Teachers' responses to the cuts' in AHIER, J. and FLUDE, M. (Eds) *Contemporary Education Policy*, London, Croom Helm.

WOODS, P.E. (1979) *The Divided School*, Routledge and Kegan Paul.

WRIGHT-MILLS, C. (1970) *The Sociological Imagination*, Harmondsworth, Penguin.

Teacher Careers in the Comprehensive School

Patricia J. Sikes

Introduction *pattern/trend*

In recent years teacher morale has frequently been characterized as low, and still falling. Teachers claim, and research confirms (Kyriacou and Sutcliffe, 1979; International Labour Organization, 1981; Edelwich with Brodsky, 1980) that teaching is a particularly stressful job. Teachers say that they are dissatisfied and that their careers are no longer meeting their expectations in terms of prospects, job security, working conditions, job satisfaction and status. The major areas to which they attribute their dissatisfaction are, as the teachers quoted below noted:

— Cuts in educational spending; promotion prospects; the inevitable wrangle each year over pay; the brain washing of the public by the media and politicians that many of the problems in society are due to problems in school. (male, age 30, scale 2)
— Changing attitudes within society; a decline in parental support for schools. (male, age 40, scale 4)
— The difference in attitude and behaviour of the children (who are) far more likely to question discipline and who are more aware of what they consider to be their rights. (female, age 35, scale 1)
— Change-over to comprehensive education from selective. (male, age 33, scale 1)
— Comprehensive reorganization; mixed ability teaching; larger schools. (male, age 40, scale 4)

In short, falling rolls and contraction following quickly upon rapid and extensive expansion have resulted for many teachers in dramatically reduced promotion prospects, job insecurity and curricular and organizational change, all of which have had a negative influence on teacher morale, commitment and motivation (see Briault and Smith, 1980; Bush, 1980; Dennison, 1981; Fiske, 1979; Hunter and Heighway, 1980; Whiteside and Bernbaum, 1979). Cuts in spending mean limited resources, even at a basic level and there are few signs that the situation will improve in the foreseeable future (Dennison, 1981; Hunter and Heighway, 1980; Bush, 1980). Teachers claim that their social status has fallen (Hargreaves, 1980), and that 'the standards of today's society conflict with standards of many teachers' (male, 42, scale 4), with 'parents less likely to support schools in all aspects of work and community' (male, 40, scale 4). Calls for accountability and the raising of standards (plus recent moves to give responsibility for the education and training of young people to agencies other than the school) can only be seen as reflecting a public and official view that teachers are failing to do their job adequately (see Hunter, 1981).

With comprehensivization, many teachers found that they were in jobs for which they had not originally applied. Thus, the majority of schools developed as comprehensives with a high proportion of their staffs having initially been recruited to a different type of school. Whereas the expressed aims of comprehensives have tended to be unspecific, phrased in terms of 'equality of opportunity' and the 'development of the full potential of the child' (see Ross, Bunton, Evison and Robertson, 1972), the selective schools were characterized by distinctive functions and philosophies. Generally, grammar schools were oriented to achieving success (that is, exam passes) in academic subjects, while secondary moderns had the task of preparing less academically motivated pupils for working life. Thus, the emphasis in grammar schools tended to be on the discrete subject, and in the secondary modern on social relationships and social control.

Teachers faced comprehensivization with mixed views (see Riseborough, 1981). Many were apprehensive about whether they could cope with a wider range of pupil ability, motivation and behaviour, and some were concerned that they might lose the satisfactions they gained from a particular type of work with a particular group of pupils (see Richardson, 1973). However, the undreamt of career prospects and job satisfactions that were to become available within the enlarged academic or the newly formalized pastoral care/disciplinary structures could offset some of these anxieties. For comprehensive schools offered increased promotional opportunities to some teachers.

The rationale usually put forward for the pastoral care/disciplinary system is that it guards against the potentially negative effects of a large impersonal school on the individual child. D. Hargreaves (1980) however, suggests that there was another equally important reason and that the development of the system provided a career structure for the ex-secondary modern teacher who would be at a disadvantage in competing with better qualified grammar school teachers for senior academic posts. The major consequence for the teacher of this dual structure is that

> It seems that in making a decision about whether to seek promotion on the pastoral side or whether to seek it on the curricular side people may feel that they have unwittingly labelled themselves as relatively strong or relatively weak in their subject specialism. Equally the decision to go one way rather than the other seems to carry with it an implication that one is either predominantly interested in one's subject or predominantly interested in children. (Richardson, 1973, p. 130)

The dual system would appear to be perpetuating the grammar/ secondary modern divide. Yet teachers do not only experience this divide in terms of their objective career within the scale post system, but also in terms of their subjective career, which is the 'moving perspective in which the person sees his life as a whole and interprets the meaning of his various actions and the things which happen to him' (Hughes, 1937). Thus differentiated as 'academic' (grammar) or 'pastoral/disciplinary' (secondary modern), teachers can have different commitments and motivations, different aims and values, look for different satisfactions and experience teaching in terms of different teacher cultures. But this is not all. Research has indicated that schools can develop and be organized in very different ways (Reynolds and Sullivan, 1981), and that they differentiate teachers yet further in terms of their own particular internal hierarchical structures (Hargreaves, 1967; Lacey, 1970; Taylor, 1963). These structures, which can be formal and linked to the salary structure, or informal and concerned with non-teaching activities and responsibilities (see Lacey, 1970, in particular) tend to reflect the orientations, priorities and concerns of those responsible for the management of the school. If a school is in effect managed by the head — who Riseborough (1981) suggests, is the 'critical reality definer' — or by a small executive team, and if teachers are differentiated and have limited opportunity to participate in policy and decision-making, the staff, as a group, is less likely to share aims and values. Teachers were differentiated in the selective schools but they were united insofar as they were members of a community with specific aims and distinctive values which they could identify and to which they could respond. The comprehensive school often lacks this kind of central focus and sense of purpose. Teachers, pupils, parents, employers, society, all have different expectations of what the school should be doing and of how it should be doing it, and these various views make the development of a united consensual community with a positive outlook and ethos, difficult.

Research, in particular the work of Rutter *et al* (1979) and Reynolds and Sullivan, (1979; 1981) has pointed to the important effect that the characteristics of the school as a social institution — in other words, its ethos — have upon pupil outcomes in terms of academic achievement, motivation, commitment and behaviour. It seems that in those schools where there is a relatively high level of agreement concerning aims, the ethos is positive and pupil outcomes tend also to be positive. Teacher outcomes can be expected to be similarly affected. The evidence which I shall present suggests that they are.

Data and method

This chapter is based on data collected in the course of two unconnected but substantively related investigations. These were as follows: i) research into how secondary school teachers have perceived, experienced and adapted to the reduction in promotional opportunities brought about by falling rolls and contraction. Over 1100 teachers working in thirty-one schools throughout England and Wales (a representative sample of the secondary school and teacher populations) were involved in the study which employed techniques of triangulation[1] and took a multi-method approach to data collection (using questionnaires, relatively unstructured interviews and case studies of schools and individuals); and ii) a project which looked at teacher careers using life history method, involving approximately forty-eight teachers of art and science.

The Schools

Almost immediately I began fieldwork in schools, I found, as did Nias (1980), that teachers' job satisfaction and career plans depend to a large degree upon their perceptions and hence experiences of the managerial context provided for their teaching. Although decisions about when, how, with what provision of facilities and resources, and what form comprehensive secondary schooling should take, were generally made by politicians and administrators, it was the teachers, and particularly the head and management staff who chose and were responsible for implementing organizational arrangements and designing the curriculum of the reorganized school. The management of reorganization was therefore a significant influence on teacher careers, for it would seem that, as Hunter and Heighway hypothesize, 'the prime (but not only) source of higher morale and motivation lies initially within the school itself rather than with central government or local authority centres' (1980, p. 484).

My research supports such findings. However, two schools in particular stood out. These schools are polarized in terms of how reorganization was approached and implemented, management style and strategy, teacher adaptation to reorganization, what teachers say about working in the school, atmosphere, ethos and morale. They represent extreme cases and can therefore be regarded as ideal types to which other schools may approximate.

The schools shared a number of characteristics. Each had been founded in the middle ages, and until reorganization, were locally prestigious grammar schools. Their present headmasters had been in post throughout the transitional phase and both initially had similar ideas about comprehensive schools as communities in which all members, teachers at least, were involved in policy- and decision-making. In only one case however were these ideas recognized as approaching realization.

Bahram School

In June 1981 Bahram School had a roll of 1350, a staff of 90, including the head, and had been a 14–18 comprehensive for eleven years. Compared with other schools included in the study, a far greater percentage of the staff at Bahram indicated that they were satisfied with their job[2] and that their job satisfaction was dependent on their working in that particular school:

> I work in a school which I believe is excellent, therefore my responses are in a sense governed by that. In most schools that I know of I would be extremely discontented. (male, age 35, scale 3)

I think I work in an exceptional situation. Most schools seem awful, narrow limited factories. I find it difficult to imagine gaining the same satisfaction outside Bahram. (male, age 31, scale 2)

Those who said that their job satisfaction had increased were more likely than teachers elsewhere to mention the school as the influential factor. This was not all. Further promotion, in particular if it meant leaving the school, tended to be less important.[3]

Within the right school position in the hierarchy is not significant. (female, age 31, scale 1)

If one's school is flexible in job definition and engenders a high sense of involvement, then promotion becomes much less important as a stimulus. (male, age 36, scale 3)

To move from my current place of employment to another school would be difficult because of the set-up in this school as regards democracy, freedom and responsibility for staff and students. Until other schools adopt similar roles there will not be a great urge to 'further one's career' or to develop a career within teaching. (male, age 27, scale 3)

In their references to involvement, freedom and responsibility teachers touch on what seems to be the significant feature of Bahram. Teachers explained that participation in policy- and decision-making in curricular, organizational and administrative areas was open to and expected of them all. At the same time all were expected to teach and, compared with many schools, senior staff had heavy teaching time-tables. For example, the headmaster, who took his coffee breaks in the staffroom of which he was a full member on reciprocal Christian name terms, was also a junior teaching member of a subject department. Teachers say that full staff involvement in all areas of school life led to:

A more congenial working environment with better staff relationships. (female, age 23, scale 1)

A strong sense of support from colleagues, and mutual respect. (male, age 42, scale 3)

The tradition and nature of this active participation can be traced back to the way in which the school's reorganization was managed. In 1965, in anticipation of comprehensivization, the present head was appointed to what was a very traditional, 400 pupil, rural grammar school. The headmaster for the previous twenty-one years had been an 'autocrat' and it was only under the temporary one-term headship of the deputy head that staff meetings were introduced. Teachers responded enthusiastically to them and the new head built on this enthusiasm by setting up sub-committees to discuss the nature and relevance of various received, accepted and to date unquestioned areas of school life, such as the house system, and prefects. In 1967 when it was confirmed that the school would become comprehensive in two years time, he formed three working parties to cover and investigate social and academic organization and the sixth form. The committees were briefed to report back in a year's time. The head emphasized that while he held ultimate power of veto, he hoped that all decisions would arise out of discussion among those whom they would affect. In the event he says that he never had to use his veto.

Given those responsibilities the teachers set out to find out as much as they could about comprehensive education: 'We read voraciously and visited other schools. We gave up a lot of time after school, at weekends and during holidays. Commitment was very high' (headmaster).

The commitment and vision of the head was shared by the staff[4] and was to lead to the development of an integrated community school. Changes and adaptations were accepted as necessary. Teachers say that the committee system made it possible for them to explore and negotiate the nature and range of possible adaptations and to be aware of the implications. There was no change for its own sake. Traditions which were important in the grammar school but inappropriate in a comprehensive, such as prize-giving, were slowly phased out; those which were valued were kept or modified. For instance, while it was the ultimate intention to phase out prefects they continued for some years, although their role changed somewhat and they became, to quote the head, 'sheep dogs' instead of 'bulldogs'.

But the teachers did not want a school based on either the grammar or secondary modern model. They did not want:

> a body of men and women divided by function, university degree and experience ... there should be no divisions. [The committees were] unanimous that all members of staff should be able to teach in all parts of the school, if subject and timetable demands made this possible. (deputy head).

The stages on the way towards this aim of a united staff and an integrated community of pupils and teachers (and local people) have taken various forms: people have stopped wearing academic gowns; there has been a move towards subject integration, and mixed ability classes have become the rule; Mode III examinations are favoured (examination results are average and above for the area); craft and practical subjects have assumed an important position in the core curriculum; although there is a pastoral/disciplinary and a curricular structure, each teacher is fully involved in each area; members of the local community are able to join in classes; teachers as well as pupils are encouraged to develop their abilities to the full and to use them for the benefit of the whole community. Although, as the deputy head put it, 'the creation of one united staff was a little more painful and lengthy than some had bargained for, and in the first six hectic months the day-to-day business clouded and sometimes obscured the view and warped the perspective', it would seem that there has been a large measure of success:

> [I have become more satisfied with teaching because of] 'being in a school where students are respected and treated well. And working in a way that uses my experience and abilities well'. (female, 36, scale 4)

> [because] 'I've started teaching in a school less obsessed than most with mean-minded inanities, with a smooth institutional ride, with controlling and squashing'. (male, age 34, scale 3)

> [because there are] better staff relationships; more involvement with students, especially with regard to their social and emotional development. (female, age 23, scale 1)

> [because of the] compatible ideas of colleagues. (male, age 35, scale 3)

> [because it is a] school with an ethos I agree with; sympathetic senior staff; an open staffroom; student response. (male, age 34, scale 3)

> I was fortunate in my career to go to a school which took a real responsibility for the development of the staff. I was helped to grow from a down-trodden teacher of domestic science in a grammar school to head of house in a large comprehensive — and hence to counselling. Some schools help staff to grow. Some schools in my observation, do not. (female, age 44, scale 4)

In some ways Bahram has been especially fortunate. For instance the school moved into new buildings which pre-empted an 'attitude of condescension or resentment on the part of the grammarians towards that "unselected" threequarters of the community which had been permitted to intrude' (headmaster). The size of the staff had to be increased and it was possible to recruit sympathetic teachers. The tradition has now been established that all appointments and promotions are made with staff consultation and discussion after candidates have spent a full day (at least) in the school to ascertain that they really want the job. This situation means that, in contrast to majority opinion in other schools, promotions are believed, by and large, to be equitable.[5] (This may be contrasted with the situation described by Ball, in this volume.)

The school is characterized by a strong sense of purpose, of membership, and pleasure and pride in belonging which is shared by pupils and teachers alike. Compared with teachers in other schools who complained about pupil attitudes and behaviour, the teachers at Bahram emphasized the good relationships they had with pupils. This they attributed to involving pupils and respecting them as people and giving them responsibility within and for the community; this is an area for future development — 'students are too much left out of the present machinery' (headmaster).

Laneham Grammar School

Compared with Bahram, Laneham Grammar School represents the opposite extreme. On my first visit to the school the headmaster's greeting was: 'I don't know why you've come here. You won't get a typical impression'. And when I told the teachers that I was investigating teachers' career experiences and was particularly interested in motivation and job satisfaction, the general response was a guffaw and comments to the effect that I 'wouldn't find much there'. I was very surprised, once they knew why I was in school, by the number of teachers who approached me to tell me about the circumstances that made a career at Laneham Grammar School a dissatisfying experience. Individual teachers described general staff commitment and morale as very low and their impressions were supported by the overall picture provided by responses to the questionnaire.[6] Disaffection was attributed to one or both of two factors: i) comprehensive reorganization, mentioned by 29 per cent of responding teachers, and ii) the headmaster and management team, mentioned by 42 per cent; 16 per cent mentioned both. Although these factors are inter-related, for the sake of clarity in describing a complex situation, I propose to consider them separately.

Reorganization at Laneham Grammar School

Before reorganization, in 1973, Laneham Grammar school had a good local reputation with a long academic tradition supported by a high external examination pass rate, and a sixth form of 300 plus. There had been a high level of active resistance on the part of a substantial proportion of the staff and the local community to the changing of the school's status, yet nothing came of proposals to go independent and nor was the LEA willing to allow the school to continue to be selective.

All teachers who have experienced reorganization could say with this man: 'It's not the same job that I started doing ... and it's not the job I set out to do' (male, age 37, scale 4). The ex-grammarians at Laneham Grammar School had been trained and had set out to teach academic subjects to able, motivated pupils; they could not longer do this:

> Teachers trained for years at university to pass on specialist information to eager pupils can no longer hope to impart what they know for more than a small percentage of their time (if at all). I know from experience that I shall never see a single O level class. I may never teach another A level group. Yet this school has over 1000 pupils. Instead I shall try to help a few while drowning in a mob of disruptive and hopeful leavers. (male, age 47, scale 4)

> I think it's a rotten job now. I would like to be out of it but I'm probably too old to change ... I did my first, what, fifteen years or so here in the grammar school ... which required certain skills and I reckoned that I had got those skills fairly nicely developed, I was doing O level examining at the time ... I'd got the job of O level preparation of good kids absolutely taped. I, I reckoned I was virtually as good at doing 'A' level ones as well. And you see, from being there the whole thing was reorganized and I found myself just, just talking to noddies most of the time. There are days of the week when I can come in here and I know before I arrive that I'm, the people I talk to

aren't going to be one little bit better for my presence during the whole day. So I suppose you might say the first thing is, job satisfaction has just more or less disappeared. (male, age 44, scale 2)

According to the head there has been great reluctance to relinquish or modify the tradition of teaching for academic excellence on which the grammar school prided itself. Consequently, he says, hostility and a mood of non-cooperation and non-acceptance has been directed towards the aims and curricula associated with the comprehensive ideal. From the teachers' viewpoint, because comprehensive schools are comprehensive, their jobs have been diversified: 'Teachers in schools spend too much time in the role of parents, social workers, baby sitters, cafeteria managers, policemen, psychologists, etc. etc. (male, age 39, scale 4). And they are 'having to do jobs that really shouldn't be expected of us' (male, age 42, scale 4). This means that there is less time available for them to do what they see as being the real job of teaching. The following quotations which are representative of the view of the ex-grammar school teachers, indicate what this should be.

I would like to see academic work given greater prominence in schools. I think we are failing the more able pupils. I think pastoral work carries too much status and should be reduced in quantity. I hold firmly to the view that no pupil should be allowed to disrupt another pupil's education. We need many more sanctions for disruptive pupils. (female, late 40s, scale 3)

Each school should have an overall policy of curriculum and standards and work towards all staff adhering to the school's policy. Example: children with problems at home should leave their problems behind them as they enter school in the morning — a matter of self control. They seem to be excused bad behaviour because 'the poor little thing's Mum has run off' etc. (female, age 49, scale 1)

Although the second comment does sound very unsympathetic it reflects the generally held opinion that schools are for work, and for work only. By adding pastoral functions the aim of academic achievement cannot be pursued so single-mindedly, and nor is it valued so highly. By implication, with comprehensivization and the growth of the pastoral structure, the ex-grammar school teachers lost status and were to some extent deskilled. Unlike the teachers at Bahram they have not, on the whole, developed new aims to replace those which have become inappropriate and thus, for many of them, 'Comprehensive reorganization has produced a mediocre mish mash in education. Schools have lost their dignity and identity' (male, scale 4).

Some teachers did leave at the time of reorganization, most of them going into the independent sector. Various commitments and personal investments made it psychologically and emotionally as well as practically difficult for others to consider moving. There was a clique of approximately ten who have tried to leave but had been unsuccessful, usually because of their age. These people described themselves as discontented and very unhappy and said that they were 'serving time', only looking forward to their retirement. Younger teachers hoped that promotion would take them away,[7] and they were prepared to consider horizontal as well as vertical career moves.

When the school was reorganized a number of promotion posts became available. Not unusually, appointments to these posts became points of contention contributing to disharmony and dissatisfaction (see Lacey, 1970; Riseborough, 1981; Lyons, 1981). As Lyons suggests was often the case during reorganization (1981, p. 63), hoping to obtain goodwill the head said that he had promoted as many people as he felt he could to new or vacated posts. He now regrets this, feeling that in many instances jobs are inadequately performed, while those who were not promoted are resentful and have consequently reduced their effort and commitment. From the teachers' perspective, common opinion and experience was that those who deserved promotion were generally passed over. By contrast with the teachers at Bahram who are involved in appointments and promotions, staff at Laneham Grammar School tend to see promotion as a relatively inequitable business.[8]

Because at Laneham Grammar School promotions and appointments were managerial tasks (and Conway's work (1980) indicates that they are usually perceived as such, it seems pertinent to go on to consider what was the most frequently mentioned cause of teacher dissatisfaction.

For example, as one teacher put it: 'I should imagine that you've come across quite a bit of feeling that people who have the real ability to make decisions in this place are moving in directions which most of the staff resent.' (male, age 30, scale 3A). Indeed I had. It seemed that there was a breakdown in communications between the head and his management team and the teachers:

[There is a] lack of understanding shown by the head and some deputies, of the difficulties encountered while teaching. Failure must be due to individual teachers or departments because the 'system' is right. (male, age 32, scale 4)

[There is a] lack of sympathy at a senior level [which] makes good morale and therefore the highest educational standards increasingly difficult to achieve. (male, age 30, scale 3B)

I was told, and so it proved, that I would never see the headmaster in the staffroom or even in the corridors, because he spent all his time in his room. Comments such as the following were common:

[This school lacks] positive leadership by the headmaster. (male, age 46, scale 2)

I think if there had been leadership over the eight years since we went comprehensive this would be a good school. (male, age 30, scale 3C)

At the same time the head was often described as an administrator, with the inference that this was an inappropriate role:

Humanity has disappeared; the attitude of senior staff is now one of management. (female, age 48, scale 3)

I think the place is probably run by an administrator rather than a teacher ... I think you need someone whose sympathies are with the kids and the staff, rather than with administration and putting things on paper and following correct procedures all the time. (male, age 30, scale 3A)

Some indication of what was meant or understood by 'administrator' is given in the following observation:

I think if the headmaster was to take a more active interest, not only in the running of the school but in his staff ... I would like to see him maintaining standards, doing it himself rather than delegating. Mind you, I have heard that a definition of a good manager is one who doesn't have anything to do because he's delegated it all; and that means the smooth machine is running smoothly – but I'm sure that's only in administration. (male, age 32, scale 2)

This teacher touches on what is probably the crux of the problem at Laneham Grammar School. The headmaster explained that when the school went comprehensive he wanted to introduce a participative style of management. The ex-grammar school teachers, however, did not

Patricia J. Sikes

see involvement in policy- and decision-making as part of their role. They could or would not see that their participation would facilitate the development of a new community with its own appropriate traditions and of which they would be responsible, contributing members. They refused to relinquish their old traditional grammar school community, and saw the head as weak and ineffectual, not at all the sort of authoritarian patriarch they expected and wanted. Eventually they found that they were unable to sustain their reality in the face of totally changed circumstances. In addition, partly because they had not been willing to widen their experience and increase their knowledge by taking advantage of in-service courses designed to introduce teachers to comprehensive teaching they were also in a situation for which they were ill-prepared. By the time the reorganization had actually taken place, the head had decided that he was wasting his time trying to persuade teachers to adopt an alternative approach, and consequently had started to act on his own and in consultation with his management team.

Thus, paradoxically, there are within the school a group of teachers, generally those from the grammar school, who feel that the head delegates too much, and a group (of usually younger teachers) who believe that they are not consulted enough. Examples of the views second group are as follows:

> I feel that everybody's views should be sought and I think that can be done ... if there was more general participation of all teachers in decisions in the school. (male, age 29, scale 1)

> I have not been in teaching very long, so my experience of teaching as a profession which has/is changing is limited. My experience is largely as expected. My dissatisfactions with the job are not unexpected. They concern the hierarchical structure within schools which hinders any discussion and participation in both the wider 'political' educational issues, and their practical implementation in schools. (male, age 25, scale 1)

Teachers in this group also tend to think that what participation there is is purely cosmetic. As Conway has put it, they are likely to feel that 'participation was objectively real but subjectively false' (1980, p. 213; and see also Hunter, 1981; and A. Hargreaves, 1981). For example:

> Over the years there's always been an attempt to make it seem as though you're involved in it, but when it comes to the crunch the decision's always been made despite your views, or despite the whole staff's views. For example, at one time the thing was

260

to have a working party for everything, you know, every problem. And one year we had a working party on the curriculum options to be given to the 4th and 5th years. And so a group of us worked, you know, regularly, once a week, after school, finding out an option scheme that would take into account career demands, what the kids wanted to do, what they might do, things like that. And after months of work we presented these options which had been really carefully worked out. They were changed by the headmaster to what he wanted and just, you know 'these are our ideas', or 'this is what I want and this is what's going through'. And then, the following year when somebody grumbled about them he said 'Well, we had a working party into it last year'. And yet the options as they stood were nothing to do with the ones the working party decided on. (male, age 30, scale 3C)

The situation at Laneham Grammar School is the product of differentiated aims, values and teacher cultures, conflicting realities, misunderstandings and mistrust. Of course, it may well be that criticism of the lower ability intake and of management style are defensive strategies used by individuals who are unable to cope with the demands comprehensive schools make on them (see Elbaz, 1983, p. 122, who hypothesizes that some teachers use their subjects as defences). And similarly group complaints and criticisms do contribute to a sense of unity in adversity[9] (and perhaps serve the school as a cathartic outlet). Nevertheless, there does not seem to be any positive, purposive ethos at the school, and many disillusioned teachers work there. Their careers have, in their estimation, been blighted, if not totally spoilt. A typical assessment of the state of affairs is illustrated in the following quotation:

I would say that in 1973 when we went comprehensive they had a very good staff and everybody was very hard working. But as time has gone on morale has gradually fallen so that a lot of people have no longer the same enthusiasm, and this must, *must* affect standards. (male, age 30, scale 3C)

Individuals — Two Case Studies

The cases of Bahram and Laneham Grammar Schools illustrate how atmosphere, ethos and ultimately outcomes, can be influenced by the ways in which staff respond to reorganization. I shall now look briefly at how two teachers, one ex-grammar, the other ex-secondary modern, experienced amalgamation and comprehensivization. What it meant for and to them and how they adapted to it did not only affect them personally; as is always the case, there were implications for their school.

Mr Count (retired, previously head of science, senior teacher scale, at 'Roman School')

Mr Count had always wanted to be a teacher: 'I liked the atmosphere of school, in the grammar school particularly. It was quite a traditional place [and I thought that] I would like to work in this sort of atmosphere. This was why I wanted to graduate. I didn't want to work in what was then an elementary or primary school, I wanted to work in a grammar school [with a] sort of academic, cloistered atmosphere'. Having obtained his degree and a teaching qualification, Mr Count got a post in a school that was 'very traditional. It was an old established high school which had been developed into a grammar/technical school, but the influence of the non-grammar streams hadn't really made itself felt; they had more or less superimposed on them the traditional elements of the former high school ... there was a lot of tradition and a lot of atmosphere which I liked very much, and the staff were tremendous'. After four years he left for promotion: 'It was a marvellous experience, it really was. It is hard to understand. I think eventually the idea of having your own department initially outweighed the fact that I wasn't necessarily going to a school which had the tradition that I'd enjoyed.' (He went to a relatively new technical grammar school.) As he recounts it,

> Then, when I got here I found that it was a school virtually in the making ... We had to more or less establish traditions ... they were largely staff based but some came from the pupils ... We didn't sit down and say "What traditions are we going to establish?", but the first thing we had to do was establish an academic tradition. People came here to work and therefore we had to offer them suitable courses ... The atmosphere was one of work mainly. Then the other things grew quite naturally.

The 'other things' included social events, sports days, concerts, codes of conduct and behaviour, a reputation for technical subjects and a house system 'modelled on the Public School as much as possible, or the traditional grammar school'.

The aim of that, apart from creating the right atmosphere, ...
was also to convince people outside that we weren't a second
rate school, that we were a school that was heading for
advanced work and high academic standards, and this is what
we achieved in the mid-60s. It took us about five or six years to
achieve a good school but we definitely made it ... This was
inspired by the headmaster ... He had a very clear idea of
where he wanted his school to go and the standards he wanted
... he could communicate these to people ... he was an
absolute inspiration ... the appointments to the staff were
people who he thought would have [not only] the qualifications, but also the agreement with his ideas to put them into
practice.

And then the school was amalgamated with its corresponding
girls' school. This amalgamation meant the end of the specialized
technical orientation, but as both staff and pupils at each school had
essentially the same values, after two or three years a new community
with its own traditions began to emerge. Although he regretted the
change Mr Count approached it pragmatically and in many respects
enjoyed this period, because as head of faculty he was responsible for
working towards and building up new traditions and standards.

Then, after eight years the school was reorganized. For Mr Count
this meant that:

there was the addition of people further and further down the
academic scale. Now that meant that I was getting involved,
even in a classroom situation, in a forty minute period, half was
spent organizing the kids and getting them settled down and
this sort of thing, and the rest of the time was spent hopefully,
on the subject, and I didn't like that. *And it wasn't going to get any
better as far as I was concerned.* You see, if you go back to my
original requirements for a school, that I liked the traditional
academic atmosphere, that had *gone*, and also the original ethos
of the school, which was technical and applied science ... the
academic ethos had been diluted considerably and I didn't like
this.

His response, the way he adapted to the change, was to take early
retirement, at the age of 53. Perhaps in the extent to which he embraced
his role as an academic grammar school teacher, in his almost total
investment of self in the culture of the grammar school, Mr Count is
atypical. However, it is because his experience provides an extreme and

therefore clear illustration of what comprehensive reorganization meant for many teachers and also because it can be considered in the light of the situation at Bahram, that it has been used here. Both at Bahram and Mr Count's second school, staff (and pupils) built up a community, a tradition with a distinctive positive culture and ethos. What Mr Count says points to the importance of a central focus and shared aims. For him these were united by and manifested via the head. Perhaps this was so at Bahram, although there the brand new school also served an important function in giving substance to the future. For Mr Count and his colleagues, such a central focus was lacking when their separate grammar and secondary moderns were amalgamated. Reorganization happened to them, they had little part in planning for it and few welcomed it. Working on a split site exacerbated the differences between the staffs and made unification even more difficult. The staffs lost their distinctive cultures and there was no central figure or goal which was strong enough to unite them and overcome the physical, philosophical and practical/technological divisions between them.

Mr Baden (head of art, scale 4, 'Roman School')

Mr Baden was the only teacher from the secondary modern that amalgamated with Mr Count's grammar school who became a head of department in the comprehensive. He says that he only got the post because the head of department at the grammar school retired at the time of reorganization. Despite his subsequent promotion, from scale 3 to 4, and because of reorganization, he says that he has become increasingly dissatisfied with his job. In particular he attributes his changed career perception and experience to the following aspects of reorganization:

- He feels that the head (who was deputy head at the grammar school) has attempted to model the new school on the traditional grammar school and that the academic ethos associated with this type of school is totally inappropriate in a comprehensive because it is divisive. He gives the example that staff who are entitled to, are expected to wear academic gowns at official school functions; he is a graduate but he attends in a suit (see also Riseborough, 1981).
- Mr Baden teaches art. At the secondary modern art had

status, but now, because of the dominant academic orientation, it has become a marginal subject. The work of the art department receives very little recognition, except on those occasions when the head wants visitors to see 'nice' displays. Mr Baden says that he occasionally 'rebels' by putting up pictures all around the school but that on the whole he has tended to withdraw.

— Mr Baden saw his role as a teacher as being about 'encouraging kids to realize their full potential, whatever that might be' and relationships were very important. Working on a split site made it much more difficult to establish a sense of community and belonging and to develop relationships. Furthermore, with the emphasis being on examination success, less time is available for and less value is placed on such activities (see Hargreaves 1982; Riseborough, 1981). Mr Baden very much regrets and misses the distinctive community, sense of purpose and the ethos which characterized the secondary modern.

Around the time of reorganization, quite by chance Mr Baden became involved in founding a business. Over the years this has expanded and it now provides him, not only with extra cash but also with the job satisfaction that he had had but lost in teaching. Even now, however, he can still 'get excited by and lost in his teaching'. He says it is because he 'juggles his interests' (see Woods, 1981), because he is not totally reliant upon teaching for job satisfaction, that his actual teaching has not suffered (see Riseborough, 1981, p. 363).

Discussion

Although the majority of schools have been comprehensive for some years[10] the consequences of reorganization continue to be a significant influence upon school ethos and teacher cultures (see Hargreaves, 1980). The dissatisfactions of Messrs. Count and Baden and of the teachers at Laneham Grammar School result from the differentiation that seems to have been engendered by the way in which reorganization was managed at their schools. This differentiation seems to have been particularly apparent in two areas. Firstly, the way in which the majority of comprehensive schools were organized and developed required that a relatively high proportion of staff should take on managerial tasks. While little work has been done on how teachers have adapted to these new aspects of their role, it does seem that; (a) they feel that they are inadequately prepared to take on managerial and personnel tasks. As one teacher put it 'Part of my job at the moment is management, management of people and I feel totally untrained for it at times ...' (male, age 40, scale 3, head of house), and (b) an 'Us' versus 'Them' situation, as existed at Laneham Grammar School easily develops. The effect of this can be that 'There's very little group feeling in the school, well, I suppose what group feeling there is "us against them" ... them are the hierarchy. It's just "they're gonna try to make us work and we're gonna sit here and not do anything"'. (male, age 25, scale 1 — not from Laneham Grammar School.) Yet as the experience of Bahram shows, if teachers are involved and can see a role for themselves in policy- and decision-making this negative conflict need not necessarily arise.

The second major area of teacher differentiation is that of teacher streaming. Teacher streaming in the comprehensive secondary school has been well documented (see Monks, 1968, p. 72, Robertson 1970, pp. 94–5; Allen, 1971, pp. 17–20; Benn and Simon, 1972, pp. 318–20; Bunton, 1972, pp. 195–9; Ross *et al*, 1972, pp. 57–61; Bellaby, 1977, p. 82, Riseborough, 1981). Few authors, however, have paid any attention to how it is experienced by the individual teacher or to the potential consequences for their role performance. Riseborough has demonstrated how ex-secondary modern teachers in the comprehensive can feel 'proletarianized' (p. 363) because of their relatively low status in terms of traditional subject and qualification hierarchies. This was Mr Baden's experience. This young teacher expects it to be hers:

> There's a feeling now in the reorganization [to take place a term after she said this] that people in our position [at the secondary modern], who are as equally qualified nowadays as the staff at the grammar school are going to get the plebs because 'we've got the experience with them'. (female, age 25, scale 1)

In this chapter I have attempted to show that reorganization can be just as traumatic an experience for ex-grammar teachers. They too feel that they get the less able pupils and that they are no longer able to do what they consider to be their job. For both groups of teachers the root of dissatisfaction is essentially the same. Comprehensives have often failed to create a coherent consensual set of values and shared aims. 'Academic' teachers aim for academic excellence and 'pastoral' teachers aim to enable pupils to become well adjusted, socially confident and competent. Commitments are not directed to the good of the group of teachers and pupils which is the whole school. There is fragmentation and the individual becomes the focus of attention (see Hargreaves, 1979). Schools and teachers have lost any corporate sense of commitment, identity and purpose.

It is interesting to note that teachers who have detailed career plans tend to be perceived as having the 'wrong' attitude because their commitment is seen to be to their own advancement, rather than to the benefit of pupils and the school as a whole. People with the 'right' attitude put pupils and schools first. Teachers say that the majority of those who worked in grammar and secondary modern schools had the right attitudes, but that this altered with the introduction of comprehensive schools and the proliferation of scale posts. Because promotion was available teachers wanted it for themselves and commitments shifted from the community to the individual. There is evidence to support this argument for, while teaching has traditionally been seen as a vocation with all the implications of self sacrifice that this type of commitment is perceived to involve (see Nias, 1980) it seems that contemporaneously the majority of teachers do not have a vocational-type orientation (Ejiogu and Herries-Jenkins, 1980) which tends to support Woods' (1981) speculation that in the current climate a bureaucratic type of individualized commitment will come to the fore, if it has not already done so.

Conclusion

As a career, teaching does not appear to be particularly satisfactory.[11] To date, schools have relied heavily upon teacher goodwill and commitment. This can hardly be expected to persist if teachers are unable to identify with the institution in which they work; furthermore, if they come to feel that their contributions and their skills are no longer valued they are even more likely to withdraw motivational investments from the job. This is a particularly important point when considered in association with the fact that due to falling rolls school staffs are likely to become static, with teachers growing old together. If low morale, commitment and effort characterize a staff, change to a more positive outlook is likely to be difficult to effect, for the chances are that incoming teachers will eventually adopt the cultural norms of

Patricia J. Sikes

their school. Thus, as Hargreaves says, 'The challenge for the comprehensive school is the challenge for the teachers and it is the critical test
of their professionalism' (1982, p. 233).

Acknowledgements

The research into secondary school teachers' perceptions of and adaptations to reduced promotional opportunities was undertaken whilst I
was receiving an SSRC postgraduate award. I would like to thank Peter
Woods and David Sheard for their help and constructive criticisms. But
most of all I would like to thank the teachers on whose experiences this
chapter is based.

Notes

1 Following Denzin's typology (1970), the types of triangulation used in the
study were: time triangulation — insofar as teachers of different ages and
career stages took part; space triangulation; combined levels of triangulation; methodological triangulation; and, in terms of the conceptual
framework which oriented the study, theoretical triangulation.
2 On a 7 point scale with extremes labelled 'extremely satisfied', through
'neutral' to 'extremely dissatisfied' teachers were asked to rate their present
level of overall job satisfaction. As many as 83 per cent of responding
teachers at Bahram expressed overall satisfaction. The mean percentage for
satisfaction for all schools in the sample was 58 per cent and the range for
satisfaction was 11.5 per cent to 100 per cent. Two schools had higher
scores but in each case the number of respondents was small.
3 On a 7 point scale with extremes labelled 'extremely important' to
'completely unimportant' teachers were asked to indicate the extent to
which promotion was important to their future job satisfaction. Taking the
first three categories as indicating importance, 54 per cent of teachers at
Bahram rated promotion to be of some importance to them. The mean
percentage for all schools was 56 per cent, and the range from 25 per cent to
79 per cent.
4 At this time it was relatively easy — in an objective sense — for teachers to
get jobs. It can therefore be assumed that those who did not share the same
basic aims would choose to leave. Admittedly they would probably not be
able to obtain work in another grammar school but they could go to a more
conventional school than Bahram promised to become. In the event, one
teacher left because of the reorganization.
5 Teachers were asked to indicate whether in their experience the right
teachers got promotion: always, generally, sometimes or never; 59 per cent
of the whole sample said sometimes and 39 per cent generally. At Bahram

32 per cent said sometimes and 68 per cent generally. A number of people did add the comment 'at this school'.
6 See note 2. 35 per cent of responding teachers at Laneham Grammar School indicated that they were dissatisfied as compared with 8 per cent at Bahram. The mean percentage for dissatisfaction for all schools in the sample was 24 per cent and the range for dissatisfaction was 65 per cent (at a school which was closing) to 8 per cent.
7 See note 3; 67 per cent of teachers at Laneham Grammar School said that promotion was important for their future job satisfaction.
8 See note 5; 76 per cent of teachers at Laneham Grammar School said that the right teachers sometimes got promotion, and 18 per cent that they generally did.
9 It is interesting that although Laneham Grammar School had the third highest percentage of dissatisfied teachers, it also had an above average overall satisfaction rate, with 62 per cent of teachers indicating that they were satisfied overall with their job. The reason for this is that only 3 per cent were neutral. The mean percentage for neutrality for all schools was 17 per cent (9 per cent were neutral at Bahram) and the range was from O (at a school with a very small sample) to 35 per cent. It should be borne in mind that teachers were asked to indicate their overall satisfaction with teaching; thus factors other than those connected specifically with Laneham Grammar School such as job security, holidays, intrinsic satisfactions, etc. would also be considered.
10 See DES (1983). In 1965 there were 1180 grammar schools and 3500 secondary moderns. By 1970 there were 975 grammar schools, and 655 secondary moderns in 1974. In January 1981 there were 200 grammar schools and 380 secondary modern schools; it is estimated that at the time of writing (1983) there are fewer than 200 grammar schools.
11 See notes 2 and 6. Only 58 per cent of teachers were satisfied overall with their jobs. And their answers must be considered in the light of present economic circumstances.

References

ALLEN, A. (1971) 'Are teachers streamed?', *Where*, 53, pp. 17–20.
BELLABY, P. (1977) *The Sociology of Comprehensive Schooling*, London, Methuen.
BENN, C. and SIMON, B. (1972) *Halfway There*, Harmondsworth, Penguin.
BRIAULT, E. and SMITH, R. (1980) *Falling Rolls in Secondary Schools* (Parts 1 and 2), Slough, NFER.
BUNTON, W.J. (1972) 'Does streaming teachers lead to better examination results?', *Where*, 70, pp. 195–8.
BUSH, T. (1980) 'Contracting schools: problems and opportunities', in BUSH, T., R. GLATTER, J. GOODEY, and C. RICHES, (Eds) *Approaches to School Management*, Milton Keynes, Open University Press.
CONWAY, J. (1980) 'Power and participatory decision-making in English

schools', in BUSH, T., R. GLATTER, J. GOODEY, and C. RICHES, (Eds) *Approaches to School Management*, Milton Keynes, Open University Press.

DENNISON, W.F. (1981) *Education in Jeopardy: Problems and Possibilities of Contraction*, Oxford, Basil Blackwell.

DEPARTMENT OF EDUCATION and SCIENCE (1981) *Statistics of Schools*, London, HMSO, January.

DENZIN, N.K. (1970) *The Research Act in Sociology: A Theoretical Introduction to Sociology Methods*, London, The Butterworth Group.

EDELWICH, J. with BRODSKY, A. (1980) *Burn-Out: Stages of Disillusionment in the Helping Professions*, New York, Human Sciences Press.

EJIOGU, A.M. and HARRIES-JENKINS, G. (1980) 'Marginal professionalism: a study of teachers' work values' *Durham and Newcastle Research Review*, IX, 44, Spring, pp. 74–89.

ELBAZ, F. (1983) *Teacher Thinking: A Study of Practical Knowledge*, London, Croom Helm.

FISKE, D. (1979) *Falling Numbers in Secondary Schools — Problems and Possibilities*, North of England Educational Conference.

GLASER, B.G. and STRAUSS, A.L. (1967) *The Discovery of Grounded Theory*, Chicago, Aldine.

HARGREAVES, A. (1981) 'Contrastive rhetoric and extremist talk; teachers, hegemony and the educationist context', in BARTON, L. and S. WALKER, (Eds), *Schools, Teachers and Teaching*, Lewes, Falmer Press.

HARGREAVES, D.H. (1967) *Social Relations in a Secondary School*, London, Routledge and Kegan Paul.

HARGREAVES, D.H. (1977) 'Durkheim, deviance and education', in BARTON, L. and R. MEIGHAN, (Eds) *Schools, Pupils and Deviance*, Driffield, Nafferton Books.

HARGREAVES, D.H. (1980) 'The occupational culture of teachers', in WOODS, P. (Ed) *Teacher Strategies*, London, Croom Helm.

HARGREAVES, D.H. (1982) *The Challenge for the Comprehensive School: Culture, Curriculum and Community*, London, Routledge and Kegan Paul.

HUGHES, E.C. (1937) 'Institutional office and the person', *American Journal of Sociology*, 43, November.

HUNTER, C. (1981) 'Politicians rule OK? Implications for teacher careers and school management', in BARTON, L. and S. WALKER, (Eds) *Schools, Teachers and Teaching*, Lewes, Falmer Press.

HUNTER, C. and HEIGHWAY, P. (1980) 'Morale, motivation and management in middle schools' in BUSH, T., R. GLATTER, J. GOODEY, and C. RICHES, (Eds) *Approaches to School Management*, Milton Keynes, Open University Press.

INTERNATIONAL LABOUR ORGANIZATION (1981) *Employment and Conditions of Work of Teachers*, Geneva, International Labour Office.

KYRIACOU, C. and SUTCLIFFE, J. (1979) 'Teacher stress and satisfaction' *Educational Research*, 21, 2, pp. 89–96.

LACEY, C. (1970) *Hightown Grammar: The School as a Social System*, Manchester, Manchester University Press.

LACEY, C. (1977) *The Socialization of Teachers*, London, Methuen.

LYONS, G. (1981) *Teacher Careers and Career Perceptions*, Slough, NFER.

MONKS, T.J. (1968) *Comprehensive Education in England and Wales*, Slough, NFER.

NIAS, J. (1980) 'Leadership Styles and Job Satisfaction in Primary Schools', in BUSH, T., R. GLATTER, J. GOODEY, and C. RICHES, (Eds) *Approaches to School Management*, Milton Keynes, Open University Press.

REYNOLDS, D. and SULLIVAN, M. (1979) 'Bringing schools back in' in BARTON, L. and R. MEIGHAN, (Eds) *Schools, Pupils and Deviance*, Driffield, Nafferton Books.

REYNOLDS, D. and M. SULLIVAN, (1981) 'The comprehensive experience' in BARTON, L. and S. WALKER, (Eds) *Schools, Teachers and Teaching*, Lewes, Falmer Press.

RICHARDSON, E. (1973) *The Teacher, The School and the Task of Management*, London, Heinneman Educational.

RISEBOROUGH, G.F. (1981) 'Teacher careers and comprehensive schooling: an empirical study', *Sociology*, 15, 3, pp. 352–381.

ROBERTSON, T.S. (1970) 'The school curriculum and pupil welfare', in MONKS, T.G. (Ed) *Comprehensive Education in Action*, Slough, NFER.

ROSS, J.M., BUNTON, W.J., EVISON, P. and ROBERTSON, T.S. (1972) *A Critical Appraisal of Comprehensive Education*, Slough, NFER.

RUTTER, M., MAUGHAN, B., MORTIMORE, P. and OUSTON, J. (1979) *Fifteen Thousand Hours*, London, Open Books.

TAYLOR, W. (1963) *The Secondary Modern School*, London, Faber and Faber.

WHITESIDE, T. and BERNBAUM, G. (1979) 'Growth and decline: dilemmas of a profession', in BERNBAUM, G. (Ed) *Schooling in Decline*, London, Macmillan.

WOODS, P. (1981) *Careers and Work Cultures*, Milton Keynes, Open University Press.

WOODS, P. (1981) 'Strategies, commitment and identity: making and breaking the teacher role', in BARTON, L. and S. WALKER, (Eds), *Schools, Teachers and Teaching*, Lewes, Falmer Press.

The Political Devaluation of Comprehensives: What of the Future?

Colin Hunter

It has been a reasonable claim throughout this century for people to believe that their contemporary scene was unique and especially significant. Today we can not only claim this but point to recent qualitative changes — especially in the political and educational fields — that could dominate the trend of change for some years to come. This short essay tries to put this qualitative change into perspective, particularly with regard to the development of the comprehensive schools. It argues that the political and educational consensus which gave birth to that system has been broken, and that increasingly decisions have been made in the educational field by politicians on the basis of economic criteria. Case study material shows how this has already detrimentally affected the working conditions of teachers and pupils in the schools.

Sunshine Days

The extent of the change in the place of education in the national scene can be highlighted by recollecting the change in schooling conditions since the 1960s. It was the time of the great reports (Crowther in 1959, Newsom in 1963, Robbins in 1963, Plowden in 1967, etc.) in which the progressive ideals of liberal Conservatives and radical Labour Party politicians tended to converge in their search for the maximization of talent. Kogan (1971) makes an interesting aside after quoting Edward Boyle's famous sentence in the forward to the Newsom Report. This stated 'The essential point is that all children should have an equal opportunity of acquiring intelligence and developing their talents and abilities to the full'. Although Boyle confessed to being uncertain as to the origin of this dictum it first appeared in Anthony Crosland's *The Conservative Enemy* (1962).

Together in the mid-1960s Crosland and Boyle presided over the benign consensus which was the basis of the organizational implementation of the comprehensive system. In a period of growing GNP it was possible to support the two potentially opposing objectives; that secondary schooling should work towards creating greater social justice and equality within society *and* be an investment in creating a more efficient workforce. Indeed there was such a strong consensus for the new system that Harold Wilson could change his 1963 (opposition) promise that grammar schools would be abolished 'only over his dead body' to his 1965 (Prime Ministerial) pronouncement that comprehensives were 'grammar schools for all'.

Support for the consensus came from sociological and psychological evidence that the tripartite system was wasting the nation's talent in a tight economic situation. The 11+ system was deemed to be inefficient and invalid in that it was based on the assumption that intelligence was a given innate ability which remained fairly constant and could be objectively tested. The environmentalists identified intelligence as a social construct and argued that a child's attainment at 11 years was largely the product of its environment and experiences and could well change radically thereafter. But perhaps a more potent political basis for eliminating the 11+ was the head of steam that was building up from the disenfranchised middle class parents whose children were not selected to go to grammar school because of the lack of places, and who suffered from the obvious lack of parity and esteem of secondary modern schools.

So the expansion of the education system begun by Eccles (1956–62) and Boyle (1962–64) took a quantitative and to some extent qualitative step forward with the Labour government of 1964–70. The 11+ was abolished, the beginnings of the comprehensive system instituted, education priority areas were installed, the expansion of further and higher education begun, a massive increase in teacher training was undertaken to reduce class sizes to 30, and discussions for the raising of the school leaving age were initiated (see for example Bellerby (1977) CCCS (1981) Evetts (1973) Simon (1971)). Also during this period the teaching profession achieved some kind of hold on curriculum development. This was seen in the positive sense in the majority teacher control of the newly instituted Schools Council of 1965, and in the negative sense by the demise of the DES Curriculum

Study Group. This was the DES committee made up of a number of HMIs, administrators and educational experts that had been set up to identify, analyze and publish accounts of curriculum development in schools (see Kogan, 1978, p. 63). The determined opposition by the Teacher Associations, on the basis of the possibility of the control of educational content by central government, was instrumental in establishing the alternative model of the teacher dominated Schools Council. It was also the time when demands for smaller classes, higher salaries and secure conditions of service for teachers were met to a great extent (see Burke, 1971; Coates, 1972).

From the vantage point of the 1980s, the period 1965 to 1970 seems to be a golden age for those involved in education. The popular image was that education was 'a good thing'. It helped to bring greater equality and a fairer society and it was an investment to substantiate the economic development in the 'white heat of technology'. The important cornerstone of this whole educational and policy-making edifice was comprehensive reorganization. This was both politically and educationally significant; it was the crucial link in substantiating the gains made in the progressive primary school system and in providing a basis for those to be realized in the expanding higher education sector.

In the 1980s the picture has changed out of all recognition. Not only is the comprehensive system with other sections of education being starved of resources, but its status and adequacy are being questioned to the extent that private school alternatives are being given public support (through the assisted places scheme); the central government initiatives in curriculum and examination planning are taking responsibility away from teachers, and the National Training Initiative for vocational training of unemployed 16 year olds is being wrested from the education system and is using resources which many teachers claim could be better used in a partnership between schools and industry. An attempt to understand this process of devaluation and its effects on teachers in schools is presented here in order to clarify some of the choices which are open for the future development of comprehensive schooling.

A System Born in Compromise

The outline sketch above of the political and educational context of the beginning of the comprehensive system was legitimated at an ideological level (Crosland said 'Our belief in comprehensive education was a product of fundamental value judgments about equity and social division'), and depended on its practical vindication in terms of economic outcomes which were subject to variables which lay well outside the purview of education. The contradictions in this situation became only too obvious in the context of the 'Great Education Debate'. However, there was a further discrepancy between the ideological objectives and the practical implementation of the system which was born in compromise. Firstly, there was compromise between the DES and the LEAs. Circular 10/65 'requested' local education authorities 'to submit plans for their areas on these lines within a year'. The lines concerned were six types of schools including all-through 11–18 schools, three types of two-tier schemes; sixth form colleges and middle schools. There was no clear-cut definition of comprehensive schooling. As Crosland argued:

> There's no question but that we had to have options. For one thing, the legacy of existing building compelled it — it meant for example that a lot of areas *had* to have a two-tier system. And secondly there was no clear consensus on which type of organization was best on merit — all-through comprehensives or the Leicestershire system or what. So there was no alternative to allowing options. (Kogan, 1971, p. 188)

A further set of compromises was pushed onto LEAs in the circular. There was a very limited capital allowance for new schools and most of it was used for altering old buildings. Also the LEAs were required to consult with governing bodies, teachers, and to some extent parents before reorganizing schools in a locality. To a great extent the ethos of many of the new comprehensive schools depended on which of the contributing schools were successfully assertive in maintaining its own ideology. Some schools started with a largely grammar or secondary modern bias. The circular also urged the local authorities to negotiate with voluntary aided schools and persuade them to join in their comprehensive schemes and also to enter into discussions with direct grant schools. The latter proved very difficult to do and the binary public-private system was virtually untouched by the reorganization.

A third element of compromise was on the notion of selection. It was this — in the 11+ form — that was under attack, though no definition or clarification of selection beyond the abolition of the 11+ was given. It was left to individual schools, or authorities, to define it for themselves. It was possible therefore for 'selection' to occur between the interim two-tiered variety of comprehensives; this could be based on examinations and/or teacher reports and/or parental choice. Forms of selection also took place within schools in various organizational systems ranging from strict streaming through setting to different banding arrangements, to open mixed-ability (see Ball, 1981). Given these compromises in the original requirements, and the lack of common philosophy to adhere to or aim for, and the extent of the enthusiasm of the particular local authority (among elected members and/or officers) towards the reorganization, and the variety of local conditions prevailing, it is no wonder that there is such a wide diversity of comprehensive school models, not only between local authorities but within them.

Within the busy period from 1965 to the early 1970s most teachers in the comprehensive system were more occupied in reacting to the organizational demands of reorganization and of ROSLA than in forging new directions of approach. When two schools are amalgamated there is much at stake in the jockeying for positions and in not losing the culture of the school to which you have belonged — be it grammar or secondary modern (see Hargreaves, 1980; and Sikes and Ball in this volume). There was also during this period the struggle for better wages which resulted in the Houghton Committee's recommendation for substantial increases for teachers in January 1975. While all this turbulence was going on two fundamental aspects of the existing education system remained virtually unchallenged. First, the examination system; in the mid-sixties, the tertiary formation of GCE, CSE and non-examination streams had been instituted. The discussion which ensued centred on the possible combinations of the two 16+ examinations. The basis of the rules which evaluate the pupils and their work through marks, tests, examinations and reports remained unquestioned. So Witkin's (1974) criticism continued to apply in that 'it is assessment by examination that binds schools to the locus of authority with hoops of steel' (p. 72).

The second area that went largely unchallenged was the *process* of teacher training. The *content* of the burgeoning courses in the mid-sixties to the early 1970s was increasingly influenced by the progressive ideology — which included the participatory elements of discovery learning, the pupils being an active partner in their own education, and the social aspects of schooling being given at least equal weighting with the cognitive aspects. The *process* of teacher training however, remained authoritarian and paternalistic. The students were largely treated as passive recipients of knowledge and progressive ideals in the professional training involved in becoming a teacher. Success still depended to a greater degree on academic results rather than classroom compe- tence (see Lacey, 1977; Hunter, 1980). The keys to the definition of professional competence remained firmly in the hands of the traditional gatekeepers. Even given the change in organization in secondary schooling it was not surprising that when the students were initiated into full-time teaching the 'theory' of the revamped courses was invariably found inadequate in the reality of the classroom. It was easier for newly-qualified teachers to adopt the more authoritarian coping strategies of many of the more experienced colleagues.

Taken together the practical compromises of the DES and the local authorities, and the fudging of the selection issue, plus the hidden agenda of teacher survival in the turbulence of reorganization (usually into larger schools), and ROSLA, the maintenance of the examination system and the lack of change in the socialization of teachers strongly mitigated against one of the main legitimizing ideologies of the comprehensive system — that of greater social justice and equality. It is suggested here that progressive education did not make great inroads from the primary system to the secondary system. Nor did the organization of the new comprehensive schools become any more open and participative for either teachers or pupils. (For a case study on this last point see Hunter (1979) where it is argued that participation in comprehensive schools really only meant an increase in consultation.)

It is therefore not surprising that Ford (1969) in an early study of comprehensives questioned whether any fundamental changes had been achieved by reorganization, and Neave (1975) largely based his arguments about the legitimacy of the comprehensives on examination results being no worse than in the tripartite system. The number of comprehensives continued to expand however, even under the Con- servative direction of Mrs Thatcher, who, three days after becoming Secretary of State for Education in 1970, announced that she was reversing the Labour policy requiring local authorities to advance towards complete comprehensive education.

The Turning Point

Paradoxically, the comprehensive system came under greater pressure from the Labour administration of 1974–79 than from the previous Conservative government. It was at this time that one of the two main legitimizing ideologies of the comprehensive system — the argument that they would contribute to economic efficiency — came to the fore. The year 1974 is a focal date in identifying the change of emphasis. After a previous winter of strikes by power workers and miners and a three-day week, two general elections were fought and won by Labour. It was the year too of local government reorganization. It was also the year when the world-wide rise in oil prices dug deep into the economic foundations of the British economy. Previously the national economic cake had been enlarged (though the total wealth was not redistributed) to finance the growth of public expenditure — including the education services. The economy however was dependent on cheap energy sources. When the oil prices rose this fundamentally affected production costs, real growth was stymied and inflation rose.

There was an immediate deceleration in the growth of public spending, and Crosland's statement that 'the party's over' was aimed in particular at the high levels of public and local authority spending an education. The initial reaction of teachers was one of hostility and outrage. Indeed between 1974 and 1977 teachers in London came out on strike many times. But the militancy of the early days of cuts in growth (as opposed to later cuts in real terms) slowly dissipated with the reduction of employment possibilities for teachers (due to falling rolls) and the increasing energy required to absorb the effects of declining resources. Teachers found themselves isolated, for the alliance between politicians, education theorists and teachers had split wide open.

Theorists had already begun to challenge the idea that more investment in education helped equalize educational opportunites and argued that even when it did, social mobility was little enhanced (see for example Boudon's *Education, Opportunity, and Social Inequality*, 1974). And the socio-cultural arguments of the early 1960s, which linked educational achievement directly with home background, were being reasserted. Jencks's study *Inequality* (1972) insisted that only a small part of the inequality of incomes could be explained by number of years of education, and that the output of schools was dependent to a great extent on input (the family background) rather than the through-put of school experience. In the mid-seventies there was a great divide in the sociology of education between those interested in the minutiae of classroom experience (Hammersley, Woods, Delamont, Furlong *et al*) from a phenomenological and interactionist approach, and those who, through a macro approach (mostly neo-marxist), saw education as reproducing capitalist divisions and hierarchies in society, (Bowles and Gintis, Bourdieu, later Bernstein *et al*). The interesting thing about

the two approaches was that neither of them was obviously amenable
to practical policy implementation in the same way as the work of
Halsey, Husen, Douglas, Vaisey etc was in the 1960s. The first dealt
with intra-school activity, the latter challenged and opposed the power
structure which maintained the establishment. The axis of agreement
on comprehensive school goals and values that had existed between
teachers and academics was broken. And indeed educational researchers
played their part in undermining the position of the teachers. Politicians too had begun to distance themselves from teachers. The Conservatives, in opposition, were constructing a substantial populist
approach with their pleas for greater parental choice, fortified by the
re-emerging standards debate (kept alive by the Black Paper writers
between 1969 and 1975, for example, Boyson, 1972). This debate
developed further after Neville Bennets' (1976) survey in Lancashire,
which questioned the effectiveness of progressive teaching.

Also, in 1976, Thameside local authority won its case against the
government not to implement comprehensive reorganization; and this
was the year of the William Tyndale case, and the year Fred Mulley,
Secretary of State for Education, furnished Prime Minister Callaghan
with the HMI 'Yellow Book' which voiced concern about standards in
comprehensive schools. This provided the basis for the October speech
by Callaghan at Ruskin College in which he wrested the populist mantle
from the Conservatives and publicly identified his concern about
standards, raised the question of assessment of performance, directly
challenged the accountability of teachers and brought to the centre of
debate 'the needs of industry'.

In the January of 1977 the new education minister, Shirley
Williams, directly confronted teachers at the North of England Conference with new demands. The progressive alliance of the 1960s had been
severed. The education budget of £6 billion would no longer increase in
real terms and there should be redeployment of resources, both teachers
and buildings, released as a result of the falling birth rate. But, Shirley
Williams argued, a quantitative standstill must be accompanied by a
qualitative improvement in 'standards of achievement in schools, about
discipline, about the quality of teaching'. She added: 'The juxtaposition
in our country of one of the longest periods of compulsory education in
the world with a poor record of low productivity, low growth, low
investment and indifferent design and marketing skills must make us all
reflect'.

There is here, and in the Green Paper of 1977 *Education in Schools*,
almost a total emphasis on the ideology of economic efficiency to the

neglect of that of social justice. Indeed it could be argued that the crisis helped to identify the contradictions which underlay these goals. If social justice is based on bringing people together through cooperation, economic efficiency emphasizes differentiation through contest. It was the latter ideal that was used to legitimize cuts in educational spending as well as put pressure on the autonomy of teachers.

Accelerated Devaluation of Education

But if the process of changing the requirements of comprehensive schooling and the place of the teacher had begun with the Labour government it was quantitatively and qualitatively accelerated by the incoming Conservative government of 1979 whose thinking was dominated by the needs of monetary economic policies. The present government has influenced the comprehensive system in two ways. The first is through the effect of the economic individualism and anti-statism of the new Conservative ideology. The other, slower to proceed but quickly gaining ground, is the way in which central government is imposing itself on social issues within a social author-itarianism (see Hall and Jacques, 1983). In many respects these trends are complementary in their effects but it is the economic aspects which are considered first.

To a great extent it has been the Department of Environment rather than the DES which has had the most direct impact on the comprehensive school teacher. This arises from the new form of local government funding, introduced by the 1980 Local Government Planning and Land Act (No 2) (for a detailed review of its working and effect on education, see Hunter, 1983). In order to control the amount of local authority spending, the block grant system has been devised to calculate the requirements of each local authority based on the provi-sion of a standard level of service. Unit costs are given for each service with some allowances being made for variables such as size, type and sparsity of population (53 per cent of this total is based on the calculation of educational need). If the authority spends over this amount, then the government will hold back some of its grant. The new complicated system, continually being developed, has not worked exactly as planned by the government in the three financial years from 1980–81 to 1982–83, but it has been clear that the tighter the grip on the spending, the less flexibility local authorities have had in their allocation of resources. This marks a clear shift in the power relationship between local and central government towards the latter. The intention to continue with this process was announced in the Queen's Speech (22 June, 1983) where the government indicated its intention to legislate to determine rate limits for selected local authorities, and to adopt a reserve power to set limits for all authorities if necessary.

The effects of this shift of control on schools have been marked. Between 1974 and 1980 education officers in local government had tended to trim the whole range of the budget, but the cuts from 1980–81 on have resulted in significant inroads being made into the education service. Since a position of acute scarcity of resources has been reached, the cuts have increasingly been made by councillors in line with political priorities. In practice this has meant they would make the cuts which would entail the least public opposition or those which could remain most conveniently hidden. This tended and still tends to result in a constant series of pragmatic, short term tactical manouevres rather than any longer term strategy based on educational criteria. In the largest section of the local authority revenue budget there is in fact little manouevre for cutting if the councillors do not wish to sack teachers, or if they shy away from the unpopular community exercise of closing schools. What has tended to happen is that the superstructure of education has to work in a context of fewer resources and support facilities.

As an example of this process I recently participated in a special governors' meeting of a comprehensive school. The education chairman and schools committee chairman were both present, together with the chief officers for secondary schools, further education and buildings. The meeting was called to ask for the agreement of the authority to go ahead with a major building initiative in the school. The plans for this had already been drawn up and costed in detail over the past three years. The school was built as a secondary modern in the early 1940s, and had acquired, as numbers grew, a large number of temporary buildings (housing 450 out of 1000 pupils). There was a backlog of basic repairs, the specialized science facilities were short by four laboratories, art and woodwork rooms physically inadequate, PE facilities chronically under-resourced, maths accommodation had been deplored by HMIs in their June 1982 visit, two washbasins in the boys' lavatories served 520 boys, and subjects such as technology, drama and agriculture were not being developed in the curriculum because of lack of facilities. As we toured the building the case on educational grounds appeared unanswerable. Given the attitude of the present government to capital under-spending in the financial year 1982–83, it seemed reasonable that the £2 million building plan could be financed on a rolling programme of two to three years.

Nonetheless, the unanswerable education arguments could be, and were, answered on political grounds. The chief building officer said at one point:

> I have great sympathy with your case. There is no doubt that your floor area is a little short. I recognize too that the quality of the building and the distribution and balance of facilities are all wrong. However, until I receive contrary instruction from my political masters I can only take as my guide of need the minimum DES requirements of total area of teaching space for the numbers of pupils present. This can be made right with the minimum of spending.

The education chairman (Conservative) interposed:

> We are dealing really with screening needs and chronic over-crowding over all the district. Until we get the roof problems solved we cannot spend our limited amount of money on large projects. Also we cannot rely on the government's attitude to capital spending being as encouraging this year. It varies from year to year and we do not get advanced warning.

It is this latter consideration which makes it difficult for local authorities to plan ahead, especially as indications for extra spending are usually only given at a time in the financial year which makes it impossible to begin and complete major programmes. The practical result of this exercise on going to press is that there will be yet another extra temporary classroom erected, one science laboratory will be built, in-filling a space between two present classrooms (as a minor works project), and the boys' toilet plumbing system will be overhauled. None of the major points which dogged curriculum planning has been answered. The buildings remain inadequate for the development of the core curriculum, as well as computer education and sports, social and resource centres. Nor is this an isolated case. The cutback in real terms in public expenditure has severely affected the comprehensive system to the extent that basic requirements are often at risk. In May 1981 Northamptonshire and Surrey parents challenged the education minister as to whether the education service offered by their secondary schools was capable of fulfilling the requirements of the 1944 Education Act. In October that year a Peterborough comprehensive head advised parents that he believed the school was now operating illegally under the 1944 Act because it could not provide the books and equipment to maintain education standards.

These may be celebrated media cases, but they illustrate the gradual erosion of resources which affect the system. And while this process is unfolding still greater demands are being placed on the schools. The above school has been required to open in the evenings and weekends for community use; to open in the summer holidays for unemployed teenagers; the sixth form numbers have increased by 20 per cent between 1982 and 1983; and as a result of oversubscription by parents there is no let-up on the pressure of numbers at the lower end of the school. In addition, as a member of the tertiary commonwealth in conjunction with further education colleges and other schools, this school has its part to play in the new Youth Training Scheme; and in line with the recent Warnock Report it has tried to achieve the integration of some physically handicapped pupils, without any extra resources. With cuts in office, laboratory and groundstaff as well as in capitation, and with a rise in teacher/pupil ratios, there is an increasing strain imposed on the staff, who attempt not only to maintain attainment — but try to change the approach of the school to fit the needs of a changing society and to respond to the growing problem of youth unemployment. The fact that the Young Engineer of Great Britain 1982 was a pupil of the school is a superficial indication that, in spite of rather than because of, the government and local authority policies, good practice in many aspects is maintained in the school. But it is a rearguard action; the question remains as to how long relevant standards can be maintained in present circumstances.

At the beginning of 1982 Bradford head teachers (representing all 24 comprehensives) publicly issued a reasoned but pointed report on the effect of staffing and financial cuts on their schools. Some of the points they make could be relevant to many authorities. They point to the higher staffing ratios of 1 to 19.5 for years 3 to 5, and 1 to 14 for years 6 and 7 which have been used as the basis for staffing cuts in most schools. Class sizes have therefore risen, setting reduced, and those children with special learning needs have been specifically affected. The effects have also been felt in the curriculum; 'subjects which by their very nature must be taught in classes below average size are being particularly badly hit'. These turn out to be vocational subjects including boys' crafts, domestic science, art, technical drawing and physical education. 'The position of the second language, even up to O level, is in jeopardy'. ... 'Subjects which are highly desirable but not seen as essential in terms of examination requirements are being reduced' (for example, music and sixth form general studies). Minority subjects in the sixth form and the numbers in optional groups in O level and CSE are affected. 'There is no doubt that it is affecting the balance of subjects which is available and which will limit career opportunities in some cases.'

Also the class contact ratio, which is a measure of the amount of time staff spend with classes, exceeds .8 in all upper schools, and is between .85 and .9 in a significant number of schools. This constitutes a significant reduction in non teaching time and the Head's comment, 'There has been a noticeable increase in the strain and tension amongst staff, affecting health, increasing absence through illness, and no doubt, though far less easy to pinpoint, reducing efficiency in the classroom'. The Bradford report goes on to say:

> All schools report a noticeable reduction in the number of voluntary duties which staff are undertaking. There are fewer football, netball, hockey, basketball and rugby teams. There are fewer theatre visits and lunchtime clubs and societies. The staff who have traditionally undertaken these duties have not with-drawn vindictively; they enjoy this work and the contact outside the classroom with the children. In many cases, these are some of the reasons why they were attracted to the profession. All of their time and energy is now given to their primary role as subject teachers. They can give no more.

Other points on staffing cuts which are discussed in detail, are: their effects on tutorial systems; the lessening amount of non teaching time for heads and senior staff (many deputy and year heads teach up to three-quarters of the timetable and heads up to half a timetable); a decrease in inservice courses attended in school time because of the effects on other teachers; and reduced opportunities for staff to develop links with local industry and education welfare services and other supportive agencies. The authority's temporary appointment policy is severely criticized — that is, only giving one year contracts to some new staff in order to retain flexibility in modifying the staffing budget should further cuts be required. The effects on motivation of the teachers and the lack of continuity of teaching for courses of more than one year are only two of the many points raised against their practice. The policy of opening senior posts only to other teachers in the authority is regarded as potentially stultifying, and the effects of the cutting of ancilliary staffing levels in school offices, science and practical subjects, and ground staff are commented upon. None of the schools now have a full time librarian. And a telling point is made in the observation that the majority of the comprehensive schools did not have a matron: 'This would not be tolerated in any factory employing one thousand+ people'.

The devaluation of the schools with regard to the fall in the rate of capitation is then presented:

1   Since 1975 (seven years) Bradford's Upper School capitation has increased by 59 per cent for 13–16 year olds (from £11.76 to £18.70) and by 63 per cent for 16–19 year olds (from £16.92 to £27.60).

2   The increase has been smallest over the last four years, from 1978–81; for lower school pupils the rate has risen from £16.00 to £18.70, an annual rate increase of 4.2 per cent and for post-16 the increase has been £22.50 to £27.60 at an annual rate of 4.5 per cent.

3   In real terms since 1975 there has been a decline of at least 27 per cent in spending capacity, with a higher figure for the last four years. Over the same period general price inflation has been of the order of 200 per cent.

A catalogue of stationery and equipment and their rising cost between 1979 and 1982 are shown and 'in all cases the annual rate of increase is at least double the improvement in the capitation rates and this is particularly devastating in three main areas — paper for writing on, equipment for experiments and materials for practical subjects'. But not only has there been a decline in the purchasing power of capitation, but extra demands on it — insurance, transport, repairs of photo-copiers, washing machines etc, even the rental of public telephones in schools are now to be paid from capitation. The level of basic resource materials for use in the classroom has 'starkly declined'. Three examples from different schools are given: 'Many departments have not bought a new text book for three years'; 'In 1977 each pupil had a separate text book for woodwork, metal work and technical drawing. In 1981 there is one book amongst five pupils'; and 'The head of modern languages here is forced to use books which in his former authority would have been thrown away'.

The effects on teaching approaches for assignments, individual learning, homework, etc. are obvious:

The corollary of the restriction on the content and organization of lessons and learning is the consequent misuse of teacher time just when class size and ancillary secretarial support are at their worst levels ... there is a tendency to cope through basic didactic methods and often these are inappropriate and frustrating to teacher and taught alike ... teachers know that their pupils are receiving a secondary service with restricted opportunities, and the lack of consequent job satisfaction is damaging to morale as they spend far too much of their time on 'coping chores' to close the gap caused by an expenditure of less than 2p per pupil per lesson.

At the same time the authority is requiring innovation in such areas as multicultural relevance and community education, and the forward-looking 16–19 policy which involves links between upper schools and colleges. Schools are tending to borrow heavily from the financial provision for the main and statutory years in the lower part of the upper school for this latter development. The discrepancy between the level of funding for MSC and similar schemes and that allowed for schools is well noted. The report ends, almost bitterly:

A 13 year old entering an upper school now will find fewer adults, poor maintenance of the fabric, inadequate furniture and a restricted curriculum. There will be less practical work, fewer games activities, no books to take home, less stimulation in lessons and few contacts with the community. The examination courses to be encountered may well be inappropriate and the preparation for them less thorough than expected. This most unsatisfactory state of affairs is to be expected with the completely inadequate level of capitation, averaging considerably less than 10p a day per pupil, and much of that diverted to non class-focused purposes. As adults, we need better reasons than are presently perceived for offering such a miserable provision to our youngsters. We should not need the headmasters' conference, the voice of the independent sector, to tell us that more than nine-tenths of our children are educated in a sector that is only *partly maintained*.

The Future

The future under the present Conservative administration does not appear to offer any change in the trends outlined above. The White

Paper of March 1981, which outlined the government's expenditure plans for 1981–82 to 1983–84, stated

> The government remain committed to the objective of maintaining and improving the quality of education. In the present economic situation it has however been necessary to restrict the aggregate level of public expenditure on all services including education to what the country can afford at the present time. The government accept that this will have some impact on educational provision but believe that local authorities and their other partners in education will wish to secure the maximum educational value for money within the substantial resources which will continue to be at their disposal.

The cuts in expenditure have been implemented, but the Secretary of State, Sir Keith Joseph has refused to acknowledge that there are any direct links between the cuts and the quality of education in schools, though he did concede that there could be 'limited damage' to some schools. The now publicly published HMI Reports which have claimed a link between cuts and quality of education have either been ignored or repudiated. Indeed the public are given the impression that resources in education are improving. The recent Conservative Manifesto (1983) states, 'This country is now spending more per child in schools than ever before, even allowing for price rises. As a result, the average number of children per teacher is the lowest ever. Exactly how the money is spent, and how schools are run, is up to local education authorities' (p. 29).

This remarkable statement with its let out clause for complaints, is based on the selective use of statistics. The decline in school rolls is substantial, but as the DES circular 2/81, *Falling Rolls and Surplus Places*, points out, government expenditure plans 1981–84 assume that 700,000 school places will have been taken out by March 1983 whereas in reality only 250,000 have been (see the Secretary of State's announcement in *Education*, 1 January, 1982, p. 5). Even in the latest DES figures, costs per pupil head are calculated on the assumption that a total of 470,000 places have been taken out. Furthermore the cost of the assisted places scheme and help to the private sector are taken into consideration. It is assumed throughout that money earmarked in the block grant for schools is totally spent on them. This is not always the case as local authorities still have freedom to spend the total grant as they see fit.

But as mentioned above there are two major thrusts of present government policy. First, economic liberalism and anti-statism and the support of privatization. The economic impact of this on public expenditure has already been discussed as it affects the comprehensive system. The other element of government policy is distinguished by what Hall and Jacques (1983) call 'authoritarian populism' or the strong state syndrome. This is confined to social issues such as race, law and order, the family and education. A flavour of this is evident in the Conservative Manifesto:

> We shall switch the emphasis in the educational welfare services back to school attendance, so as to reduce truancy ... We shall encourage schools to keep proper records of their pupils' achievements, buy more computers, and carry out external graded tests.

Other aspects include the parental choice of schools, the statutory publishing of examination results, and the spirited defence of church schools and independent schools. An education voucher scheme is still under consideration — a pilot study was agreed in February 1983 whereby the vouchers would be transferable to the private sector if parents were willing to top up fees where necessary. Some kind of repayment of grant from higher education students is still being actively considered by Keith Joseph. But in a policy of increasing intervention, there are five areas where comprehensives are affected directly.

1 The use of the ministerial veto on local authority, tertiary or 16 to 19 schemes if they involve the closure of schools 'of proven worth' in the eyes of the minister. In the Manchester reorganization scheme this involved three schools with large sixth forms in a largely middle class section of the city, and in Wiltshire two grammar schools were 'saved' in this way. Croydon and Durham are two other examples where locally formed plans to meet the challenge of falling rolls have been similarly dismissed by central government.

2 With the virtual demise of the Schools Council and the setting up of the two government bodies to advise on examination and curriculum reform, there is potential for a significant shift in the balance of curriculum planning between the teaching profession and central government. The most recent proposal (in the Queen's Speech, 22 June 1983) is that the support grant equivalent of 0.5 per cent of education expenditure (£47 million) would be held back. The government would then seek bids from local

authorities for the money to be spent on important initiatives as defined by the DES.

3 The continued exhortation of Keith Joseph for the sacking of incompetent teachers and the March 1983 White Paper, *Teaching Quality*, and the continual pressure on teacher unions to link salary increases with conditions of service, are the basic approaches for ensuring increased teacher accountability.

4 The emphasis on the comprehensive school incorporating aspects of the market economy — parental choice etc. — and the support of the private education sector as discussed above.

5 The spectacular growth of the Manpower Services Commission.

This last point raises a whole set of issues related to the future development of comprehensives. The crucial point is that the training of individual youngsters above the statutory school leaving age has largely been taken out of the education field. Large sums of money are being redirected away from schools (the MSC budget for 1981–82 was £1,340,000,000). And responsibility for vocational education is being taken out of the hands of the DES and given over to the Department of Employment.

Other Alternatives?

At the present time the future development of comprehensive schooling appears to be limited by the political status given to education, by the decreasing resources available, and by increasing encroachments by central and local government into those areas of autonomy left to teachers. But the future only seems so bleak if teachers and educationalists employ their energies in simply reacting to present policies and circumstances.

The social context of comprehensives will alter radically in the coming decade. New technology will increasingly make an impact on individual life-style, and there will be intense public discussion of the 'definition of work' and the social problems created by long term under-employment, with its particular consequences for school leavers. There will undoubtedly be increasing problems in trying to reconcile ecological and economic needs, and there will be long term pressures on the funding of public services for an aging population. Movements organized around issues such as racial and sexual equality, industrial democracy, community politics and nuclear disarmament are also beginning to challenge the basic assumptions of today's society. These issues in turn are linked to debates concerning the balance between representative and participative democracy, and central versus decentralized power structures, including the relationship between central and local government.

Education is affected by, and potentially involved in, these issues. If that involvement is to be taken seriously there needs to be a reappraisal of the principles of schooling — and especially of comprehensive schooling. Do we still accept the wide and probably conflicting goals of social justice and economic efficiency? Are we, as teachers, agents of social control or do we actively prepare youngsters to change society? Do we concentrate more on teaching pupils *what* to think or *how* to think? What is the balance required between training and education?

The responses to these questions will have direct implications for the practice of schooling and may result in significant changes in the definition of the teachers' role; the degree of openness in the organization of schools; the content and form of the curriculum (as Hargreaves, 1982, argues); the development of the examination system and/or assessment profiles of pupils; and the degree of involvement that pupils have in the planning of their education.

Perhaps teachers and educationalists have reacted too passively to the external constraints on education for too long. If this passivity continues, the future for schools is likely to prove frustrating, with important decisions being taken elsewhere. A more pro-active response, involving making links and alliances within the community, local authorities, parliament and the trade unions, could enable schools to play their part in the formulation of post-industrial society. For the moment it remains to be seen whether we develop the role of, or accept the devaluation of, the comprehensive school system.

References

Bahro, R. (1982) *Socialism and Survival*, London Heretic Books

Ball, S.J. (1981) *Beachside Comprehensive*, Cambridge, Cambridge University Press.

Bellerby, P. (1977) *The Sociology of Comprehensive Schooling*, London, Methuen.

Bennet, N. (1976) *Teaching Styles and Pupil Progress*, London, Open Books.

Boudon, R. (1974) *Education, Opportunity, and Social Inequality*, New York, John Wiley.

Colin Hunter

BOYSON, R. (Ed) (1972) *Education: Threatened Standards*, Enfield, Churchill Press.
BURKE, V. (1971) *Teachers in Turmoil*, Harmondsworth, Penguin.
CENTRE FOR CONTEMPORARY CULTURAL STUDIES (1981) *Unpopular Education: Schooling and Social Democracy in England since 1944*, London, Hutchinson.
COATES, R. (1972) *Teachers' Unions and Interest Groups Politics*, Cambridge, Cambridge University Press.
CROSLAND, A. (1962) *The Conservative Enemy*, London, Cape.
EVETTS, J. (1973) *The Sociology of Educational Ideas*, London, Routledge and Kegan Paul.
FORD, J. (1969) *Social Class and the Comprehensive School*, London, Routledge and Kegan Paul.
HALL, S. and JACQUES, M. (1983) *The Politics of Thatcherism*, London, Lawrence and Wishart.
HARGREAVES, D. (1980) 'The Occupational Culture of Teachers' in WOODS, P., *Teacher Strategies: Explorations in the Sociology of the School*, London, Croom Helm.
HARGREAVES, D. (1982) *The Challenge for the Comprehensive School: Culture, Curriculum and Community*, London, Routledge and Kegan Paul.
HUNTER, C. (1979) 'Control in the comprehensive system', in EGGLESTON, J., *Teacher Decision-Making in the Classroom*, London, Routledge and Kegan Paul.
HUNTER, C. (1980) 'The politics of participation — with specific reference to teacher–pupil relationships', in WOODS, P. (Ed) *Teacher Strategies*, London, Croom Helm.
HUNTER, C. (1983) 'Education and local government in the light of central government policy', in AHIER, J. and M. FLUDE, *Contemporary Education Policy*, London, Croom Helm.
JENCKS, C. (1972) *Inequality*, New York, Bask Books.
KOGAN, M. (1971) *The Politics of Education*, Harmondsworth, Penguin.
KOGAN, M. (1978) *The Politics of Educational Change*, Manchester, Manchester University Press.
LACEY, C. (1977) *The Socialisation of Teachers*, London, Methuen.
NEAVE, G. (1975) *How They Fared*, London, Routledge and Kegan Paul.
SIMON, B. (1971) *Intelligence, Psychology and Education — A Marxist Critique*, London, Lawrence and Wishart.
WITKIN, R. (1974) *The Intelligence of Feeling*, London, Heinemann.

Notes on Contributors

Stephen Ball is Lecturer in Education and Director of Research in the Education Area, University of Sussex. He is the author of *Beachside Comprehensive*.

Robert G. Burgess was trained as a schoolteacher and taught in comprehensive schools before doing educational research. He is a Lecturer in Sociology at the University of Warwick and author of *Experiencing Comprehensive Education*.

Carol Buswell is Senior Lecturer in Sociology at Newcastle upon Tyne Polytechnic and has published several papers based on full-time research in a northern comprehensive school.

Brian Davies is Professor of Education in the Centre for Science and Mathematics Education at Chelsea College, London. He is author of *Social Control and Education* and Director of a large-scale study of mixed–ability teaching in London schools, soon to be published.

Lynn Davies has taught in junior and secondary schools in Mauritius and Malaysia as well as this country and now teaches Sociology of Education in the Commonwealth Unit of the Education Faculty of the University of Birmingham. Her main research and publications have been on deviance and sex roles in school.

Martyn Denscombe is Senior Lecturer in Sociology at Leicester Polytechnic. He is a qualified teacher and his published research has focused on teacher and pupil control strategies in secondary schools.

John Evans taught in comprehensive schools before embarking on research into mixed–ability teaching methods at the London Institute of Education. He is Lecturer in the Department of Physical Education at Southampton University.

Ivor Goodson taught history in comprehensive schools (including both Countesthorpe College and Stantonbury) before taking up a post as Research Fellow at the University of Sussex where he is now Director of the Schools Unit in the School of European Studies. He is the author of *School Subjects and Curriculum Change*.

Colin Hunter was a teacher and youth tutor for eight years before moving into higher education. He is now Senior Lecturer in the Sociology of Education at Leeds Polytechnic. He has been a city councillor in Bradford and his research is concerned with politics and education.

Lynda Measor has taught in schools, colleges and universities in England, Sweden and Nigeria and has been involved in research into education in the USSR. She is currently a Research Assistant at the Open University, working on teachers' life histories.

Sheila Miles has taught in primary and secondary schools and colleges of education and has held an Open University studentship. Her research is on the transition from school to work. She is a Research Associate on a teacher education project at the University of Cambridge.

Patricia Sikes is a qualified teacher and has worked as a Research Assistant on the 'Race' project at the Centre for Applied Research in Education. Her own research focuses on the motivation and morale of mid-career teachers and she is presently a Research Assistant at the Open University.

Peter Woods taught in schools for 14 years before joining the Open University where he is now Reader in Education. His research has concentrated in particular on the perceptions and strategies of pupils and he is author of *The Divided School* (a case study of a secondary modern) and *Sociology and School*. His current research is concerned with teachers' careers.

Paul David Yates is an anthropologist with a particular interest in Indian culture. He has made a study of Asian immigrant children in a British comprehensive and is now researching the development of childrens' conception of money. He is Lecturer in Education at the University of Sussex.

Index

LIVERPOOL POLYTECHNIC LIBRARY
I M MARSH CAMPUS
BARKHILL ROAD, LIVERPOOL L176BD